Public Relations Ethics

Public Relations Ethics

How to Practice PR Without Losing Your Soul

Dick Martin and Donald K. Wright

BUSINESS EXPERT PRESS

Public Relations Ethics: How to Practice PR Without Losing Your Soul

First published in 2016 by
Business Expert Press, LLC
222 East 46th Street, New York, NY 10017
www.businessexpertpress.com

ISBN-13: 978-1-63157-146-6 (paperback)
ISBN-13: 978-1-63157-147-3 (e-book)

Business Expert Press Public Relations Collection

Collection ISSN: 2157-345X (print)
Collection ISSN: 2157-3476 (electronic)

Cover and interior design by S4Carlisle Publishing Services
Private Ltd., Chennai, India

First edition: 2016

10 9 8 7 6 5 4 3 2 1

Printed in the United States of America.

Dedication

For my former colleagues at AT&T,
from whom I learned so much
and whose friendship I will always cherish.

—Dick Martin

For hundreds of students I've had the pleasure
of teaching public relations ethics at
Boston University and other institutions.

—Don Wright

Abstract

This book represents a practical guide to ethical decision making tailored specifically to the needs of public relations students and practitioners. Co-authored by a corporate public relations officer of deep experience and a widely published public relations ethics scholar, the book thoroughly explores both ethical theories and their practical applications.

With emphasis on the analysis of contemporary cases, the authors guide readers in building personal frameworks for ethical reasoning, enabling them to (1) recognize the ethical issues at play in public relations practice, (2) analyze the conflicting duties and loyalties at play in ethical situations, and (3) justify their decision and/or counsel in terms that others will understand and ultimately accept.

The book fills a gap in the currently available literature on the subject, most of which lacks either theoretical grounding or practical application. Unlike other books that focus on the broad field of ethics in "communication" or "mass communication," this book focuses solely upon public relations ethics. It cites illustrative cases spanning a wide range of public relations functions that involve several of the world's largest public relations agencies as well as a number of their clients.

As the authors consider questions of right and wrong, good and bad, they explore ethical theory from the times of the ancient Greeks through the period of the Enlightenment and into modern-day scholarship, including the emerging field of feminist ethics.

The authors examine the works and writings of Socrates, Plato, Aristotle, Immanuel Kant, Jeremey Bentham, and John Stuart Mill along with more contemporary ethics scholars such as Kenneth R. Goodpaster, John Rawls, Lawrence Kohlberg, John B. Matthews, W. D. Ross, Virginia Held, Carol Gilligan, Marilyn Friedman, and Alasdair Macintyre. They review the work of Daniel Kahneman, Amos Tversky, and Jonathan Haidt, among others, as they examine how behavioral psychology affects ethical decision making. They also touch upon those who have made significant contributions to the literature of public relations ethics including Tom Bivens, Shannon A. Bowen, Kathy Fitzpatrick, Dean Kruckeberg, Patricia Parsons, and Brad Rawlins.

Throughout much of the book the authors focus extensively upon the role of the public relations practitioner including exclusive interviews with such prominent leaders as Harold Burson, Robert Dilenschneider, and Richard Edelman. They also extensively review ethical codes of conduct as well as topics such as character, virtue, reason, duty, justice, and ethical decision making.

Although the authors do not advocate a specific ethical approach, they attempt to give readers sufficient grounding in the major theories of normative ethics to identify the strengths and weaknesses of each and to construct their own frameworks, appropriate to their circumstances.

To update readers on cases and issues discussed in this book, and to help all public relations people stay abreast of current ethical questions, the authors have started an online conversation. Please join the discussion at http://Updates.PRethics.com.

Keywords

Ethics, Public Relations, Corporate Communication, Character, Reason, Social/Corporate Responsibility, Ethical Reasoning, Justice, Duty, Virtue, Care, Consequences, Deontological Ethics, Utilitarian Ethics, Teleological Ethics

Contents

Acknowledgments

Writing a book is a lonely process. Writing a book about public relations ethics has the added complication of inviting cynical snickers. So the authors are especially grateful for the support of their spouses and a few generous friends who assisted in the research. Among the latter, Harold Burson, Robert Dilenschneider, and Richard Edelman deserve special mention for giving us so much of their valuable time. Mike Paul shared his experience counseling senior executives on ethical issues. Reynold Levy kindly agreed to read an early draft of the book and offered a number of insightful and helpful suggestions.

Tara Craig and Sady Sullivan of the New York Public Library kindly made a transcript of Arthur W. Page's reminiscences available to us. Shelly and Barry Spector helped us navigate the stacks in the Museum of Public Relations as we explored the careers and ideas of early practitioners like Edward Bernays and Ivy Lee. George Kupczak opened the doors of the AT&T Archives to us so we could plumb the writings of James Drummond Ellsworth and Arthur W. Page. Denise Sevick Bortree, executive director of the Arthur W. Page Center at Penn State University helped us track down speeches given by Arthur Page and Walter Gifford. Paul Lieber generously shared his own research findings on public relations practitioners' patterns of ethical decision making and led us to even more recent work. And Don Stacks shepherded our manuscript into publication with singular care and attention. Finally, as this book's bibliography clearly indicates, we benefitted greatly from the prior work of scholars and practitioners across the millennia. Obviously, any errors in interpretation or application are solely ours.

CHAPTER 1

Introduction

The topic of ethics presents both a challenge and an opportunity to public relations practitioners. In a world where far too many consider "public relations ethics" an oxymoron, those who practice public relations frequently must deal with diverse ethical dilemmas. Yet few practitioners have developed frameworks for making ethical judgments.

Noting that public relations practice offers "unique and challenging ethical issues," the Public Relations Society of America (PRSA) encourages its members to "protect and advance the free flow of accurate and truthful information." Through its Member Code of Ethics, PRSA also encourages "informed decision making through open communication" and urges public relations people to strengthen public trust in the industry.[1]

Ethics involves questions of moral behavior and the difficult choices people face when trying "to do the right thing." It concerns moral principles that govern human behavior and the moral correctness of specified conduct. Ethics scholar Richard Johannesen (1983) says ethical situations are multifaceted and usually arise when a *moral agent* (the one making the ethical decision) commits an *act* (either verbal or nonverbal) within a specific *context* with a particular *motive* directed at an *audience*. Johannesen stresses that each of these factors need to be taken into account before passing judgment on the outcome of any moral scenario.

Steven R. Van Hook (2011), who has both practiced and taught public relations, points out the public relations department often is the "ethical heart" of most organizations. Public relations ethics scholar Thomas Bivens (2006) notes people seek accountability and "want to know who is

---

[1] The PRSA "Member Code of Ethics," last revised in 2000, is available online at: http://www.prsa.org/aboutprsa/ethics/#.U_t_FFZRzwI. Accessed Sept. 4, 2015. For an interesting history of the PRSA code, see Fitzpatrick, K. (2002, Feb) "PRSA Code of Ethics Moves From Enforcement to Inspiration" at: http://connection.ebscohost.com/c/articles/6048100/history-prsas-code-ethics-moves-from-enforcement-inspiration. Accessed Sept. 4, 2015.

responsible for certain actions and who is accountable for the consequences of those actions" (p. 19). Van Hook notes that even though "many people perceive public relations to be something less than respectable," those responsible for internal and external communications in an organization control the flow of both good and bad news to employees, customers, stockholders, and other strategic stakeholders. He also notes public relations people are part of organizational decision making.

About This Book

This book represents a practical guide to ethical decision making tailored specifically to the needs of public relations students and practitioners. We do not spend much time on the day-to-day ethical issues every white-collar worker faces, whether mundane or serious—from whether it's wrong to bring pens home from the office or to sleep with a client or boss. Rather, we focus on issues arising from public relations' role within society, especially the potential to abuse techniques of communication, persuasion, and advocacy.

We trace the development of ethical theory from the ancient Greeks to modern time to give the reader an understanding of the principles that underlie current standards of behavior. But the book's major emphasis is on *practical application* of these theories and principles through the analysis of contemporary cases. Our goal is to guide readers in building a personal framework for ethical reasoning that will enable them to do the following:

- *Recognize the ethical issues at play in the practice of public relations*, including those inherent in business decisions that do not directly involve the public relations function.
- *Analyze the conflicting duties and loyalties at play in these situations*, as well as the likely consequences to all affected publics, so they can choose the best option in their own practice or counsel their clients in their decision making.
- And, finally, *justify their decision and/or counsel in terms that others will understand and ultimately accept.*

Our book fills a gap in currently available literature on the subject, most of which lacks either theoretical grounding or practical application. Unlike other books that focus on the broad field "mass communication," this book focuses solely upon public relations and cites illustrative cases spanning a wide range of its functions.

Although we do not advocate a specific ethical approach, we attempt to give readers sufficient grounding in the major theories of normative ethics to identify the strengths and weaknesses of each, and to construct their own frameworks, appropriate to their circumstances.

The Importance of Ethics

Public relations counselor Bob Dilenschneider has represented a third of the Fortune 500 companies and, from that vantage point, he has concluded that ethics has never been more important. "The desire to succeed at any cost is washing over the world in a relentless wave, flying in the face of ethics and integrity," he warns. "It takes strong willed people to resist it, and there are fewer strong-willed people today than there used to be."[2] Governments have issued stacks of new regulations and imposed layers of additional oversight in response to corporate scandals. And misconduct by leaders of institutions from our colleges and churches to our sports teams and news organizations has severely rocked public confidence. That may be why the 2015 Edelman Trust Barometer shows "an evaporation of trust across all institutions" not only in business but also in government, media, and nongovernmental organizations (NGOs).[3] The practice of public relations is not immune from these forces. In fact, it could be complicit.

Although few have ever perceived public relations to be a highly ethical industry, in recent years its reputation has taken serious hits thanks in no small part to the actions of a few prominent practitioners. For example, Hill & Knowlton prepped the Kuwaiti ambassador's daughter to give false testimony before a Congressional committee in the run-up

---

[2] *Source:* Conversation with Robert Dilenschneider on March 10, 2015.
[3] The Edelman public relations agency has been surveying the public's level of trust in various institutions since 2000. The 2015 survey cited here is available at: http://www.edelman.com/2015-edelman-trust-barometer/. Accessed Sept. 4, 2014.

to the first Gulf War.[4] Ketchum and ConAgra tricked food bloggers into eating Marie Callender's frozen food when they thought they were dining on meals prepared by noted chefs,[5] and two FleishmanHillard executives were jailed for fraudulently billing the Los Angeles Water Department.[6] Not to mention an abundance of unpaid internships that some say are unfair to public relations students, especially when the agencies bill clients for their time.

Theoretical Foundations

According to ethics scholar J.C. Callahan (1988), the formal study of ethics can be divided into four subareas: meta-ethics, descriptive ethics, normative ethics, and applied ethics. **Meta-ethics** concentrates on what morality is by examining the meanings of ethical terms, the nature of ethical judgments, and various types of ethical arguments. **Descriptive ethics**, also known as **comparative ethics**, studies what people believe about morality. **Normative ethics** provides the foundation for decision making through the development of general rules and principles of moral conduct. **Applied ethics** is concerned with using these theoretical norms to solve real-world ethical problems.

The study of ethics can provide a framework for making difficult moral choices at every stage of the decision-making process, from identifying and analyzing ethical issues to weighing and justifying options to resolve them. Inevitably, this process will reveal conflicts among *competing* values and interests. The study of ethics cannot always settle such conflicts, but it can

---

[4] The tearful testimony of the Ambassador's daughter is available on C-SPAN. See http://www.youtube.com/watch?v=LmfVs3WaE9Y Accessed Sept. 4, 2015. Hill & Knowlton's role in preparing her testimony is described in chapter 10 of *Toxic Sludge Is Good For You* (Stauber, J. and Ramdon, S., 2002, Common Courage Press, Monroe, Me.) excerpted online at PRWatch, http://www.prwatch.org/books /tsigfy10.html. Accessed Sept. 4, 2015.

[5] The Gawker website gleefully reported the incident. See Hamilton Nolan, H. (2011, September 7). ConAgra forced to apologize for tricking bloggers into eating ConAgra food, http://gawker.com/5837896/conagra-forced-to-apologize-for-tricking-bloggers-into-eating-conagra-food. Accessed Sept. 4, 2015.

[6] See Spano, J. (2006, May 17). Dowie, aide guilty on all counts in bill scam. *Los Angeles Times*. http://articles.latimes.com/2006/may/17/local/me-dowie17. Accessed July 22, 2015.

provide the tools to unravel them by clarifying such concepts as truth, fairness, respect, integrity, and loyalty. That not only makes it easier to live with our choices but it also makes justifying them easier. As many public relations practitioners have discovered, knowing how to justify an ethical decision is almost as important as the decision itself.

Normative Ethics

Most of the scholarly research exploring public relations ethics has focused on normative ethics. As described in more detail in later chapters, the study of normative ethics has historically concentrated on three areas: *virtue* (ethical behavior depends on moral character), *duty* (actions are right or wrong in themselves), and *consequences* (results determine whether an action is right or wrong).

As we explain in Chapter 3, the study of **virtue** ethics can be traced back to ancient Greece where Socrates (c. 470–399 BCE) said virtue could be identified and practiced. His disciple, Plato (c. 428–348 BCE) encouraged moral conduct even in situations where responsible behavior might be different from societal norms. His student, Aristotle (c. 384–322 BCE) stressed that moral virtue frequently required difficult choices (Blackburn, 2001). This Greek interest in virtue has been credited by some for developing a school of thought concerned with the nature of goodness and self-discipline as advocated by Epictetus (c. 55–135 AD), who stressed individuals must be responsible for their own actions (Plaisance, 2014).

Deontology, or the study of duty-based ethics, judges people by their actions regardless of the consequences and is discussed in greater detail in Chapters 5 and 6. Deontologists believe acts are moral or immoral by their very nature regardless of consequences or outcomes.

This theory's major advocate was Immanuel Kant (1724–1804) a German philosopher who authored the *categorical imperative,* a moral principle he considered absolute and unconditional. For example, he believed it required people to tell the truth even if it resulted in harm to others (Hinman, 2012). At the core of Kant's ethical thinking was his strong belief humans never should treat other people as a means to an end.

Public relations ethics scholar Shannon A. Bowen (2004) sees considerable relevance for public relations in Kant's thesis and has proposed a theoretical model for ethical decision making in public relations that is based upon Kant's categorical imperative and James E. Grunig's two-way symmetrical model of public relations.

Teleology, or the study of consequence-based ethics, focuses on the end result of an act or a decision. Teleological ethics has two basic approaches, *ethical egoism* and *utilitarianism*. Ethical egoists make decisions based on what result is best for their own self-interests. This philosophy dates back to Epicurus (c. 342–271 BCE), who advocated people should do those things that would lead to their own satisfaction.

Utilitarianism, which is covered more completely in Chapter 7, is an ethical philosophy that fosters whatever is best for society as a whole, endeavoring to provide "the greatest happiness for the greatest number." Jeremy Bentham (1748–1832) is recognized as the founder of utilitarianism, a theory also advocated and promoted by John Stuart Mill (1806–1873). More modern versions of utilitarianism focus on either acts or rules. *Rule utilitarianism* is concerned with what rule or action, when followed, will maximize the greatest good for the greatest number. *Act utilitarianism* places little value in precepts, claiming rules such as "thou shalt not kill," "never lie," and so forth only provide rough directions for ethical experiences.

Ethics and Individual Public Relations Practitioners

Kenneth F. Goodpaster and John B. Matthews (1989) claim the desire for ethical behavior has deep roots in the actions of individual people who wish to act responsibly. As one of us has explained previously, this endorses the notion that some individual public relations people might elect to be ethical while others might not (Wright, 1996). As we explain in greater detail in Chapter 11, most people understand clear-cut differences between good and evil, right and wrong, and similar dichotomies. However, when ethical decision making comes down to the bottom line, the final arbiter in separating right from wrong or good from evil is the free will of the individual decision maker.

Goodpaster and Matthews maintain that the notion of ethical *responsibility* has three meanings: who is to blame, what has to be done, and what we think of someone's moral reasoning. The first meaning of responsibility concerns who is the cause of an action or event, (i.e., who is answerable for it). The second meaning concerns what standards or social norms one should be following. This most often occurs when individuals are responsible to others: lawyers to clients, physicians to patients; or, in the communication context, journalists to their readers and public relations managers to their organizations, their clients, or the public at large. The third meaning reflects our judgment that an individual has made reliable and trustworthy moral decisions.

Ethics and Decision Making

The topic of ethics has attracted a good deal of attention throughout the public relations field over the past few decades perhaps because practitioners frequently are bombarded with many diverse ethical situations and too few of them have developed frameworks for making ethical judgments. Ethical decision making depends on both the decision-making process and on the decision makers—their experience, intelligence, and integrity.

Much of the applied communication and ethics literature centers on the role of the decision maker in ethical behavior, and an important aspect of many public relations jobs is trying to help management make business decisions that have ethical implications. In this process, the ethical question might be whether or not to *do* something as much as whether or not to say something. Unfortunately, for some it is easy to say nothing and later blame the unethical results on somebody else's decision. When he was Chairman and CEO of the Bank of America, Dick Rosenberg told an audience of corporate public relations professionals, "We don't shoot people for bringing us bad news; we shoot them for delivering it too late."[7] This view suggests that public relations executives who can head off serious problems before they blow up in the company's face, surface in the news media or blogs, or ruin an individual's reputation are two steps ahead of the game.

---

[7] Rosenberg, R. (1991, Sept. 20). Remarks to the San Francisco Academy. San Francisco, CA.

Unfortunately, the people who make the decisions in American business do not always possess responsible moral judgments. Psychologist and management consultant Saul Gellerman (1998) lists four reasons why managers do things that ultimately can inflict considerable harm on their organizations. They are as follows:

1. A belief that the activity is within reasonable ethical limits—that is, that it is not "really" illegal or immoral.
2. A belief that the activity is in the individual's or the organization's best interests and that the manager would somehow be expected to undertake the activity.
3. A belief that the activity is "safe" and will never be found out or publicized.
4. A belief that because the activity helps the organization the company will condone it and even protect the manager.

Harvard business school professor Kenneth R. Andrews (1989) contends that ethical decisions require three qualities that individuals can identify and develop. These are given below:

1. Competence to recognize ethical issues and to think through the consequences of alternative resolutions.
2. Self-confidence to seek out different points of view and then to decide what is right at a given place and time, in a particular set of relationships and circumstances.
3. "Tough-mindedness," which is the willingness to make decisions when all that needs to be known cannot be known and when the questions that press for answers have no established and incontrovertible solutions (p. 2).

Some Basic Questions

As we said earlier, most people understand the clear-cut differences in moral choice. They can recognize and decide what is good or evil, right or wrong, honest or dishonest. Nevertheless, many in our society assume that communication practitioners believe they can act unethically as long as they resolve conflicting claims in their own hearts and minds. That perception may reflect the fact that most people—in and out of public relations—do often rationalize questionable behavior. For example, one way or another, most people break some law at least once a day. The speed limit is 65 miles per hour but a person drives 72 ("everyone's doing it; it would be unsafe to do otherwise"). People jaywalk ("no traffic, why walk to the corner and then back?"). Healthy people sometimes park their cars in places reserved for handicapped drivers.

Furthermore, merely breaking the law is not necessarily equivalent to acting unethically. Sometimes *adhering* to the law can be unethical, as examples of Martin Luther King, Jr., and Mahatma Gandhi illustrate. Drawing the line is not always cut and dry. And in some situations deciding what is ethical can be perplexing. For example, food industry consultant Ron Paul (1994) pointed out that, although the fast-food industry is frequently called unethical for producing meals high in fat and cholesterol and encouraging obesity, nobody forces people to eat its products. However, sociologist George Ritzer (2014) suggests economic realities might force lower income families to eat unhealthy fast food. Complicating matters further, in recent years, retailers have been accused of "vanity sizing," by changing labels on "extra-large" sized clothes to "large" or "medium" so customers will ignore the reality they are gaining weight. Is that unethical?

Public Relations Codes of Ethics

As we address in greater detail in Chapter 12, one way public relations associations have responded to ethical concerns is with formalized codes of ethics. However, as public relations scholars Scott Cutlip, Allen Center, and Glen Broom (1985) have argued, the enforcement of these codes of conduct is uneven and infrequent. Also, as James E. Grunig and Todd Hunt (1984) explain, many public relations people do not belong to professional associations and have no membership obligations to uphold codes of ethics.

Mini-Case[8]

The case of a noted Detroit-based public relations person clearly illustrates the lack of enforcement quotient. In 1986, Tony Franco, the President and CEO of Anthony M. Franco, Inc., Detroit's largest independent public relations firm, held the highest elected office in PRSA. Today that position is called, "chairman" but in 1986 it was "president." Mr. Franco enjoyed a strong reputation for social responsibility and charitable giving. For example, he donated $1.2 million to St. Joseph Mercy Oakland Hospital in Pontiac, Michigan. But a number of concerns surfaced after a petition was filed accusing him of various violations of PRSA's Code of Ethics during his presidential year. Rather than face possible disciplinary action by the PRSA committee responsible for managing the association's code of conduct, Mr. Franco immediately resigned his membership in PRSA, including the presidency. But if he had been a medical doctor, an attorney licensed to practice law, or someone from most of the other more traditional professions, he could not have so easily avoided scrutiny of his actions and being found guilty of violating the code of conduct probably would have led to some kind of professional suspension. However, since his occupation was public relations, Mr. Franco continued to practice and his agency remained highly successful. He retired in 1994 and sold his firm, passing away in 2002. Today the Franco Public Relations Group is Detroit's most successful, independent public relations agency.

Public Relations and Professionalism

The Franco example provides a good transition into the final point we will address briefly in this first chapter: the question of whether or not public relations is a "profession," and whether or not those who practice public relations are "professionals." Scholarly literature has plenty to say about defining a profession. Medicine and law lead the list of the most

---

[8] This mini-case was developed from "A quarter century of contributions." *Crain's Detroit Business.* May 2, 2010. Accessed September 4, 2014, at http://www. crainsdetroit.com/article/20100502/SUB01/100439980/a-quarter-century-of-contributions.

elite of the "traditional professions" (Williams, 2008, January 6). Scholars such as A.M. Carr-Sanders and P.A. Wilson (1933), Everett C. Hughes (1965), Myron Liberman (1956), and Morris L. Cogan (1955) generally include the clergy. Lieberman (1956, pp. 2–6) claims eight criteria distinguish professions from occupations:

1. A profession must perform unique and essential services.
2. It must emphasize intellectual techniques.
3. It must have a long period of specialized training to acquire a systematic body of knowledge based on research.
4. It must be given a broad range of autonomy.
5. Its practitioners must accept broad, personal responsibility for judgments and actions.
6. It must place greater emphasis on service than on private economic gain.
7. It must develop a comprehensive self-governing organization.
8. It must have a code of ethics which has been clarified and interpreted by concrete cases.

It would be difficult to argue public relations meets all of these requirements. For example, there is no comprehensive self-governing organization for public relations as there is for medicine and law. At best and in actual practice, public relations is what Abraham Flexner (1915, June 26) termed a "semi-profession," an occupation that meets some, but not all, of the criteria for a true profession. But rather than considering some occupations "professions" and others "trades," we contend the question of professionalism should be asked in terms of individuals and not entire groups of people practicing an occupation. This is to agree with Howard M. Vollmer and Donald L. Mills (1966) who advocate their concept of "professionalization" pointing out there are some practitioners of every occupation who act as professionals and there are others who do not, something we will explore more fully in the following chapters.

Although there are "public relations professionals" who function effectively and ethically, there also are people who practice public relations in a less than professional manner. That is why throughout this book we rarely use the term "public relations professional" to identify those who work in public relations, preferring terms such as "practitioner," or "manager."

In the end, what separates public relations professionals from mere practitioners is an abiding concern with the very topic of this book—how to practice their craft without losing their souls. One dictionary definition of "soul" is "a person's deeply felt moral and emotional nature."[9] Anthropologists might characterize such feelings as evolutionary adaptations to enhance group survival in a threatening world; believers, as the God-given spark of immortal life. But atheist and believer alike recognize the deepest of those feelings in our lifelong search for meaning.

New York Times columnist David Brooks calls the search for meaning "one of the few phrases acceptable in modern parlance to describe a fundamentally spiritual need." But he cautions it is not the "warm tingling" we get when we feel particularly significant and meaningful. "If we look at the people in history who achieved great things," he points out, "it wasn't because they wanted to bathe luxuriously in their own sense of meaningfulness. They subscribed to moral systems—whether secular or religious—that recommended specific ways of being, and had specific structures of what is right and wrong, and had specific disciplines about how you might get better over time."[10] That is the source of true meaning.

It is the search for meaning that separates professional from practitioner. Practitioners find meaning in whatever enhances themselves, whatever produces that tingly feeling. Professionals find meaning *outside* themselves. John Gardner perhaps described it best:

> *Meaning is not something you stumble across, like the answer to a riddle or the prize in a treasure hunt. Meaning is something you*

---

[9] Merriam-Webster Online Dictionary. (n.d.). http://www.merriam-webster.com/dictionary/soul

[10] Brooks, D. (2015, January 5). The problem with meaning. *New York Times.* http://www.nytimes.com/2015/01/06/opinion/david-brooks-the-problem-with-meaning.html. Accessed July 22, 2015.

build into your life. You build it out of your own past, out of your affections and loyalties, out of the experience of humankind as it is passed on to you, out of your own talent and understanding, out of the things you believe in, out of the things and people you love, out of the values for which you are willing to sacrifice something.[11]

We hope in these pages to connect you with some of humankind's experience in exploring these questions of right and wrong, good and bad. We hope to put you in closer touch with your own values and beliefs. And in the process, we hope to give you the opportunity to discover the true meaning of your practice of public relations.

---

[11] From "Personal Renewal," a speech John Gardner delivered to McKinsey & Company in Phoenix, AZ., on November 10, 1990. See: http://www.pbs.org /johngardner/sections/writings_speech_1.html. Accessed July 22, 2015.

CHAPTER 2

Is Public Relations Inherently Unethical?

Edward Bernays is widely considered the "father of public relations," but his daughter Anne feels few sisterly impulses toward the trade. "Public Relations has got to be the longest four-letter word of the 20th century," she has written. "I see it as a powerful and often useful device but one far more like a gun than a hammer." She considers public relations people "the tireless, not to say somewhat paranoid, guardians of our economic, financial and social status quo." She notes public relations enables corporate interests "to control the masses' behavior without their knowledge," through a maneuver her father termed "the engineering of consent, a bone-chilling phrase if there ever was one." In short, Ms. Bernays considers public relations "un-American."[1]

Indeed, whether used as noun or verb, the term "PR" carries so many negative connotations, we have studiously avoided its use in this book. But before tackling public relations ethics head-on, we should consider the bedrock question implicit in Ms. Bernays's assessment—is public relations inherently unethical? Are ethics and public relations mutually exclusive, like ethical embezzlement?

Any occupation can be practiced unethically. Health care professionals are generally regarded as highly ethical. They have topped the list since Gallup started surveying people about the ethical standards of various occupations back in 1999.[2] Yet there are more nurses and doctors in

---

[1] Ms. Bernays expressed these thoughts about public relations in her review of Stuart Ewen's history of the practice. Bernays, A. (1996, December 1). Review of PR: A social history of spin (by Stuart Ewen). *Los Angeles Times.* http://articles.latimes.com /1996-12-01/books/bk-4546_1_stuart-ewen. Accessed July 22, 2015.

[2] Gallup's latest poll on the ethics of different occupations was in 2013. See Gallup. (2013, December 13). http://www.gallup.com/poll/166298/honesty-ethics-rating-clergy-slides-new-low.aspx. Accessed July 22, 2015.

jail than public relations people. Forty-five nurses and doctors were convicted of serial murder between 1970 and 2006 (Yorker et al., 2006). But no one is saying the practice of medicine is inherently unethical. With just two public relations people serving time in recent years (for overbilling the City of Los Angeles Water Department), public relations has to rank as one of the most law-abiding occupations around.

Of course, not everything legal is ethical. To many, public relations operates in the dimly lit corners of commerce through whispers, innuendo, and misdirection. And because it works best when unseen, it naturally raises suspicion. People tend to be wary of any occupation dedicated to making them think or act in a certain way. Popular conceptions of public relations range from the relatively benign, as in ginning up publicity, to the more nefarious, as in spreading disinformation. On a good day, public relations is frivolous; on a bad day, evil.

Social Criticism

A long line of philosophers and social critics see more evil days than good. Writer and political activist John Stauber (2002, pp. 100–101), for example, tells the story of a phone call he received from a representative of the Water Environment Federation who was alarmed when she heard he was writing a book about the public relations industry entitled *Toxic Sludge Is Good for You*. She explained that sewage sludge is not toxic when properly treated and it is not called sludge anymore. It is now called "biosolids, a natural organic fertilizer." In fact, she said, the Environmental Protection Agency had funded an educational program to convince farmers to spread it on their fields. Indeed, the Water Environment Federation—formerly known as the Federation of Sewage Works Associations—had run a contest to come up with a name for treated sludge that can legally be used as fertilizer. They even managed to get the new name into the dictionary without any reference to this "sludge" business.[3] "There really is a campaign telling us toxic sludge is good for us," Stauber marveled.

---

[3] Dictionary.com (n.d.) lists the definition of "biosolids" as follows: bi-o-sol-ids. [bahy-oh-sol-idz] plural noun, nutrient-rich organic materials obtained from wastewater treatment and used beneficially, as for fertilizer.

No wonder public relations people are known as "spin doctors," "flacks," "handlers," and "fixers." One academic study suggests the average American considers most public relations practitioners "smart, friendly liars."[4] Another indicates seven out of ten people do not trust public relations people.[5]

Compounding the problem, anyone can hang out a shingle offering to provide "public relations" services. "The whole PR industry is lambasted for the actions of the least of us," agency CEO Richard Edelman warns. "The democratization of the media means a lot of people are doing our kind of work without being steeped in the industry's history, culture, and standards. That's a reputational problem; worse, we have to be careful that everyone in the industry doesn't sink to the lowest common denominator."[6] There is reason to fear that may already be happening.

As a result, even authentic public relations practitioners go by as many aliases as a Florida swampland developer. They are variously "reputation managers," "public affairs officers," "information directors," "communications consultants," or "relationship managers." Many at the top of the field have even abandoned the moniker entirely, christening themselves "Chief Communications Officers" or "CCOs" to grease their way into the suite of corporate chiefs who reign over finance, law, marketing, and other corporate domains.

One scholar suggests this rebranding reveals a disconnection between what public relations people claim to do within an organization and the chores they actually perform. Fiona Campbell (2010), a graduate student in communications at the University of Hertfordshire, interviewed public

---

[4] Two professors at Texas Tech University came to this conclusion after polling public attitudes about public relations. See Watson, G. (2014, October 27). Survey: Public relations reps are knowledgeable but also unethical. *Texas Tech Today.* http://today.ttu.edu/2014/10/survey-public-relations-reps-are-knowledgeable-but-also-unethical/. Accessed July 22, 2015.

[5] A survey commissioned by industry publication *PRWeek* came to this conclusion. See Griggs, I., & Aron, I. (2015, March 19). PR in the dock: Nearly 70% of the general public does not trust the industry. *PRWeek.* http://www.prweek.com/article/1339167/pr-dock-nearly-70-per-cent-general-public-does-not-trust-industry (Subscription required). Accessed July 22, 2015.

[6] *Source:* conversation with Richard Edelman on April 30, 2015.

relations people while looking for a thesis topic. She heard a recurring theme in the stories they told—a lot of general managers were sticking public relations people with the task of cleaning up when a business decision went wrong or had bad consequences. Needing to believe in their client organization, but unable to justify it to themselves, much less to others, Campbell concluded public relations practitioners suffer from an "endemic" case of cognitive dissonance. "They carry the pain of their organization's misbehavior," she wrote, "with no realistic way to unload it."

Media Skepticism

Other observers are less sympathetic and give public relations people no credit for at least being well intentioned. Nancy Solomon, a reporter for public radio in New York City, once described crisis communications as "obscuring facts and protecting your client."[7]

The highly respected *Economist* magazine has accused public relations people of issuing "tendentious bumf" for more than a century.[8] The late David Carr, *New York Times* columnist and Boston University journalism professor, called it "slop."[9] Whatever, it nicely characterizes the news media's attitude toward public relations people and what they do. It is a relationship marked by mutual dependency and mutual contempt. Journalists resent having to deal with "handlers" and "mouthpieces." Public relations people regard journalists with a mix of fear and envy.

Journalists and public relations people are always on a perpetually recurring first date. Even when, over time, they become comfortable with each other as individuals, they are suspicious of each other's motives. The journalist wants a story; the public relations person wants it to be favorable to the client. Those do not have to be mutually exclusive

---

[7] Ms. Solomon was discussing efforts by New Jersey governor Chris Christie's public relations staff to distance him from accusations he had a hand in closing lanes to the George Washington bridge to punish a local mayor for not endorsing his candidacy for re-election. March 27, 2014.

[8] See Rise of the Image Men. (2010, December 16). *The Economist.* http://www .economist.com/node/17722733. Accessed July 22, 2015.

[9] See Carr, D. (2012, January 29). A Glimpse of Murdoch Unbound. *The New York Times.* http://www.nytimes.com/2012/01/30/business/media/twitter-gives-glimpse-into-rupert-murdochs-mind.html

goals; but they almost always get in each other's way. One of us became good friends with a prominent financial columnist. In researching this book, we asked him what ethical principle he thought public relations people followed. "Don't get caught," he said. This, from a friend.

Indeed most journalists work hard to maintain emotional distance from public relations people. "Public relations people work on behalf of corporations, to further those corporations' interests," writes Hamilton Nolan, the longest-tenured (and most acerbic) writer at the Gawker website.

> *"If your sympathy for the PR person stifles your impulse to criticize the PR person's client, then the corporation wins. This, indeed, is what companies are buying with all of that money that they spend on spokespeople: human sympathy. …if journalists stop pointing out the craven, dishonest nature of PR, we are not doing anyone any favors. That would be doing exactly what the corporations want."*[10]

If journalists have a siege mentality toward public relations people, it may be because according to the U.S. Department of Labor, they're outnumbered nearly five to one. Plus, their salaries are an average 40 percent lower.[11] And thanks to the Internet, they no longer control access to a brand's customers. This creates an extraordinary opportunity for public relations practitioners, but it also presents an ethical dilemma. "In a world of dispersed authority and democratized media," agency CEO Richard Edelman told us, "PR practitioners have greater responsibility to check their facts with third party experts, because we are no longer always going through a reporter's filter."[12]

Poisoning Public Discourse

Some criticism of public relations reflects more than concern about factual accuracy, as important as that is. Some social critics believe large

---

[10] Nolan, H. (2014, June 12) Do PR people deserve our sympathy?, Gawker http://gawker.com/do-pr-people-deserve-our-sympathy-1589842837

[11] See: "Occupational Employment and Wages, May 2014," U.S. Bureau of Labor Statistics, Washington, D.C., March 25, 2015. http://www.bls.gov/news.release/pdf/ocwage.pdf

[12] *Source:* conversation with Richard Edelman on April 30, 2015.

corporations use public relations to accumulate and exercise political, social, and economic power. Public Relations enables them to control the agenda of public discourse and the framework within which it takes place. Rather than fostering open debate on matters of public interest, public relations seeks to nip emerging issues in the bud, before they *become* the subject of broad debate. Failing that, it tries to redirect or obfuscate the discussion by raising side issues or reframing the question. And, of course, whenever possible it tries to accomplish all this through trusted third parties in a strategy called "Third Party Endorsement" (Bowen et al., 2010). In all these ways, corporations have systematically undermined democracy and created a consumer society that worships false images and harbors unattainable, self-centered aspirations. In this battle, advertising has been the visible artillery; public relations, the black ops.

That's why critics and activists like Naomi Klein (2001, May–June) have attempted "a radical reclaiming of the commons." When they say they want to "take back the streets," they really mean they want to wrest control of their lives from embedded corporate interests. Ironically, in furtherance of that goal, they have no compunction about using the very public relations techniques they consider so unethical in the hands of corporations. Public relations in the service of economic, ecological, and social justice, they believe, is no vice. Public relations is not inherently unethical, just the powerful corporations that use it to serve their greedy self-interest.

But other critics take an even dimmer view of public relations. For example, sociologist and philosopher Jürgen Habermas (1984, 1987; see, Wehmeir, 2013) believes corporations and politicians have so dominated and reshaped the "public sphere" individuals are little more than human pinballs, careening off unseen flippers and bumpers. He considers public relations an instrument of the privileged. And he believes it is a twisted instrument, even in more virtuous hands. Habermas says strategic communication between any organization and its publics is conscious deception, since its "strategic purpose" is always hidden and seldom amenable to meaningful change or compromise.[13]

---

[13] Habermas explained his theory of "communicative action" in two books. *The Theory of Communicative Action: Volume 1, Reason and the Rationalization of Society*

At best, corporations pollute the public sphere with pseudo-events and phony sound bites. At worse, they subvert the very process of reasoned, respectful discourse. And even when they appear to be making concessions in response to criticism, it is all part of a cynical exercise to maintain their dominance by undermining their opponents' arguments (Weaver et al., 1996). The individual—even individuals acting in concert—are no match for corporations. It's simply not a fair fight; it's socially irresponsible.

Respected public relations scholars like Jacquie L'Etang (2004, pp. 53–67) have even questioned the morality of so-called "corporate responsibility programs," whose aim might be to "look good," without actually "being good" in a morally stringent way. Considerations of self-interest suck the ethical virtue out of an act, turning it into a purely reciprocal transaction. Furthermore, she suggests that in all its functions, "the ethics of public relations are to a large degree governed by its paymasters," making the suggestion that public relations is the "conscience of a company" hopelessly naïve.

Hidden Persuasion

Many critics maintain that, even when public relations practitioners are open about their persuasive intent, they use techniques with an element of deceit. They do not simply present alternative arguments. They exploit cognitive processes that bypass rational thought and manipulate people on an emotional and symbolic level, treating them as mere tools in achieving a purpose that may not even be in their own interest. As a result, public relations, by its very nature, has an alienating effect.

To many public relations people, that seems to condemn the practice by giving it more credit than it deserves. But critics know that influencing people's behavior can be as simple as how a question or issue is phrased. For example, psychologist Daniel Kahneman has been studying how we make decisions for more than 50 years. In one experiment

---

(Beacon Press, 1984) and *Theory of Communicative Action: Volume 2, Lifeworld and Reason—A Critique of Fundamentalist Reason* (Beacon Press, 1987). For an excellent summary of his views, see "Habermas, Jurgen and Public Relations," Stephen Wehmeir, pp. 410–411, *The Encyclopedia of Public Relations*, edited by Robert Heath, Sage Publications, 2013.

(2011, pp. 436–437), he asked participants to imagine that a deadly disease affects 600 people. There is a treatment, but it is risky with a 33 percent chance of saving all 600 people and a 66 percent chance of saving no one. Nearly three-quarters of the participants still thought it was a good bet. But when he changed the odds to a 33 percent chance that no one would die and a 66 percent chance that they all would, the number agreeing dropped to 22 percent.

The outcomes, of course, are identical. But the second version exploited the fact that people naturally want to avoid risk. Frame an argument to highlight risk and you are playing a winning hand. Kahneman and his research partner Amos Tversky called the phenomenon "risk aversion," and it is just one of a catalog of cognitive illusions that distort our perception of reality and skew our judgment.[3] For example, we have a natural tendency to make decisions based solely on the information at hand (availability bias), to discount evidence inconsistent with preconceived notions (confirmation bias), and to give greater weight to the first data we uncover (anchoring bias). Many of these mental shortcuts are evolutionary adaptations that enabled our ancestors to survive in snake-infested jungles, but have nothing to do with logic. With all this, Kahneman and Tversky put a stake in the heart of *homo economicus*, the notion that people always act in their own rational self-interest. As bounty for dispatching that hoary myth, Kahneman received the Nobel Prize in economics in 2002. (Tversky had passed away before the prize was awarded and was not eligible.)[14]

Economists might have been late to the party, but public relations practitioners have been paying attention to the work of cognitive and social scientists for more than a century. Edward Bernays, a nephew of Sigmund Freud, was an avid student of the latest thinking in psychology and sociology. Hired by the American Tobacco Company to increase the

---

[14] Kahneman and Tversky first presented their theory in a scholarly article. See Kahneman, D. and Tversky, A, (1970, March–April), Prospect Theory: An Analysis of Decision Under Risk, *Econometrica*, Vol. 47, No. 2, pp. 263–292. Available online at http://pages.uoregon.edu/harbaugh/Readings/GBE/Risk/Kahneman%201 979%20E,%20Prospect%20Theory.pdf. Kahneman later expanded on this and other "cognitive illusions" in his best-selling book *Thinking Fast and Slow* (Farrar, Straus, & Giroux, 2011).

number of female smokers, he consulted a psychoanalyst who told him cigarettes were an unconscious symbol of male dominance, specifically the penis. So Bernays arranged for a group of debutantes to march in New York's Easter Parade smoking cigarettes, which he billed as "Torches of Freedom." The resulting newspaper publicity associated smoking with the suffragette movement to secure a woman's right to vote (Brandt, 1996). Ultimately, Bernays made it respectable for women to smoke. His practice of "engineering consent" was based on painstaking research into the public's deepest attitudes and desires. He "created news," leveraging symbols and feelings the public is predisposed to embrace.

Was it manipulative? Certainly. Was it unethical? Bernays, who lived to be 103, apologized later in life for his role in promoting tobacco products. But you will decide how ethical his techniques were for yourself in the following pages. As corny as the "Torches of Freedom" might seem today, many public relations critics see Bernays's strategies reflected in the tradecraft of today's public relations practitioners.

Impact On Democracy

But even setting particular techniques of persuasion aside, Stewart Ewen (1996, pp. 409–410) asks a series of questions at the very end of his history of public relations that get at the heart of the issue:

- Can there be democracy when public agendas are routinely predetermined by "unseen engineers"?
- Can there be democracy when the tools of communication are neither democratically distributed nor democratically controlled?
- Can there be democracy in a society in which emotional appeals overwhelm reason, where the image is routinely employed to overwhelm thought?

Ewen posed those questions in 1996, when the Internet was just leaving the lab and making its way into people's homes with the raucous sound of dial-up connections. One might ask whether much has changed in

today's hyper-networked broadband society, where everyone is a potential publisher and consumers have near total control of the information
that reaches them.

Questions of Right and Wrong

Public relations, by definition, is bound up in questions of right and
wrong. By its very nature the practice involves an exchange between two
parties that is almost always intended to affect one party's attitudes or
behavior. Every professional public relations person we have known strives
to act ethically. None of them think of themselves as liars and cheats. Yet,
a surprising number share a rather cynical view of their industry. According to a 2010 study, nearly three-quarters say, "PR people *lie* in the course
of their work." Only about a third said, "The PR industry is fundamentally honest."[15] And, truth be told, at some point, even the best of us blunder
into unethical territory without realizing it, usually at the end of a series of
small compromises that can each be justified on its own merits. For example, outright lying is seldom an issue, but shading the truth so clients
are in the best possible light is standard operating procedure.

Ironically, many public relations people like to think of themselves as
the consumer's advocate within their companies, whether adopting an
outsider's perspective or trying to recast *corporatese* into everyday speech.
At their most pious, they fancy themselves the "corporate conscience;" in
day-to-day practice, they like to play devil's advocate. But only a rare few
are in the room when policy is set and major decisions are made. We
believe public relations people *should* be in that room. But they should
not expect to get there on the strength of their title or writing skills. They
have to earn a place at the decision-making table by demonstrating a rig-
orous approach to ethical reasoning in a business context.

In practical terms, that often means overcoming the cognitive illusions Kahneman and Tversky (1970) warned about. For example, we
naturally have greater empathy for people close to us than for strangers.

---

[15] Sundhaman, A. (2010, February 3). PR professionals believe "spin" is entrenched
in industry, survey shows. *PRWeek*. http://www.prweek.com/article/981450/pr-
professionals-believe-spin-entrenched-industry-survey-shows. Accessed July 22, 2015.

We are hesitant to rock the boat by questioning long-standing conduct that appears to be accepted or at least condoned by the people closest to us. We give greater weight to the most recent data we saw or to the data that is easiest to get. And, our attention is selective, quick to focus on information that confirms our beliefs, and blind to anything that contradicts them.

The sheer pace of corporate life magnifies the power of these gut instincts and cognitive distortions. Under the pressure of client expectations and in the rush of events, we are more inclined to ask, "will it work?" than "is it right?" Introspection is not prized. Few reflect on the import of their decisions and actions. In fact, many executives pride themselves on never looking back once they have taken action. Not only is there no time, there is not much to gain. Postmortems are a sure sign you are dead.

Besides, acting ethically is not easy. It can cost a sale, a promotion, or even one's job. It can ruin friendships, build a reputation of school-marmy-ness, and alienate the powers that be. Compromises can be very seductive, especially if "everyone is doing it." As one failed entrepreneur who was sued for bankruptcy fraud put it, "Let's face it, if it were easy to be ethical, more people would do it more often" (Latman, 2012, p. 124).

Ethical Tools

Furthermore, were most public relations people given the opportunity to consider the ethical implications of their behavior, they would have very few tools with which to work. Most corporate ethics courses focus on understanding a published *code of conduct*. That is fine as far as it goes. But companies like Enron and WorldCom had beautifully written values statements and codes of conduct. Still their leaders wound up in jail, most of their employees without jobs or pensions, and their investors with zip.

As one might expect, the major public relations associations do a fair job of articulating ethical standards relevant to the practice—e.g., honesty, loyalty, and fairness. But they provide little guidance in balancing competing standards. For example, the Public Relations Society of

America (PRSA) defines "loyalty" this way: "We are faithful to those we represent, while honoring our obligation to serve the public interest."[16] Well, what if the client's interests conflict with the public's? Which is more important—loyalty or fairness? Truth or privacy? And how do you define truth? Is it everything that can be said on a subject or just the parts that suit the client? When is it allowed, required, or wrong to reveal confidences? Are ethical principles the same everywhere around the world or do they vary by culture?

Even on a topic as practical as slipping a few bucks to a reporter to get better coverage, referred to as "Pay For Play" or "PFP" in the business, the PRSA is curiously ambivalent, first taking a hard stand that it is improper, then hedging a bit, declaring, "There are gray areas, in that definitions of ethical impropriety may vary widely between industries, countries and individuals, and PFP is condoned and expected in many cultures."[17]

The PR Council, formerly known as the Council of PR Firms, an association of the largest public relations agencies in the United States, encourages its members to put their employees through an ethics course of its design. But when presented with a truly thorny dilemma, the recommended solution is to check with a "senior agency executive." But what's the senior executive to do?

In the workshops we have taught over the years, we have discovered that, while public relations people know something like lying is unethical, even the most senior and experienced have great difficulty explaining *why* with any precision. And it is amazing how elastic concepts such as truth, respect, fairness, and loyalty can be. If you cannot explain *why* something is wrong, the likelihood you will recognize it—much less avoid it—declines precipitously. And the likelihood you will interpret it rather loosely increases even more steeply.

But every major public relations crisis of recent years was rooted in an ethical lapse. Even problems that started as an Act of God became a

---

[16] The PRSA "Member Code of Ethics" is available online at: http://www.prsa.org /aboutprsa/ethics/#.U_t_FFZRzwI. Accessed Sept. 4, 2015.

[17] PRSA. (2009, October 9). *Ethical Standards Advisory PS-9.* http://www.prsa.org /AboutPRSA/Ethics/EthicalStandardsAdvisories/Documents/PSA-09.pdf. Accessed on July 22, 2015.

crisis because someone did not act ethically. Take Carnival Cruise Lines. An engine fire is an accident. But when it happens multiple times, you have to wonder if the company is not acting imprudently without due care for its customers.

Ethical Theory

Few senior public relations executives have studied ethical theory. And if they have, it is probably a distant memory that carries much less weight than the pressures of meeting budget, satisfying demanding clients, and getting through the day without acid reflux. What public relations people at every level need is a framework for reasoning that will help them recognize an ethical issue when it arises and then analyze it in terms of their own values, professional responsibilities, and the consequences for everyone affected. Research has shown that people typically make poor ethical decisions when they are under pressure. Unfortunately, public relations is a demanding occupation and ethical dilemmas are stressful by definition. But having thought through a framework for ethical reasoning beforehand can help alleviate the stress and make it easier to make good decisions.

That said, we are not presumptuous enough to pretend we have solved all the mysteries of right and wrong in the practice of public relations. Much of the time, the ethical choices public relations practitioners face do not involve choosing between good and bad, but between terrible and worse. Even most of the conclusions in this book are provisional, awaiting the discovery of new insights into human behavior and a clearer unraveling of intertwined duties, motivations, and consequences. We believe that, while the principles of ethics and morality are unchangeable and universal, our human understanding of them is fragile and evolving.

Summary

Ethics have forward motion. What we considered "settled" three centuries ago—or in some instances, three decades ago—is no longer thought to be true. Some parts of the developing world are decades behind others in their understanding of such basic issues as the fair treatment of women. Meanwhile, some parts of the developing world are decades ahead of developed countries in their understanding of the common good and the sacredness of the environment.

So this is less a catechism of right and wrong in the practice of public relations than a guide to constructing a framework for figuring it out in the heat of battle. We cannot promise that applying the lessons in this book will always produce the one, infallible and universally accepted answer to every ethical dilemma. But it will enable thoughtful readers to explain and justify their decisions. And that may help bring some logical consistency to the sequence of ethical decisions they make. These days, that would be a major advance. It might even help answer the question we asked at the beginning of this chapter. Is public relations inherently unethical?

In the next chapter, we will explore the ethical principles that have guided people in living a "good life" for millennia. We will ask how age-old concepts like "virtue" and "character" are relevant to modern life and, in particular, to the practice of public relations. That too will require some historical perspective. We won't go back quite so far in the history of public relations, but we will consider how the practice evolved through the 20th century, noting subtle changes in purpose as it responded—and contributed—to social change.

CHAPTER 3

Virtue and Character

From the time our ancestors dropped from the trees and began walking across the savannah on two legs to the day our great-grandchildren post their first Tweet, our understanding of ethics will have followed a circuitous path from gut to brain.

Our ancestors developed an evolutionary adaptation that enabled them to live relatively peacefully in small, cooperating groups—rudimentary feelings that delighted or disturbed them and that they came to identify with right and wrong, good and bad. Harming another human being—generally wrong. Caring for younger or weaker members of the tribe—generally right. Dividing hunting spoils fairly—good. Freeloaders who do not pull their weight—bad.

Over time, different religions and civilizations elaborated and codified these gut feelings, giving them greater specificity, nuance, and authority. But they retained a striking commonality. *The Golden Rule*, for example—"Do unto others as you would have them do unto you"—shows up in practically every major religion and is the basis for Judeo-Christian ethics.

Historical Development

Nevertheless, a few obstinate souls refused to settle for "the gods ordained it" as justification for ethical precepts. They wanted to understand *why* it is wrong to lie, cheat, steal, or murder. Like their contemporaries who sought to understand the reasons behind the changing of the seasons and the movements of the stars, they wanted to unveil the organizing principles of ethical beliefs.

Coincidentally, the sixth to second centuries Before the Common Era (BCE) saw a flourishing of ethical thought in east and west. For example, in what is now Nepal and India, a prince-turned-monk named Guatama Buddah, or the Enlightened One (c. 563–483 BCE), taught that a good life followed a "Middle Path" between self-indulgence and self-mortification. In China, an itinerant scholar named Kong Fuzi, "Master Kong," or as we know him, "Confucius" (551–479 BCE), taught that a good life was built on the practice of virtue, righteousness, and humaneness. And in Athens a small city-state on the Ionian Peninsula, three successive generations of Greek scholars plowed the same philosophical fields over a period of roughly 150 years.

Western Ethical Thought

In exploring the meaning of a good life, Socrates (c. 470–399 BCE), Plato (c. 437–347 BCE), and Aristotle (c. 384–322 BCE) gave us an entire system of thinking about life's biggest questions. And in the process, they shaped more than two millennia of Western civilization, which will be the primary focus of our ethical exploration.

Born to families of means, Socrates, Plato, and Aristotle were free to spend time in the *agora*, or covered market, arguing about the meaning of life. Eventually, they changed the market from a place to sell vegetables, olive oil, and animal hides to a marketplace of ideas—the first *lycea*, the progenitor of today's universities. Plato was Socrates's prize student; Aristotle, his. And all three were dedicated to the love of wisdom, in Greek, φιλοσοφία or "philosophy."

Not surprisingly, they each spent a lot of time discussing the nature of what is "good." Socrates, in particular, thought something is "good," not because the gods say it is, but because it helps make us better and happier people. We no longer needed to seek divine revelation to understand what is good or bad. We could figure it out.

Socrates was not dissing the gods. On the contrary, as interpreted by Plato, he believed God created the world following a perfect blueprint, but he used imperfect material. Thus, the world—and each of us—is flawed, but we have the potential to perfect ourselves according to the original blueprint. Plato believed that is the goal of ethics.

Although Aristotle disagreed with many of Plato's ideas, he picked up on his ethical inquiry, asking in particular, "What defines a good life?" Almost everything he came up with turned out to be a means to something else. Honor, pleasure, money, or any other good he could imagine was only desirable because it led to something else he called εὐδαιμονία. Eudaemonia was originally translated as "happiness," but is now considered to mean our flourishing as human beings.

Only human flourishing, or *eudaemonia*, is an end in itself and not a means of attaining some other good. To Aristotle, it was the ultimate purpose of life, the goal by which a life should be measured. Of course, that led to another question—how could we achieve true happiness, the kind that isn't just a way station to something else? Aristotle concluded it required a lifelong habit of making the right choices, and he called those good habits "virtues."

Virtue and Purpose

The link between virtues and purpose is a key element of Aristotle's ethical theory. In fact, in Greek, Aristotle's very name derived from αριστος (*aristos*), meaning "best" and τελος (*telos*) meaning "purpose." As Aristotle understood them, virtues were not simply moral states, as in being honest or generous. They were qualities of all sorts that help their possessor fulfill his, her, or its potential. So in an Aristotelian sense, height is a virtue in a basketball player; speed, in a horse; sharpness, in a knife. Think of **virtue** as a synonym for "excellence in attaining purpose." For Aristotle, virtue was always the "Golden Mean" between extremes. Courage, for example, is the happy medium between the contrary dispositions of rashness and cowardice. Friendliness lies between obsequiousness and petulance; modesty, between diffidence and boastfulness.

Aristotle considered the ability to reason the highest virtue for a human being because it is unique to our species. But he knew human beings were more than reasoning machines. He was way ahead of his time in his understanding of human psychology and actually wrote the first treatise on the subject, entitled *Para Psyche*, Greek for "about the mind or soul." He was the first to identify the struggle between the human id and ego: "There are two powers in the soul which appear to be moving forces—desire and reason.... But desire prompts actions in violation of reason" (Aristotle, tr. Hammond, 1901, p. 132).

So he understood that acting ethically would not always be easy. He realized that reason and baser appetites usually pull in opposite directions. But social order depends on self-control and delayed gratification. He also understood that people could not simply will themselves to be virtuous; it required practice. Virtues are like good habits; vices, bad habits. We have dispositions toward both, but repeatedly performing one or the other and really working at it will make them part of our character. In fact, biologist E. O. Wilson (1999, p. 269) considers "character" the internalization of virtues into "an integrated self ... strong enough to endure through trials of solitude and adversity."

Character

Character may seem like an old-fashioned quality when celebrities build careers on the distribution of sex tapes, corporate executives make soft landings in golden parachutes after steering their companies into the ground, and investors cannot seem to see beyond a quarter's earnings. But recent research (Strohminger & Nichols, 2014) suggests moral character plays an even more important role in how others see us than previously suspected. "Our identity comes more from our moral character than from our memory or intellect" notes psychology professor Nancy Gopnik. "Our moral character, after all, is what links us to other people. It's the part of us that goes beyond our own tangle of neurons to touch the brains and lives of others."[1] And proving to be of poor moral character has serious consequences. Consider the example of just one hapless CEO who was caught kicking his dog on an elevator surveillance video.[2] More than 180,000 people signed a petition to have him fired. Even his abject apology, a $100,000 donation to fight animal cruelty, and a promise to do 1,000 hours of community service with at an animal shelter could not save him. After 10 days of unrelenting criticism, his Board was forced to let him go.

---

[1] Gopnik, N. (2015, September 12). Is Our Identity in Memory, Intellect, or Moral Character? *Wall Street Journal.* http://www.wsj.com/articles/is-our-identity-in-intellect-memory-or-moral-character-1441812784.

[2] Horovitz, B. (2014, September 2). "Dog-kicking CEO out after petition," *USA Today.* http://www.usatoday.com/story/money/business/2014/09/02/centerplate-changeorg-petition-social-media-animal-abuse/14967819/. Accessed July 22, 2015.

The price of a character failing has been quantified in even starker terms. According to one academic study, companies with CEOs accused of personal misdeeds—ranging from drunken driving to domestic disputes—experience an immediate loss of 4.1 percent in shareholder value and a long-run decline of 11 to 14 percent (Cline et al., 2015).

Good character is not only the hallmark of an ethical life, it is expected by hard-nosed investors. But what really drives the Aristotelian concept of ethics is **purpose**—the goal to which virtues are directed. It comes up in the very first sentence of Aristotle's book on the subject (Aristotle, tr. Ross, 1999, p. 3).

Every art and every inquiry, and similarly every action and pursuit, is thought to aim at some good; and for this reason the good has rightly been declared to be that at which all things aim.

Contemporary Aristotelianism

Aristotle believed everything exists for a purpose. Whether something is good or bad, virtue or vice, depends on whether or not it serves the purpose to which it is directed. And, of course, he believed all virtues should support life's ultimate purpose—human flourishing.

One of the foremost contemporary interpreters of Aristotelian ethics, Alasdair Macintyre (1998, p. 187), points out that Aristotle defined virtue within the social roles of his time. "To excel is to excel at war or in games as Achilles does, in sustaining a household as Penelope does, in giving counsel to the assembly as Nestor does, in the telling of a tale as Homer himself does," he explained. Macintyre applied this concept to modern life. "The exercise of a virtue exhibits qualities which are required for sustaining a social role and for exhibiting excellence in some well-marked area of social practice," he wrote.

To Macintyre, virtue is expressed in two kinds of activity. First are those that sustain the human community, which is how we usually think of virtue. But then he adds a second category of action—excellence in "some well-marked area of social practice." By "social practice" Macintyre does not mean activity along the lines of social work or community activism, but the ordinary occupations common to modern life. "Social practices," for Macintyre, are any complex activities that take place within a social setting and have their own internal standards of excellence. In fact, to Macintyre's way of thinking, the occupations and professions of everyday life are the primary settings within which virtue and character are expressed today. This interpretation of Aristotle puts such practices as public relations—or accounting or farming—at the center of virtue ethics. So uncovering the ethical principles of public relations requires us to examine its very purpose.

The Early Practice of Public Relations

This book is not the place to get into a detailed history of public relations. But a quick survey of the practice's major phases over the last century or so reveals the multiple purposes it has embraced. Sadly, it may also shed some light on why so many people think public relations practitioners are unprincipled, obfuscating spin doctors.

Modern public relations started off innocently enough in the 19th century, following the U.S. Civil War, when the railroads made it practical to move products to market from far-flung factories and the telegraph allowed newspapers to report news happening outside their immediate area of circulation. Few saw it at the time, but those developments gave birth to a rapacious consumer market. People no longer had to deal with local artisans; they could purchase products from corporations that used the burgeoning media of the time to create homey personalities, renown, and demand for what were now their "brands."

Notable Influences on Public Relations Ethics

Phineas T. Barnum

This first wave of public relations was all about promotion, getting attention for a product, a company, or an idea. An entrepreneurial showman named Phineas T. Barnum gave the era its motto—"There's no such thing as bad publicity, as long as they spelled your name right." Though there is no evidence he ever actually said those words, his whole life was a testament to his belief in the precept.

P. T. Barnum (1810–1891) was only the second millionaire in the United States. And just 5 days before his death he wrote what could have been his epitaph: "I am indebted to the press of the United States for almost every dollar which I possess" (Brunn, 2001, p. 25). Indeed, reporters of the time were indebted to Barnum because he gave them such great copy, and public relations scholars Scott Cutlip, Allen Center, and Glen Broom (1985) anointed him "master of the press agents." For example, to drum up attention for his Broadway museum, Barnum had an elephant plow his property along the commuter tracks into New York City. That plowing pachyderm tilled the same field at least 60 times before Barnum decided the stunt had generated enough ink.

Barnum engaged in what became known as "ballyhoo," puffery that is so ridiculously outlandish—everything was "colossal" and "stupendous"—that everyone is in on the joke. Barnum himself called it "humbug," which he defined as "putting on glittering appearances ... by which to suddenly arrest public attention, and attract the public eye and ear" (Barnum, 1866, p. 21). For example, he planted letters in the New York media, reporting that an actual mermaid had passed through outlying towns on its way to Barnum's museum. Thousands of New Yorkers lined up to see her (or it) only to find something that looked a lot like the tail of a fish attached to the torso of a monkey. No matter. Barnum never claimed it was real; he presented it as the "Feejee Mermaid," a creature that medical science had not yet been able to explain.

"Happy hoaxes" like these entertained the masses and, more importantly, drew them into his dime museum. So did other attractions, like Major, the Amazing Talking Pony, that used its hoofs to answer questions like, "What's two and two." When his acts were real, he found a way to make them even more newsworthy. To generate publicity for the Bearded Lady, he arranged to be sued. To make a distant relative who was only 25 inches tall into a sideshow worthy act, he renamed him Tom Thumb and promoted him to General, complete with uniform and medals.[3]

---

[3] Barnum cheerfully and unapologetically recounted these and other examples of humbug in his autobiography. See: Barnum, P. T. (1855). The Life of P. T. Barnum, Written by Himself, Reprint ed. (2000), Champaign, IL: University of Illinois Press.

James Drummond Ellsworth

P. T. Barnum's press agentry techniques soon moved from show business to industry. The turn of the 20th century was a period of public dissatisfaction with "Big Business." A relatively small number of corporate titans operated in great secrecy, yet controlled the country's natural resources and largest industries, exerted great influence over government officials, paid extremely low wages, created monopolies to squash competition, and further enriched themselves by manipulating the stock market. It was a time of trust-breaking, muckraking, and social unrest. Many businesses felt an acute need to justify themselves to the masses.

Perhaps the neediest of them was a young company called AT&T. It was, born in 1876, at the height of robber baron era, but by 1903 found itself without patent protection and with hordes of new competitors, not to mention unrelentingly bad media coverage thanks to its poor service. AT&T's president at the time, Frederick Fish, had been a skilled patent attorney, but he had no idea what to do about the company's plight. So he was receptive when a publicity agent named George Michaelis suggested "the situation could not be made worse by a venture in publicity and it might be made better" (Ellsworth, 1936, p. 58). Fish hired Michaelis' company on the spot. That firm—the Publicity Bureau of Boston—was the first public relations agency in the country and only three years old at the time.

Michaelis turned the AT&T assignment over to James Drummond Ellsworth (1863–1940), a reporter who had bounced around newspapers from Denver to Boston until an opera singer paid him $50 for placing a story about her in the *Boston Herald*. Ellsworth suddenly realized he could make more money promoting the likes of her than chasing police cars and ambulances for stories. So he joined the Publicity Bureau and traveled the country, convincing editors to run favorable stories about AT&T and to ignore its competitors.

Ellsworth eventually left the Publicity Bureau and became a full-time employee of AT&T itself. He continued his peregrinations, traveling as much as 30 to 40,000 miles a year, impressive mileage considering it all had to be done by rail and horseback. He continued to pioneer new tactics to counter negative media coverage, some of which seem questionable today. He shadowed the company's critics on their speaking tours, circulating negative information about them. He even tried to interfere with competitors' efforts to obtain financing. In Rochester, he spent about $4,000 on ads touting AT&T's policies and service investments, discovering in the process how easily he could leverage advertising buys into favorable (and "free") news coverage. And, to influence local editors and reporters even more directly, he sponsored a contest among them for writing the best ad copy. Few of the entries were useable, but every entry received an award of some kind.

Ellsworth was by no means alone in adopting such tactics, which passed for "street smart" in the first half of the 20th century. But publicity came to mean more than placing stories in the media; it edged ever more deeply into the newsgathering process itself.

Ivy Lee

At around the same time, a number of public relations people were taking a more expansive view of the practice. Foremost among these was Ivy Ledbetter Lee (1877–1934). Like Ellsworth, Lee was a former reporter, but while publicists focused on spreading good news, Lee believed companies should explain themselves to the public in bad times as well as good. He believed information would increase public knowledge and, in the long run, that would be in a company's self-interest.

Lee had the opportunity to put that principle into practice in October 1906, when a Pennsylvania Railroad train jumped a trestle at Atlantic City, New Jersey, and plunged into a creek killing 50 passengers. The standard practice at the time was to clam up and cover up. But Lee convinced the railroad to issue a press release before rumors spread. He even invited reporters and photographers to the scene, providing a special train to get them there. Journalists and public officials praised the railroad for its openness and concern for passengers.

Lee was not always so lucky. Earlier that same year, he represented coal mine owners in eastern Pennsylvania during a bitter strike. When he sent the local newspapers daily "handouts" with pertinent facts about the strike, the editors objected. They called these new "press releases" essentially "ads" and accused Lee of trying to manipulate them. That prompted Lee to issue his "Declaration of Principles" which read in full (Morse, 1906, p. 460):

> *This is not a secret press bureau. All our work is done in the open. We aim to supply news. This is not an advertising agency; if you think any of our matter ought properly to go to your business office, do not use it.*

> *Our matter is accurate. Further details on any subject treated will be supplied promptly, and any editor will be assisted most cheerfully in verifying directly any statement of fact. Upon inquiry, full information will be given to any editor concerning those on whose behalf an article is sent out.*

> *In brief, our plan is, frankly and openly, on behalf of business concerns and public institutions, to supply to the press and public of the United States prompt and accurate information concerning subjects which it is of value and interest to the public to know about.*

> *Corporations and public institutions give out much information in which the news point is lost to view. Nevertheless, it is quite as important to the public to have this news as it is to the establishments themselves to give it currency.*

> *I send out only matter every detail of which I am willing to assist any editor in verifying for himself. I am always at your service for the purpose of enabling you to obtain more complete information concerning any of the subjects brought forward in my copy.*

As high-minded as this declaration might have been, Lee was caught more than once apparently violating it. The most notorious example occurred in 1914 when Lee was again representing coal mine operators, this time in Colorado where a gun battle between strikers and state militia left a number of miners dead. Upton Sinclair dubbed Lee "Poison Ivy," because one of his handouts claimed the strikers' deaths resulted from an overturned stove rather than militia bullets. Lee's claim was not an outright lie—in fact, while three miners and one militiaman were killed in the initial gun battle, 11 women and children were found dead in one of the many earthen storage pits dug below the striker's tent colony outside the mine. According to an exhaustive historical study of the incident, "The innocent victims had hidden in the pit to escape the gunfire and apparently suffocated when a smoky fire later swept through the compound" (Hallahan, 2002). It is conceivable that Lee was referring the source of that fire.

But he did himself no favors when he told a 1915 Congressional Commission investigating the coal mine strike: "By the truth, Mr. Chairman, I mean the truth about the operators' case. What I was to do was to advise and get their case into proper shape for them." When asked, "What personal effort did you ever make to ascertain that the facts given to you by the operators were correct?", Lee responded: "None whatever" (Ewen, 1996, pp. 80–81). The following year, Lee offered a group of railroad executives a startlingly flexible definition of "facts" (pp. 104–105):

> *What is a fact? The effort to state an absolute fact is simply an attempt to … give you my interpretation of the facts.*

To Lee, that was the heart of the matter. For information to be of any practical use, it has to be interpreted to a public that is basically preoccupied with other things. "The public is interested in their own affairs," he told his clients. "They are not very much interested in your affairs" (Ewen, 1996, pp. 47–48). Still, the study mentioned earlier maintains there is "no support for claims that Lee was intentionally *deceptive*" despite an obvious gap between his espoused principles and his actions. "This contradiction can be explained," Hallahan (2002, p. 1) notes, "by the fact that Lee worked in less than ideal circumstances." Now, there's a loophole that Aristotle may not have recognized.

For all his faults, Lee (1925) had a practical, self-interested view of public relations. He cautioned that publicity was less a smokescreen than an antiseptic.

> *Publicity must not be thought of … as a sort of umbrella to protect you against the rain of an unpleasant public opinion. Publicity must not be regarded as a bandage to cover up a sore and enable you to get along pretty well with the trouble still there. Publicity must, if your trouble is to be cured, be considered rather as an antiseptic, which*

shall cleanse the very source of the trouble and reveal it to the doctor,
which is the public. (p. 44)

To Lee's mind, William Vanderbilt was seriously delusional when he
responded to a reporter's question about train schedules by declaring,
"the public be damned."[4] In 1916, Lee warned a group of railroad executives that "You suddenly find you are not running a private business,
but running a business of which the public itself is taking complete su-
pervision. The crowd is in the saddle, the people are on the job, and we
must take consideration of that fact, whether we like it or not" (Ewen,
1996, pp. 74–75).

Edward L. Bernays

The "crowd" was precisely the target of another public relations pioneer
who hung out his shingle about this time. Edward Bernays (1891–1995)
was a nephew of Sigmund Freud and greatly influenced by new discoveries
in cognitive science, especially those that revealed the power of unconscious
thoughts and desires. For example, in his book *Propaganda*, Bernays (1928,
p. 52) revealed:

Psychologists of the school of Freud have pointed out that many of
man's thoughts and actions are compensatory substitutes for desires
which he has been obliged to suppress. A thing may be desired not for
its intrinsic worth or usefulness, but because he has unconsciously
come to see in it a symbol of something else, the desire for which he is
ashamed to admit to himself. A man buying a car may think he
wants it for purposes of locomotion. He may really want it because it
is a symbol of social position, an evidence of his success in business, or
a means of pleasing his wife.

Bernays not only believed this theory, he applied it avidly not only
to big-ticket products like automobiles, but also to such quotidian items

---

[4] Watson, E.S. (1936, November 6). The truth about that "public be damned interview." *Lake Benton Valley News.* http://news.google.com/newspapers?nid=1018&
dat=19361106&id=DbckAAAAIBAJ&sjid=zA8GAAAAIBAJ&pg=1501,734632.
Accessed July 22, 2015.

as cigarettes. Bernays was also greatly influenced by the French social scientist and anthropologist, Gustave le Bon (1895), who wrote a widely read book on the psychology of crowds. Le Bon believed the anonymity of crowds caused people to lose their sense of personal responsibility, unquestioningly following the crowd's predominant ideas and emotions, limited only by the morality and thinking of its least capable members. Indeed, le Bon compared being in a crowd for a great length of time to being under the influence of a hypnotist.[5]

Like many progressive thinkers of the time, Bernays believed the educated elite had an obligation to lead the uneducated masses, guided by what was best for the public good. To him, this was an essential element of democracy (1928, pp. 9–10). And he was unapologetic about it. Indeed, he thought the elite would police themselves, once warning, "The public relations counsel has a professional responsibility to push only those ideas he can respect, and not to promote causes or accept assignments for clients he considers antisocial" (Bernays, 1947, p. 113).

Although widely considered a Master Press Agent, in Bernays's hands, public relations was less about breathless publicity or self-serving information than about manipulating social and psychological forces to get the public (aka "the crowd") to do what he wanted. "The functions of the public relations counsel are those of a directive influence rather than a press agent," he said in one interview. "The public relations counsel in this conception does not report events to the public press, he molds them in such form that the press will of its own accord give wide and favorable publicity to the client."[6] Bernays issued news releases like his contemporary Ivy Lee, but they were less likely to describe his client's virtues and products than to promote an event that seemed only tangentially related, drawing on third party endorsements whenever possible.

---

[5] Bernays was also influenced by Wilfred Trotter (1916) who promoted ideas similar to le Bon's in his book *Instincts of the Herd in Peace and War* (London: T. F. Unwin). Trotter eventually became Freud's personal physician.

[6] From a June 26, 1928, Metropolitan Life Insurance Company publicity piece summarizing interviews with "the two most prominently mentioned public relations counsels in New York," Ivy Lee, represented by T.J. Ross, Jr., manager of the New York headquarters, and Edward L. Bernays. See the Bernays papers in the Library of Congress: http://memory.loc.gov/cgi-bin/query/r?ammem/cool:@field(DOCID+@lit(me191)).

Bernays's very first public relations campaign, undertaken when he was just 21 and editing a medical journal for a friend's father, is a good illustration of his technique. A reader submitted a glowing review of "Damaged Goods," a French play that had yet to be staged in the United States. The play dealt with sexually transmitted diseases—an issue that was considered unfit for public discussion at the time. Bernays decided to publish the review, prompting the producers of the play to hire him as a consultant. They were concerned that prudish authorities would shut the show down, which had happened to a play about prostitution by George Bernard Shaw only years before. But Bernays saw an opportunity to turn potential controversy into a cause.

He used his position as editor of the *Medical Review of Reviews* to form the "Sociological Fund Committee" and asked some of the most prominent public figures of the time to join it, endorsing the effort to stamp out sexually transmitted diseases. Those who signed up included John D. Rockefeller Jr., Mrs. William K. Vanderbilt Sr., Mr. and Mrs. Franklin D. Roosevelt, and the Reverend John Haynes Holmes of New York's Unitarian Community Church.

Endorsements and checks poured in, helping to fund a Broadway run, as well as a special performance in Washington for justices of the Supreme Court, the President's cabinet, and members of Congress. Reviews were not kind. One paper called it "dull and almost unendurable" (Axelrod, 2008, p. 91), but a newspaper editorial credited the play with "striking sex-o'clock" in America (Bernays, 1965, p. 60).

Bernays used the same techniques in a public relations career that literally spanned the century (he died in 1995 at the age of 103). In the intervening years, he promoted everything from water fluoridation (for Alcoa) and the dangers of drinking from a common cup (for Dixie Cups) to Ivory soap (for P&G). He even helped prevent the Guatemalan government from confiscating United Fruit's lands through a campaign in the United States to portray its president as a "Communist." Public pressure became so great that President Eisenhower had little choice but to come to the fruit company's rescue.[7]

---

[7] Tye, L. (2006, Fall). Watch out for the top banana. *The Cabinet.* http:// cabinetmagazine.org/issues/23/tye.php. Accessed July 22, 2015.

In all this, Bernays's strategy of indirection seldom wavered. When surveys showed women were not buying Lucky Strike cigarettes because the green package with a red bulls eye clashed with their clothes, Bernays staged a charity ball at which wearing a green gown was required and convinced the fashion industry to declare green the color of the new season.[8] For the Beechnut Packing Company, he got people to eat ham and eggs in the morning, based on a survey of doctors he commissioned to document the health benefits of a "hearty breakfast" (Colleary, 2012, July 19).[9] For General Electric, which controlled much of the country's electrical manufacturing at the time, Bernays mounted "Light's Golden Jubilee," a worldwide celebration of the light bulb on the 50th anniversary of its invention, October 21, 1929.

Leading up to the actual date, Bernays arranged for the Post Office to issue a commemorative stamp, for George M. Cohan to write a special song (*Thomas Edison—Miracle Man*), and for stories to appear in magazines ranging from the *Saturday Evening Post* to *Scientific American*. Governors and Mayors issued proclamations; museums mounted special exhibits; and schools ran essay contests. Then, on the day itself, the elderly inventor switched on a replica of the first light bulb under the watchful eyes of the president of the United States and various captains of industry gathered for the occasion (Ewen, 1996, pp. 116–118). It was all ostensibly the celebration of a great inventor; in reality, it was the celebration and near-canonization of a gigantic company. Under Bernays, public relations became an instrument of hidden persuasion or, as he termed it, the "engineering of consent."

A masterful self-promoter, Bernays did some of his best engineering on his own image. He wrote nine books on his techniques and even taught one of the first courses on public relations at New York University in 1923. Indeed, he was so successful in establishing himself as one of the field's founding fathers, helped by the fact that he outlived all his contemporaries, the very practice of public relations became identified in the public mind with his techniques of shadowy behind-the-scenes manipulation.

[8] Described by Bernays in an interview for the Museum of PR web site: http://www.prmuseum.com/bernays/bernays_1934.html
[9] Colleary, E, "How 'Bacon and Eggs' Became the American Breakfast," The American Table web site, July 19, 2012. See: http://www.americantable.org/2012/07/how-bacon-and-eggs-became-the-american-breakfast/

Around the time Bernays was in his heyday, another lesser-known public relations practitioner entered the scene. He had a single client for much of his career and wrote far fewer books, one to Bernays's nine.[10] Yet he arguably had more lasting influence. It all came about because the CEO of AT&T wanted someone to write a book about the company.

Arthur W. Page

By the end of 1926, Arthur W. Page (1883–1960) had just about reached the end of his rope in his family's publishing business. His father was Walter Hines Page, former editor of the *Atlantic Monthly* and *World's Work* magazines, and partner in the publishing house of Doubleday, Page, and Company. Young Page had joined the staff of *World's Work* immediately after graduating from Harvard, eventually becoming editor. But a continuing series of disagreements with the Doubleday family over the magazine's direction had convinced him to quit.[11] Coincidentally, as soon as he made up his mind to leave Doubleday, an old college classmate and friend, Walter Gifford, asked if Page could drop by his office and "talk to him for a minute" (Page, 1956, pp. 70–72).

Gifford had risen through the ranks of AT&T to become CEO only 2 years earlier. The ostensible reason for his invitation was because "somebody'd suggested a book about the telephone," and he wanted to know what Page thought of the idea. "Well, it may satisfy the vanity of the folks in the company ... but such things don't have much effect upon the public," Page said. "It won't do you any harm, if you want to have it. It won't do you any good either." Then as Page started to leave, Gifford startled him by asking, "Are you wedded to the publishing business?"

---

[10] Bernays wrote nine books, including *Crystalizing Public Opinion* (1923), *Propaganda* (1928), *Speak up for Democracy* (1940), *Morale: First Line of Defense* (1941), *Public Relations* (1945), *Your Future in Public Relations* (1961), *Biography of an Idea* (1965), *Your Future in a Public Relations Career* (1979), and *The Later Years: Public Relations Insights* (1986). Despite being a prolific writer of speeches for other people and a scion of the Doubleday–Page publishing firm, Page wrote a single book which only touched on public relations: *The Bell Telephone System* appeared under his authorship in 1941.

[11] Page (1956, pp. 70–72) never spelled out the nature of his disagreement with the Doubleday family, though in an oral history recorded by Columbia University he said Doubleday "wanted to leave out the more serious side of the magazine" and "move into more picture magazines and entertainment."

It seems that James Ellsworth was still running public relations for AT&T, but was ready to retire. Gifford needed a replacement and offered Page the job on the spot. "What would you think about coming into the telephone business?" he asked. As Page later recalled,

> *What was in his mind was that I'd been writing editorials about what was the duty of big business in a democracy and how should they get along, and giving them a lot of free advice.... What he asked me to do was to come to AT&T and see what I could do. So I told them that if they were serious about it—that is, I didn't want to go there as a publicity man—but if they were serious about taking that point of view as the general policy, nothing would please me more than to try to do something instead of telling everyone else to do it* (Page, 1956, pp. 70–72).

Gifford agreed and made Page an officer of the company, perhaps the first public relations officer at any corporation, reflecting their common view of public relations. In an article Gifford wrote for the *World's Work* just the previous June, (1926, pp. 166–168) he contended "the old robber barons" of industry were being replaced by a new breed of business people "who realize more accurately what the limits of their powers are, and have a much keener sense of their responsibilities to the public." In fact, he continued, "Corporations owe their success and even their existence to the good will of the public; and where their views seem to clash, the corporation must either persuade the public to its view, or alter its own." He wanted Page to lead that effort. According to John Brooks (1976, p. 173), who wrote a masterful book about AT&T's first 100 years, it turned out to be "one of Gifford's most brilliant early staff appointments." Brooks saw Page's appointment as a "brilliantly successful effort" to return the company's public relations to "the broad standard, emphasizing candid disclosure, rather than parochial propaganda" that had characterized Ellsworth's rough-and-ready tenure.

Page's first assignment was a speech Gifford would give in October 1927 at a combined meeting of the Interstate Commerce Commission and the State Utilities Commissioners in Dallas, Texas, which regulated the company. In the speech, Page had Gifford highlight what they both saw as AT&T's special responsibility: "The fact that the responsibility for such a large part of the entire telephone service of the country rests solely upon this Company and its Associated Companies also imposes on the management an unusual obligation to the public."[12]

With a few more years in corporate America under his belt, Page came to believe that obligation was not limited to the likes of AT&T. In a speech to railroad public relations people in 1939, he declared: "All business begins with the public permission and exists by public approval."[13] To his own troops, he was even blunter: "If we think at times the public jury does not give us a fair chance to tell our story, that doesn't make any difference," he told them. "In the long run I am not afraid of that, but if in the long run it were true that the public wouldn't give us a fair hearing, it would merely mean we would have to find a way to please the public without a fair hearing. We have got to please this public for it's the only public we've got—we can't change it."[14]

In the 20 years Page led AT&T public relations, he focused his department less on the task of "selling the company" and more on the "intangible and more important job" of bringing to the company the needs and desires of its customers and the general public.[15] He considered public relations a general management function and, as he promised Gifford, he concerned himself primarily with matters of policy—not simply with what the company said, but more critically with what the company *did*. By 1941, Page was one of only three operating vice presidents sitting on the company's Board of Directors. And ironically, Page eventually did write that "book about the telephone." Titled *The Bell Telephone System* (1941), it appeared the same year he joined the company's Board of Directors.

---

[12] Gifford, W.S. (1927, October). Speech delivered to the National Association of Railroad and Utilities Commissioners, Dallas, Texas. http://comm.psu.edu/page-center/resources/other-resources/page-written

[13] Page, A.W. (1939, October 27). *Industrial Statesmanship*. Speech delivered to the Public Relations Conference of the Chesapeake & Ohio Railway Company, White Sulphur Springs, VA. http://comm.psu.edu/page-center/resources/other-resources/page-speeches. Accessed on July 22, 2015.

[14] Page, A.W. (1936, December 10). *Public Relations Today and the Outlook for the Future*. Speech delivered a public relations conference of the New York Telephone Company. http://comm.psu.edu/page-center/resources/other-resources/page-speeches. Accessed July 22, 2015.

[15] Speech delivered by Arthur W. Page to the Bell Telephone System's General Operating Conference, May 1927.

Summary

Such were the early days of public relations practice in the 20th century—a struggle to define the function, as the corporations it served tried to deal with an increasingly skeptical public and government. What would Aristotle have thought of all this?

The practice of public relations would have been familiar to Aristotle, though he would not have known it by that name. As practiced for much of the 20th century, public relations would have looked like rhetoric to him, the art of persuasive speaking and writing. That was something Aristotle knew well. He even developed a system of rhetoric, suggesting its effectiveness depended on three elements—a speaker's credibility, ability to connect with an audience emotionally, and use of compelling logic. And he measured the character of the practice by its purpose—not solely its immediate goal of persuasion, but its ultimate purpose of contributing to its audience's happiness or flourishing.

In the next chapter, we will consider how public relations—as practiced by the likes of Barnum, Ellsworth, Lee, and Bernays—served that lofty purpose. We will take a deep dive into one of the most basic virtues of public relations—truthfulness. And we'll examine other virtues that have particular application to the practice.

CHAPTER 4

Public Relations of Character

There is a good chance, were Aristotle alive today, he would be energetically engaged in trying to sort out where "the good" lay in the relatively new inventions of mass media, consumer markets, and public relations.

But why would we want to consult someone who slept in his clothes, would not know what to do with a newspaper let alone a computer, and never even saw a flush toilet? If ethics has forward motion, Aristotle gave it much of its initial propulsion, and progress made since builds on his thinking. In fact, some contemporary thinkers have suggested we could do worse than to return to the Aristotelian ideal in the conduct of our modern lives. Aristotle certainly did not have the last word on the ethical practice of public relations. But it is a good place to start.

So we start where Aristotle did—with the belief that the "goodness" of any endeavor is measured in terms of excellence in attaining purpose. How closely did Ellsworth, Lee, Bernays, and Page adhere to the qualities, or virtues, necessary to achieve their purpose? What are those virtues? And what was their purpose anyway?

It is worth noting here that Arthur Page seemed to have a different purpose than the other three.[1] In fact, he made it pretty clear in his "job interview" that he was not interested in a "publicity job." From the start, he considered his new position a general management position focused on helping the company fulfill its obligations to society, as well as to its customers. With the acquiescence of his boss and his board of

---

[1] Other than the 1956 interviews for Columbia University's oral history project cited here, Page did not write a memoir. What we know of his approach to public relations must be inferred from his many speeches which are archived at Penn State College of Communications' Arthur W. Page Center: http://comm.psu.edu/page-center/resources/other-resources/page-speeches.

directors, that is precisely what he did over his 20-year career. So, in large measure, the most significant ethical lessons we might draw from his experience would best wait for a later chapter.

Ellsworth, Lee, and Bernays, however, shared a common purpose. In part, it was ostensibly to inform the public about a business (respectively the phone company, coal mine owners, and an assortment of consumer brands). In some cases, it was also to persuade the public to take a particular action (eat bacon) or to believe a certain idea (telephone competition is unnecessary; the coal mine owners are treating their employees fairly; the president of Guatemala is a Communist). We will get into a fuller discussion of the purpose of public relations in later chapters. For now, we will assume these public relations pioneers had pure intentions; that is, their goal was to help the public make better decisions.

Aristotle would have approved of that purpose. He far preferred to be governed by many farmers, shepherds, and potters acting in the common interest (the "polity") than to be ruled by any number of people acting in their own interest. The key, though, is that the *polity* has to be well informed in order to recognize the common interest.[2]

Virtue

Having stipulated pure purpose, we turn to the qualities (virtues) Aristotle would expect to see in excellent communications. Plato enumerated four cardinal virtues—**prudence, justice, temperance**, and **courage**. Aristotle, a supremely practical man, recognized that different spheres of life might require other virtues and added as many as eight to Plato's list, including **patience, friendliness**, and **truthfulness**.

That last virtue is arguably essential in any ethical communication or relationship. Telling the truth is the very first of the so-called Page Principles, drawn from Arthur W. Page's speeches and memos by the association of senior communications officers that bears his name.[3] And not

---

[2] For more on Aristotle's views on the most practical political regime, see *Book IV of Politics*, which is available online at http://classics.mit.edu/Aristotle/politics.html.

[3] The Arthur W. Page Society is an association of chief communications officers of leading corporations, the CEOs of the world's largest public relations agencies, and leading academics from the nation's top business and communications schools. The

surprisingly, considering its source, it is immediately followed by "prove it with action."

But what does it mean to tell the truth? Ivy Lee suggested that the concept is entirely subjective. One man's truth is another man's opinion. Facts have little objective reality; they depend entirely on interpretation. Lee might have advised his clients to tell the truth, but from that point forward, they were on their own. His hands were off the wheel.

We should emphasize here that truth is not the only virtue on which the ethics of public relations depend, but it is a good place to start because it is deceptively hard to pin down.

The Nature of Truth

Philosophers have been arguing about the nature of truth for millennia, about as long as they have been debating the existence of reality. Perhaps, the nonphilosophers among us can agree on a provisional definition: *truth is conformity to facts or reality,* what is termed "**veracity**." But ethicist Kirk Hanson points out that, in practice, even that straightforward notion lies on a continuum with a notoriously slippery slope.[4]

Just below actual truth—conformance to reality—is a closely related concept: *disclosed truth.* Public relations people do not have to say everything they know to be truthful. Some facts are confidential; some are irrelevant; some might even be misleading if their context were misunderstood. For example, in planning layoffs, every organization is asked to prepare multiple options. Releasing all that raw information would not tell anyone anything truly useful and could lead people to the wrong conclusions. Other times, it could be needlessly damaging. When AT&T's data networks suffered a daylong outage in 1998, the company

---

seven Page Principles are tell the truth, prove it with action, listen to the customer, manage for tomorrow, conduct public relations as if the whole company depended on it, realize a company's true character is expressed by its people, and remain calm, patient, and good-humored. Page himself didn't write these principles; they were drawn and inferred from his speeches, memos, and example by the Society's founders. See http://www.awpagesociety.com/about/the-page-principles/.

[4] The "continuum of truth" is based on a presentation Kirk Hanson made to the annual meeting of the Arthur Page Society, in September 2003. Hanson is executive director of the Markula Center for Applied Ethics at Santa Clara University.

quickly traced the problem to a technician who installed some faulty software. The *New York Post* wanted his name. But what purpose would releasing it have served? Management was responsible for providing the software, training technicians, and ensuring the procedures they followed were fail-safe. Fingering the technician would have been irresponsible.

But disclosed truth can also be so self-servingly selective as to be misleading. The late novelist-essayist Alan Harrington once compared public relations to flower-arranging. "Public-relations specialists make flower arrangements of the facts," he said, "placing them so that the wilted and less attractive petals are hidden by sturdy blooms."[5] This amounts to a well-worn technique called "spinning," which we will discuss more fully shortly.

Then there are *plausible interpretations* of facts. We say the glass is half full; you say it's half empty. Technically, we are both right. We are not arguing about how much water is in the glass, just what it means. Statistics are particularly useful in buttressing one interpretation or the other. But some believe the manipulation of numbers is a whole category of lying all to itself. Mark Twain famously said, "There are three kinds of lies: lies, damned lies, and statistics."[6]

It is said that "figures do not lie, but liars"—and some public relations people—"figure." In the right hands, numbers and graphs can be manipulated to support almost any interpretation of data. For example, we can easily establish with mathematical certainty that the average human being has one testicle and one breast. A full exposition of lying with statistics is beyond this book's intent (and its authors' capabilities). But thankfully scholars have jumped into the breach with books of their own. Among the best is a 60-year-old classic, *How to Lie with Statistics* by mathematician Darrell Huff (1954/1993). He is the guy who came up with the original "gee-whiz graph," exaggerating small differences by setting a chart's baseline to a value greater than zero (1993 pp. 62–67).

---

[5] Quoted by Auletta, K. (2007, February 12). The Fixer, *New Yorker*. http://www.newyorker.com/magazine/2007/02/12/the-fixer

[6] Twain attributed the remark to British Prime Minister Benjamin Disraeli in "Chapters From My Autobiography" which appeared in the *North American Review* literary journal on September 7, 1906, p. 471. http://www.gutenberg.org/files/19987/19987-h/19987-h.htm. The original source has never been found in Mr Disraeli's papers, however, and it is likely Twain wrote it himself.

The PRSA and the United Kingdom's Chartered Institute for Public Relations have partnered with their respective country's leading associations of professional statisticians and data analysts to publish best practice guides for using statistics in communications.[7] For more on this from a public relations perspective, see Michaelson and Stacks (2014).

Incorrect interpretations follow. For example, we know for a fact that a McDonald's Big Mac has about half the cholesterol as a three-piece serving of KFC fried chicken (75 mg versus 145 mg). Conveniently ignoring the fact that it has almost 50 percent more calories (550 versus 320), and a third more fat (29 grams versus 19 grams), we promote its lower cholesterol and claim it is better for your heart than KFC fried chicken.

Or maybe we promote our client's vodka as "gluten-free." In fact, all vodka is gluten-free, despite its earlier life as a mash of barley, wheat, or rye. But we suspect that because we have highlighted it on the bottle, some celiac victims and food purists will assume it makes a difference. The Kremlin's public relations guy in Berlin, Germany, would call all this "the tendentious presentation of facts" which is really a way of lying about lying.[8]

And then, of course, there are *outright lies*. Public relations people know they are not supposed to lie. But in a 2010 survey, while only 12 percent admitted to disseminating false information themselves, nearly three-quarters (73 percent) said they believed public relations people lie in the course of their work.[9] The survey also suggests public relations practitioners have a flexible notion of lying. Just 29 percent considered withholding information morally equivalent to lying. And

---

[7] The PRSA's guidelines are available online at http://www.prsa.org/Intelligence/BusinessCase/Documents/StatisticsBestPracticesGuide.pdf. Accessed September 5, 2015. The Chartered Institute of Public Relations' guidelines are at https://www.mrs.org.uk/pdf/CIPR%20MRS%20RSS%20Guidelines%20for%20using%20statistics%20in%20communications%20CIPR.pdf. Accessed September 5, 2015.

[8] The Kremlin's man in Berlin explained his country's propaganda in these terms to Troianovski, A. (2014, August 21). Russia ramps up information war in Europe. *Wall Street Journal*. http://online.wsj.com/articles/russia-ramps-up-information-war-in-europe-1408675046. Accessed July 22, 2015.

[9] *PRWeek* commissioned the survey. See Sudhaman, A. (2010, February 3). PR professionals believe 'spin' is entrenched in industry, survey shows. *PR Week*. http://www.prweek.com/article/981450/pr-professionals-believe-spin-entrenched-industry-survey-shows. Accessed July 22, 2015.

three quarters said public relations people have no obligation to communicate information that may damage their clients.

Truth and the Law

Some ethicists suggest we turn to the law for guidance in defining the minimal contours and limits of truthful speech. On that score, it is worth noting that the practice of public relations is one of four jobs specifically protected by the U.S. Constitution. (The others are the clergy, journalists, and lobbyists.)

It is right there in the first amendment—"Congress shall make no law ... abridging the freedom of speech." The founding fathers had individuals in mind when they banned "abridging" free speech. And since corporations are not mentioned in the Constitution, the full range of their rights has never been entirely clear, but they have always been thought to have some of the rights individuals enjoy, such as the right to due process and the right to enter contracts. And, of course, the courts have long recognized reasonable limits on individuals' free speech. It is not lawful, for example, to yell "Fire!" in a crowded theater.

Beginning in the 1970s, the Supreme Court began applying first amendment rights to corporations in a series of decisions.[10] The Court held that companies engage in two kinds of speech, each with its own set of rules and regulations, though this has become a murky area of the law for reasons we will soon discuss.

- "Commercial speech" is motivated by profit and proposes a commercial transaction.
- "Corporate speech," by contrast, deals with social or political issues and seeks to affect policy or strengthen relationships.

---

[10] The most important of these decisions were *Virginia State Pharmacy Board v. Virginia Citizens Consumer Council* (1976), *First National Bank of Boston v. Bellotti* (1978), and *Central Hudson Gas & Electric Corp. v. Public Service Commission* (1980).

Commercial Speech

The Supreme Court allows regulation of commercial speech if there is a substantial government interest at stake, such as protecting the public from harm, and the regulation is narrowly tailored to that purpose. So laws designed to protect the public from misleading claims are constitutional. You cannot say you are discounting your product 50 percent if you are selling it at the same old price. Of course, the law leaves plenty of room for what it terms "puffery," which is widely perceived as merely an expression of the seller's opinion and usually discounted as such by any prospective customers. Whether you drink Coke or not, you know there is no way to prove it is the world's most refreshing soft drink. That is puffery and gets a free pass. Similarly, Wonder Bread can claim to build strong bodies 12 ways because it adds 12 vitamins to the dough. The rest is puffery. On the other hand, Gaines Burgers dog food once claimed it provides all the milk protein a dog needs. The Federal Trade Commission (FTC) deemed that claim *deceptive* because dogs do not need milk protein, and it is misleading to suggest they do.

Linda Goldstein, a lawyer specializing in communications law, warns that many public relations campaigns face "heightened regulatory scrutiny" from the FTC, which wants to ensure that marketers disclose any "material connection" between themselves and anyone who endorses their products.[11] "Recently, the FTC's view of what constitutes an endorsement and what constitutes a material connection has become so restrictive," she warns, "that even the most benign social media campaigns could be implicated."

Goldstein cautions that encouraging customers to blog, Tweet, or post photos of a client's products could trigger the agency's endorsement guidelines if some kind of incentive is involved. Even offering a prize for the best post could cross the line. It is all explained in 21-page guidelines.[12] But that has not stopped companies like Lord & Taylor from

---

[11] Goldstein, L. (2015, December 31). Top 3 legal issues facing marketers in 2015. *Wall Street Journal.* http://mobile.blogs.wsj.com/cmo/2014/12/31/outside-voices-top-3-legal-issues-facing-marketers-in-2015/. Accessed July 22, 2015.

[12] The FTC guidelines, ".com Disclosures," were issued in March 2013 and are available online at https://www.ftc.gov/sites/default/files/attachments/pr ess-releases/ftc-staff-revises-online-advertising-disclosure-guidelines/130312dotcomdisclosures.pdf. Accessed July 22, 2015.

paying fashion bloggers to post photos of themselves in one of the retailer's new dresses. The dresses promptly sold out and, as this was being written, the retailer had not heard from the FTC. But the bloggers were on the receiving end of so much criticism, they added retroactive "#sponsored" hashtags to their posts and the retailer itself promised to act more ethically in the future, though they termed it a "process improvement."[13]

The FTC is just one of many agencies that regulate commercial speech, depending on its nature. For example, the Federal Drug Administration regulates pharmaceutical advertising to protect public safety. The Securities and Exchange Commission regulates financial communications, for example barring companies from selectively disclosing material information to favored investors.

Public relations people also have to be careful that their passion for representing their client or promoting their client's product does not deteriorate into *fraud*. Under common law, fraud is misrepresentation of a material fact with the intent to deceive. It can be saying something that is not true or failing to disclose something that is important. A *material fact* is one that a reasonable person would depend on in making a decision. And acting with reckless disregard of the consequences can constitute intent. The person being deceived only has to show they had reason to rely on the false information and doing so resulted in injury. And you cannot use "the client made me do it" as a defense. If you help a client commit fraud, you can be found just as guilty. That is why agencies typically indemnify clients for suits arising out of the creative materials they produce, such as photo releases, while they ask clients to indemnify them for claims arising from the information they provide the agency, such as product and service claims.

Corporate Speech

By comparison, *corporate speech* was once thought to have greater protection than commercial speech. Because it deals with public policy issues, it was thought to constitute opinion that contributes to the free flow of

---

[13] Beck, M. (2015, April 3). Did Lord & Taylor's Instagram influencer campaign cross the line? *Marketing Land*. http://marketingland.com/did-lord-taylors-instagram-influencer-campaign-cross-the-line-123961. Accessed July 22, 2015.

information and less vulnerable to claims of being false or misleading. But in 2003, the Supreme Court let stand a lower court decision that seemed to erase the distinction between corporate and commercial speech.

The case had to do with a series of news releases Nike issued to rebut accusations its sneakers were made in Asian sweatshops. An activist named Mark Kasky sued Nike for false advertising. Nike responded that its views on a public issue were entitled to First Amendment protection. The local court agreed and dismissed the case, but the California Supreme Court overturned the ruling, saying Nike's news releases were subject to false advertising laws. The United States Supreme Court initially agreed to review the case, but ultimately sent the case back to the trial court without issuing a ruling. The parties then settled out of court, leaving many people wondering if the distinction between commercial and corporate speech was still valid. On the other hand, according to a recent Harvard Law School study, "nearly half of First Amendment legal challenges now benefit business corporations and trade groups, rather than other organizations or individuals" (Coates, 2015, February 27). For example, in the 2010 Citizens United case, the Supreme Court seemed to expand corporate speech when it upheld a company's right to run ads advocating a position on public policy or social issues, including political candidates.[14] It was a controversial decision that is still being debated.

But there are even more immediate legal concerns for public relations people in the exercise of corporate or commercial speech. Defamation is the legal term for harming someone's reputation by spreading false information about them. In print, it's called libel; in speech, it's slander. But whatever you call it, it is trouble. In some states, it is a criminal offense. The criteria for defamation are quite complicated, differ by jurisdiction, and apply a little differently to public personalities. But as a general rule, it is always wise to make sure the expression of an opinion is labeled as such and backed up with supporting facts.

---

[14] *Citizens United v. Federal Election Commission*, No. 08-205, 558 U.S. 310. (2010, January 21). http://www.supremecourt.gov/Search.aspx?FileName=/docketfiles/08-205.htm. Accessed September 9, 2015.

Included in the right to privacy, which we will discuss in a later chapter, is the "right to publicity." Although the specifics can vary from state to state, this generally concerns the appropriation of a person's name or likeness for commercial purposes. Originally, it was designed to protect people's privacy, but these days it is also considered a property right. If there is money to be made from someone's likeness, that person has the right to control it. In fact, the right of publicity has even been extended to identifiable buildings and animals.

It is also illegal (and unethical) to use other people's creative work without getting their permission. The sheer profusion of easily clicked, copied, and pasted images on the Internet makes them seem like free goods. They are not. Someone expended lots of calories and maybe even money in their creation. To claim any of it as your own is lying. The law does allow "fair use" of copyrighted material, but as attorney Kerry Gorgone put it, "You don't get to discuss 'fair use' until you've been sued, and lawsuits are expensive."[15]

Finally, public relations people can break the law—not to mention act incredibly unethically—by padding their expense accounts or filing false billable hours. That is called lying and when it leads to the receipt of unearned compensation it is another form of stealing. The former head of FleishmanHillard's operations in Los Angeles was sentenced to federal prison for overbilling the Los Angeles Department of Water and Power for the agency's services. He had perfectly logical reasons for the way he billed the water department, but all it got him was 42 months in jail.

Truth and Public Relations

If the law defines the minimal requirements of the truth, where does that leave us in the practice of public relations? Aristotle's notion of purpose suggests a provisional definition. Veracity—or conformance to reality—hinges on the use to which a given set of facts will be put:

---

[15] Gorgone, K. (2015, June 4). The new guide to minimizing legal risks in social media marketing. *BusinessGrow.com*. http://www.businessesgrow.com/2015/06/04 /legal-risks-in-social-media-marketing/. Accessed July 22, 2015.

In public relations, telling the truth means giving people substantially all the information a reasonable person needs to make an intelligent, voluntary decision, whether buying a company's products, investing in it, working for it, welcoming it into their community, or supporting it in some other way.

That does not mean public relations practitioners need to give people *all* sides of an issue, including what opponents or competitors allege. It is fair to assume that in the free market of products and ideas, others will have an opportunity to present their side. But telling the truth does mean you can withhold material information or engage in misdirection so people ignore other points of view. If your product has side effects or the kind of flaw that might change someone's mind about it, telling the truth requires you to reveal them. Telling the truth also means doing our very best to confirm the accuracy of the information we share. And if we discover we gave people bad information—or if they draw erroneous conclusions from what we said—we do not ignore it or cover it up. We correct it and set people straight. To do otherwise is to lie.

We explore this definition further in later chapters, but for now, consider what it means in a practical situation faced by the public relations people at Kraft Foods.

Mini-case

Kraft makes a popular baking chocolate. Sometime in 2013, many home bakers noticed the packages on grocery shelves had suddenly shrunk—from eight ounces to four. But apparently in some stores, the price stayed the same. That raised the eyebrows of the *New York Times'* "Haggler" columnist, who quickly fired an e-mail to the Kraft public relations department, asking what gives.

One can only imagine what goes through your mind when an e-mail from someone identifying himself as the "Haggler" from the *New York Times* lands in your inbox, but Kraft's spokeswoman was happy (and we suspect, relieved) to tell him the price should have gone down. "The suggested retail price for the four-ounce package is $2.89," she e-mailed back, "while the suggested retail price for the old eight-ounce package was $3.89."

Perhaps, suspecting $2.89 is not half of $3.89, the Haggler dug out his calculator and crunched the numbers discovering the price per ounce actually went *up* by 47 percent. Back he went to e-mail: "Isn't this just a price increase in semi-clever disguise?" he asked. Here's what Kraft's spokeswoman said:

> *Our consumers have told us that they prefer this size over the larger size because the majority of our Baker's recipes call for four ounces or less. The easy-break bar makes it faster to melt and easier to break apart. And they can buy only what they need for a recipe, so the product is fresher.*

Fair enough, the *Times's* intrepid columnist said, but why did the price go up? After a pause, Kraft replied:

> *Our packaging change for Baker's Chocolate was driven by consumer research. Our consumers have told us that they prefer this size over the larger size because the majority of our Baker's recipes call for four ounces or less.*

"Ooo-kay," the by-now exasperated reporter persisted, "I think you said that already, but did your consumers tell you to raise the price?" Finally, after an even longer pause, Kraft's wily spokesperson said:

> *Our new four-ounce size of Baker's Chocolate is competitively priced with other brands.*

What the *Times'* columnist wrote at this point is worth reprinting.

> *The reality is that for many items, production costs have been rising. Given these circumstances, a price increase is perfectly understandable and arguably inevitable. What's odd is that few manufacturers, it seems, ever level with consumers about what might be valid reasons for higher prices.*[16]

---

[16] Segal, D. (2013, June 22). The Haggler: Halving the portion, but not the price. *New York Times.* http://www.nytimes.com/2013/06/23/your-money/halving-the-

Kraft's spokeswoman answered the question she wished had been asked—why did you change the size of the package—rather than the one actually posed—why did the price go up? Her answer did not have to ignore the company's perspective. Indeed, the Haggler wondered why so many companies fail to level about it.

Media Training

No wonder some journalists believe media relations is really just a con game. Consider what one writer for the *Columbia Journalism Review* had to say about media training: "Media training teaches people all the fancy steps they need to answer the questions they want to answer, not those of an inquisitive reporter. The result: in too many cases, instead of shedding light, interviews cloud public discourse."[17]

Indeed, most media training seems to have been inspired by a quip Henry Kissinger reputedly once made at the beginning of a news conference—"Does anyone have any questions for my answers?" It teaches spokespeople to formulate a message that serves their purpose and then to "bridge" to it no matter what they are asked. That is undoubtedly what the Baker's chocolate spokesperson was trying to do, however unskillfully.

Ethical media training helps spokespeople communicate more clearly and in ways that contribute to public discussion. One of us wrote a short book entitled *The Executive's Guide to Handling a Press Interview* early in his career. The very first tip in the book was "always tell the truth." But that advice was not prompted by any real concern for ethics; it was based on the near certainty that few lies survive close inspection or the erosion of time. Eventually, the truth comes out. And once reporters catch you lying—or even hiding the truth—they will never trust you again (Martin, 1997).

On rereading our short guide to dealing with the media, we were gratified (and relieved) to discover it primarily emphasized techniques for getting a point across, (e.g., taking the public's point of view, avoiding

portion-but-not-the-price.html?module=Search&mabReward=relbias%3Ar%2C%7B%221%22%3A%22RI%3A8%22%7D. Accessed July 22, 2015.

[17] Lieberman, T. (2004, January/February). Answer the &%$#* question. *Columbia Journalism Review.*

jargon, dealing with interruptions, and side-stepping traps like repeating loaded words). But it did not deal with the bane of modern-day communications—*spinning*—because back when our little opus was published, the word had not yet entered the lexicon. We wish it never had.

Spinning and Framing

"Spinning" is emphasizing (or deemphasizing) facts to produce a more favorable response from the spinner's point of view. It makes bad facts look good and good facts look better. The *Oxford English Dictionary* dates its usage from the mid-1970s, around the time our brief tome came out and in the politically charged wake of the Watergate scandal. Spin probably derives from the practice of hitting a ball so it twists in a particular direction and, appropriately enough, it was first applied to politicians.[18] But as the media paid more attention to business news, it was quickly applied to company spokespeople as well. Public relations people became known as "Spin Doctors." Unfortunately, spinning facts so only their best side shows not only skates on the edge of lying, it is psychologically dangerous. If you shade the truth often enough, you can lose track of it entirely.

Spinning, however, is not the same as a closely related concept—*framing*. Framing is all about defining the context within which communication will take place (Goffman, 1974). Every thought we have and every word we express is framed in some way. Framing or context is what gives words meaning. Some truths can only be seen when they appear within the proper frame. On the other hand, spinning is usually intended to conceal truth, to direct attention away from it.

Framing can tilt discussion in a certain direction. For example, calling "estate taxes" "death taxes" takes the issue out of the realm of accounting and invites the question, "Why should I pay taxes for dying?" While that frames the issue in a particular way, it is not inherently misleading. It is simply defining the issue in favorable terms to those who would like to eliminate the tax. However, like any rhetorical device,

---

[18] For an interesting discussion of the etymology of "spin," see the Oxford Word Blog at http://blog.oxforddictionaries.com/2011/09/a-journey-through-spin/

framing can be manipulative. This is especially obvious when someone frames issues differently depending on the audience being addressed. For example, Republican pollster and word-maven Frank Luntz published talking points on immigration that carried two different sets of message for candidates, depending on the audience being addressed.

"While Americans are most concerned about the economic impact of illegal immigration, crime is a close second," he told them. "Particularly in border and industrial states with heavy illegal populations, the perception of illegal immigration and increased fear of crime are closely related." The message for general audiences then should be: "Stopping illegal immigrants at the border means less crime." But when addressing Hispanic audiences, he warned, "Hispanic Americans reject the assertion that illegal immigration fosters a general culture of lawlessness." So when addressing them "Talk about 'the system' as the problem." Point out that if the immigration system worked better—if the border were more secure and the documentation process faster—people would be more likely to obey the laws.[19]

Whether such advice amounts to cynical spinning or contextual framing is open to debate. Certainly, in today's world of 24/7 media, few politicians think what they say to one group will never reach the ears of others. But that does not mean they will not slant their remarks to their audience's preconceived beliefs and interests, emphasizing different messages accordingly. *The difference between ethical framing and unethical spinning lies in one's intention, whether it is to reveal or hide the truth.*

Secrets

The flip side of telling the truth is keeping confidences—not only those of clients or employers, which should be obvious, but also those of the media and stakeholders. Tipping a favored reporter about a story another

---

[19] Luntz's advice is in a 25-page advisory issued by his firm and published on the liberal-leaning web sire, the Daily Kos. These quotes appear on page 22–24. See: Luntz, Maslansky Strategic Research. (2005, October). Respect for law & economic fairness: Illegal immigration prevention. http://images.dailykos.com/images /user/3/Luntz_frames_immigration.pdf. Accessed July 22, 2015.

journalist is pursuing may be a way to curry favor, but it is a form of theft that harms the reporter whose scoop you have helped steal and corrupts the free functioning of the media, which is a public good.

On the other hand, keeping secrets can lead to ethical problems of their own. Obviously, no ethical practitioner would hide wrongdoing. But public relations should have a bias toward open and trusting communications with all stakeholders. Practitioners should press clients to carefully weigh the tradeoffs between protecting sensitive data and giving stakeholders the information they legitimately need to make informed decisions. Often, the people most in the dark about an organization's practices and performance are its own employees. But ethicist Sissela Bok (1989) has described how organizational secrecy can inhibit its employees' judgment. Secrecy "shuts out criticism and feedback," she wrote, "leading people to become mired down in stereotyped, unexamined, often erroneous beliefs and ways of thinking" (p. 25). The same principle applies in the larger community within which public relations practitioners seek to create meaning.

Public Relations Character

Alasdaire Macintyre (1998) suggests entering a "practice" such as public relations carries obligations that go beyond truth-telling. "To enter into a practice is to enter into a relationship not only with its contemporary practitioners," he writes, "but also with those who have preceded us in the practice, particularly those whose achievements extended the reach of the practice to the present point" (p. 194). This suggests that character or virtue manifests in two ways—in the internal quality of the activity we are practicing (what he called its "internal good" or "goods of excellence") and in whatever external impact it has (its "external good" or "goods of effectiveness" (Kelvin, 1998, p. 55)).

From the perspective of internal good or excellence, ethical public relations is *not* simply a matter of following a set of rules. It also means figuring out what kind of practitioner we want to be and developing the lifelong habits to support it. It means having the courage to stretch our capabilities to their limits, the honesty to recognize our limitations, and the humility to learn from those with greater experience. It means working to improve the overall practice of public relations as an end in itself, not simply as a means to some other goal such as greater personal stature or renown.

From the perspective of the practice's internal excellence, truthfulness would certainly be at the top of any public relations practitioner's list of essential virtues. But others are also important. Ethicist Robert Solomon compiled his own list of business virtues:

> *There are a great many virtues that are relevant to business life ....*
> *Just for a start, we have honesty, loyalty, sincerity, courage, reliability,*
> *trustworthiness, benevolence, sensitivity, helpfulness, cooperativeness,*
> *civility, decency, modesty, openness, cheerfulness, amiability, toler-*
> *ance, reasonableness, tactfulness, wittiness, gracefulness, liveliness,*
> *magnanimity, persistence, prudence, resourcefulness, warmth, and*
> *hospitality* (1992 pp. 317–339).

From that list of 28 virtues, which is far from exhaustive, we can select three in addition that, in our experience, have particular application to the practice of public relations:

- **Honesty**—Honesty is an uncompromising and consistent commitment to truthfulness in word and action. It is the path to winning the trust of clients and, ultimately, of the publics they serve and on whom they depend.
- **Courage**—Public relations people are often in the position of speaking truth to power, telling them uncomfortable facts they may not want to hear. That requires self-confidence and the courage to be the bearer of bad news or the asker of tough questions.
- **Persistence**—Neither of us has ever been asked to lie in our professional life. We were never asked to hide or disguise the truth. But simply *finding* the truth was often a challenge. In a large company, information is scattered across organizations, people hoard it and dole it out as it suits their purposes, often with their own unique interpretation. It is especially difficult to distinguish what is true

from what is speculative or simply wishful thinking in the heat of a crisis. Discovering the truth requires stubborn tenacity.

A public relations counselor's job is to dig out the facts of a situation, assess their meaning, and communicate them responsibly to relevant stakeholders. A data dump is not responsible communications, nor is abdicating their interpretation to others. Effective counselors try to understand the facts from their stakeholders' points of view so they can give them all the information they need to act intelligently and prudently.

That is not as easy as it sounds. Roger Bolton knows firsthand, having practiced public relations at the most senior levels in government and at companies such as IBM and Aetna, before becoming president of the Arthur W. Page Society. "It's hard work," he wrote,

"because self-delusion can easily convince an enterprise of things that aren't really fully, objectively true, and rooting out the natural bias takes both diligence and an ability to see the world through the objective eyes of others. It also takes guts to stand up for the truth against the natural instincts of an organization to let the little lies or omissions put it in a better light than it deserves."[20]

Now ask yourself, how well did Barnum, Ellsworth, Lee, and Bernays do by these standards in the situations described earlier?

Summary

From what we have learned, the ethical quality of public relations practice should be measured against standards of excellence and effectiveness, aligned in the common purpose of contributing to people's happiness or human flourishing. If Barnum, Ellsworth, Lee, and Bernays succeeded in persuading people to do or believe something that was harmful to them, it couldn't be ethical no matter how clever or effective their technique.

---

[20] Bolton expressed this view in the Page Society Blog, PageTurner on February 17, 2015. See "Tell the truth,". http://www.awpagesociety.com/2015/02/tell-the-truth-021/, Accessed July 22, 2015.

We have seen that truthfulness is a fundamental virtue in the practice of public relations. But it is also a nuanced quality. Barnum's happy hokum skirted the edges of truthfulness but everyone was usually in on the gag. In fact, his hyperbole was part of the entertainment and arguably contributed to people's enjoyment. Few people felt cheated even when they discovered his "Feejee Mermaid" was literally stitched together. Ellsworth, on the other hand, stepped over the bounds of truthfulness when he used advertising dollars to convince editors to run his "news stories." The stories themselves may have been truthful, but their presence in the news columns was a sham, suggesting editors considered them worthy of readers' attention. Ivy Lee's concept of the truth as whatever his client believed is just as misleading. Truth is conformance to reality, not to someone's self-interested conception of it. And Bernays' efforts to convince women to smoke may have started as a harmless stunt, but it was ultimately detrimental to their health, which Bernays himself regretfully concluded late in his life.

In public relations, telling the truth means ensuring the veracity of the information you share (i.e., it substantially conforms to all the facts the public reasonably needs to make an intelligent, voluntary decision). Truth, so defined, is the bedrock of ethical public relations. And, as it happens, that also requires practitioners to develop virtues such as courage and persistence because ensuring the veracity of such facts is seldom easy.

But we have not completed our deep dive into the nature of truth. In the next chapter, we will explore two more characteristics of truthfulness—visibility and validity. And we will see the multifarious ways some practitioners have discovered and invented to dodge, bend, and hide the truth, starting with one of the biggest misinformation campaigns of all time—Big Tobacco's efforts in the 1950s and 1960s to cast doubt on smoking's harmful effects, aided and abetted by some of the nation's leading public relations firms.

CHAPTER 5

Veracity, Visibility, and Validity

Every morning, John W. Hill, a lean and wiry man with soft, blue eyes, can be observed walking from his home at 74th and Park Avenue to his office at 42nd Street and Third Avenue. He walks at least five miles a day and spends eight hours daily at his job, and often is required to put in more time. At 72 years of age, when many men are content to spend their time idling in the sun or beside a fireplace, he is actively overseeing one of the busiest and most successful enterprises in the nation.[1]

So started a biography produced by the enterprise in question—Hill & Knowlton, the public relations agency founded by the "lean man with the soft blue eyes" whose clients at the time produced 10 percent of everything sold in the United States.

John Hill (1890–1977) was a contemporary of Ivy Lee and Edward Bernays and, like them, he started as a journalist, bouncing around from job to job as a reporter or columnist for 18 years before discovering he could make a better living distributing "information" on behalf of deep-pocketed clients rather than scraping "news" together for tightfisted publishers. But unlike Lee, who claimed he trusted the public to draw the right conclusions from the information he laid before them, Hill did not think his job was done until the conclusions he wanted people to draw were firmly planted in their minds. "The end product of effective public

---

[1] Quoted by Karen S. Miller in her masterful book *The Voice of Business: Hill & Knowlton and Postwar Public Relations,* Chapel Hill: University of North Carolina Press, 1999. Her 1995 University of Wisconsin dissertation, on which the book is based, is available online at http://www.thebhc.org/publications/BEHprint/v024n1/p0018-p0021.pdf

relations," he wrote in 1958, "is ... public attitudes resulting from communication of information, facts, and management's point of view" (p. 7).

Hill was editing a trade paper and just dreaming about opening a publicity bureau when a Cleveland steel executive, distraught that his company was about to be taken over, shot and killed himself. The bank executive underwriting the takeover knew Hill and pressed him into service to convince local newspaper editors that the suicide had nothing to do with the company's financial health. Hill succeeded. The suicide story "did not reflect upon the company's financial position in the slightest degree," and the takeover went off without a hitch (Hill, 1993, p. 18).

The bank's chairman was so impressed he quickly offered Hill $500 a month to handle his firm's media relations. Hill explained he could not afford to give up his day job, but if the banker could find other clients for him, he would accept. Amazingly, the banker got on the phone to the president of one of the area's largest steel companies and told him to hire Hill. The very next day, Hill founded his small Cleveland, Ohio, "publicity bureau." With contacts like that, Hill's firm eventually worked for most of the country's major industrial companies, from Standard Oil to U.S. Steel. When the bank that originally hired him went under during the depression of 1933, Hill invited its head of advertising and public relations, Don Knowlton, to join his firm, which then became Hill & Knowlton (H&K).

Public Advocacy

In all this time, Hill's approach to public relations was more than generating publicity, disseminating information, or even persuading consumers to buy a company's products. Because his clients tended to be large industrial companies embroiled in contentious matters such as negotiating labor contracts or fending off government regulation, Hill developed an expertise in what would later be known as public advocacy. He described his role in fairly anodyne terms to a Congressional Committee investigating his steel company clients:

Basically, the job is to let the public know as much about industry's achievements as it now knows about its faults and defects. The job is

to tell the story of its services to mankind, of its ideas, of its aims, pur-
poses, and activities. Under an enlightened public relations policy,
nothing that is of interest to the public is hidden from the public
(Tedlow, 1979, p. 99).

Public advocacy really hit its stride when the two principal thorns in
industry's side—unions and government—took common cause in the
1930s. To put it in Hill's (1993) own words, "The [Roosevelt] New
Deal had drawn a bead on steel as the number-one target for labor organization" (p. 46). Hill was referring to the National Labor Relations
Act, which made the right to collective bargaining the law of the land
and was bitterly opposed by his steel company clients. Hill (1958) himself considered it a serious "erosion of management's function" (p. 22).
He opposed anything that interfered with management's right to distribute "increases of productivity" (i.e., profits) as it saw fit (p. 24). And
he set out to gain public support for restoring management's legitimate
authority. Business historian Richard Tedlow (1979) considers Hill the
leading representative of a school of public relations counselors committed to economic conservatism. "Unlike Bernays, who could work for a
union with the same aplomb with which he could work for a corporation," Tedlow notes, "Hill was a genuine ideologue of the right" (p. 98).

Indeed, Hill was so intimately involved in the steel industry's attempts to fight unionization that, in 1933, he moved to New York,
where the industry's trade association was based, leaving the firm's
Cleveland office under his partner's care. New York then became
H&K's official headquarters. The steel industry's battle against unionization was ultimately futile, but the specter of further government interference in management prerogatives was so potent, H&K became the
center for advocacy programs on behalf of a range of industries, from
steel and aircraft to butter and tobacco. Each of these efforts deserves
book-length treatment of its own, but for purposes of exploring the ethical implications of public relations advocacy, H&K's work on behalf of
the tobacco industry stands in a class by itself.

Public Relations and Smoking

Smoking has never been entirely free of criticism, whether by moralists who considered it a private vice or by fussy homemakers who objected to the odors it left on their upholstery. But, as we've seen, public relations helped make smoking more culturally acceptable and socially popular in the first half of the 20th century. Around 1950, however, a few medical journal articles began linking cigarette smoking to lung cancer. Then in December 1952, an article in *Reader's Digest*, "Cancer by the Carton," detailed the dangers for a much broader audience.[2] Appearing in what was the largest circulation magazine of the time, the article created a sensation, prompting more stories in newspapers and magazines. Cigarette sales declined for the first time in decades and so did tobacco company stock prices. By the end of 1953, the presidents of the six largest tobacco companies had had enough. They hurriedly gathered in New York City on December 10 and 11 to consider how they might defuse the situation. In the end, they decided to call in John W. Hill, who had developed a strong reputation as a "corporate confidant" and whose agency had deep experience working with industry trade associations.

Although Hill had quit smoking in the 1940s for health reasons, he felt strongly that every company and industry was entitled to effective representation. And in the last weeks of 1953, he and his team constructed a strategy that held for more than two decades. It was pretty straightforward and can be summarized as follows:[3]

1. The industry should establish a separate research committee, led by an individual of impeccable credentials, to inform the public of the facts.

---

[2] The full *Reader's Digest* article, "Cancer by the Carton," ran in the magazine's December 1952 issue (on newsstands in November). A copy is available in the Legacy Tobacco Library: http://legacy.library.ucsf.edu/tid/bcm92f00/pdf.

[3] This summary is based on a memo prepared for Philip Morris lawyer Murray Bring by John W. Hill II (no relation to the founder of H&K). See "Health and Morality: Tobacco's Counter-Claim," Hill, 1992, p. 3. That memo is part of an archive of 14 million documents created by tobacco companies about their advertising, manufacturing, marketing, scientific research and political activities. The archive was established in accordance with the industry's Master Settlement with the state attorneys general suing for damages related to smoking. The archive is hosted by the University of California San Francisco Library and the Center for Knowledge Management. See https://industrydocuments.library.ucsf.edu/tobacco/

2. The research committee should seize control of the science surrounding health and smoking by:

- Identifying scientists who are skeptical of a link between cigarettes and cancer or critical of the statistical methods used by those who claim to have found a link and

- Commissioning its own medical research into smoking and health.

3. Rather than flatly denying the health implications of smoking, the research committee will win public confidence by appearing to take the issue seriously, while emphasizing that there are still many unknowns and undoubtedly two sides to the issue.

- Instead of fanning the flames by countering every attack, the research committee should first encourage reporters to consult it if they plan to write on the issue and, should they publish unfavorable information, the committee should quietly correct it at the source.

The "research committee's" staff would consist of public relations practitioners on H&K's payroll, but Hill was adamant that its research had to be real "to give weight and credence to the committee's statements" (Hill II, 1992, p. 3). The tobacco company presidents initially claimed they had already sponsored or conducted more research than anyone without finding any connection between smoking and lung cancer, but they eventually bought into the strategy. They agreed to create the Tobacco Industry Research Committee (TIRC), fund its research, and let it speak for all of them.

H&K's Campaign

With that, Hill published a full-page ad on the first business day of 1954 to announce the formation of the TIRC. The ad, which ran in 448 newspapers across the country, was headlined "A Frank Statement to the Public by the Makers of Cigarettes." It essentially said there was no proof that smoking causes cancer but the industry would not dismiss such claims either. On the contrary, while tobacco companies believed their products to be safe, they also considered their customers' health "a basic responsibility, paramount to every other consideration in our business" (Hill II, 1992, p. 5). Therefore, the industry promised to assist in research into all phases of tobacco use and health through a committee supervised by prominent scientists.

Within six months, the TIRC had hired as its director a doctor who had once been head of the American Society for the Control of Cancer, later known as the American Cancer Society and one of the tobacco industry's most ardent opponents. In announcing his appointment, the *Wall Street Journal* described the new director as a "husky, sun-tanned man of 66" who "toyed with a pipe ... and said he avoided cigarettes because, as they burned, they threatened to singe his mustache" (Hill II, 1992, p. 7). For its part, the media accepted the sincerity of the industry's approach on face value. According to a study prepared by H&K at the time, only nine percent of the newspapers expressing opinions about the TIRC's formation were unfavorable, predicting biased research, while 65 percent were unreservedly favorable. Most importantly, from that point on, stories based on highly unfavorable studies—such as a massive American Cancer Society study—quoted doctors on both sides of the issue and usually sought the TIRC's view as well, which almost invariably boiled down to "statistical data do not provide the answers and much more research is needed before the causes of the diseases involved in the charge are known" (Hill II, 1992, p. 7).

Hill himself described his strategy's success five years later.

The accusation against the industry's chief product was based on scientific suspicion growing out of statistical studies and experiments with animals. No conclusive or clinical proof was at hand. But the industry had no thought of waiting passively upon events.

Expressing its genuine concern over the whole problem of cigarette smoking and health, it took a step unprecedented in American industry. It invited a group of outstanding scientists, each of unchallengeable reputation, to constitute themselves as a 'Scientific Advisory Board,' for the purpose of making grants to individuals and institutions into the problem.... The results of the various research projects will be reported to the public in the form of scientific papers.

Once this sound basis of public interest was established the industry was in sound position to draw some public attention to the other sides of the question. The normal American sense of fair play came to bear at this point, and the public evidently credited the fact that, despite sensational charges, the truth is not yet known and the industry itself is doing what it can to speed the availability of true and reliable answers (Hill, 1958, pp. 136–137).

Interestingly, Hill's 1993 autobiography, *The Making of a Public Relations Man*, does not mention tobacco or tobacco companies at all. Could be have forgotten his role in what *Business Week* called "one of PR's best finger-in-the-dike jobs?"[4] More likely, he anticipated that anything he said about his efforts on behalf of the tobacco industry would simply buy him a seat at the defense table when the inevitable class action suits were filed. As it happens, H&K won that seat anyway as codefendant in many of the tobacco lawsuits.

Campaign Evaluation

By most measures, Hill's strategy was successful in protecting the tobacco companies from initial reports that cigarettes might cause cancer. It worked for 10 years, which was how long it took for the U.S. Surgeon General to amass sufficient data to conclude that "cigarette smoking contributes substantially to mortality from certain specific diseases and to the overall death rate."[5] Of course, it took at least an additional decade before the Surgeon General's warning began to have a major effect on people's behavior. That is essentially an entire generation of continued employment for the industry's employees, dividends for its many shareowners, and tax revenue for all the communities in which it operated. Of course, it may also have meant a greater incidence of cancer for an entire generation of smokers. So the real question is not, "Did it work?" but rather, "Was it right?"

---

[4] The *Business Week* quote was cited in John Hill II's memo to Philip Morris lawyer Murray Bring. Hill II, 1992, p. 6.
[5] National Institute for Health. (1964). *Smoking and Health: Report of the Advisory Committee to the Surgeon General of the Public Health Service*, p. 31. Public Health Service Publication 1103. http://profiles.nlm.nih.gov/ps/access/NNBBMQ.pdf. Accessed July 22, 2015.

The minimal ethical standard we have discussed so far is one of *truthfulness* as conformance to facts, or veracity. Hill could argue that he did nothing to mislead the public. Indeed, under his direction, the industry carefully avoided blanket denials of a link between smoking and cancer; on the contrary, it maintained the question was still unresolved and pledged support in finding an answer. If anything, it urged the public to keep an open mind.

To that end, the TIRC did its best to ensure that stories about smoking and cancer presented both sides of the question, prompting one senator to observe that, "no story about the risk of smoking goes anywhere without a tobacco industry rebuttal trailing along behind, like the tail on a kite" (Hill II, 1992, p. 22). And although a former officer of the Cancer Society told *Consumer Reports* the TIRC "conducted a smart, clever campaign of constant denials and attempted diversions, such as pointing the finger at air pollution as the real villain in lung cancer," he begrudgingly added, "No one could question their ethics of operation" (Hill II, 1992, p. 22).

Ironically, in his later years, Hill himself had doubts about the ethics of at least one aspect of his public relations strategy. The TIRC did not hide who was paying its bills, but by portraying itself as an independent "research organization," it engaged in a clever bit of misdirection designed to increase its credibility and disguise its true purpose. Public relations, not research, was the TIRC's real agenda. It did very little actual research, and what it did do was clearly designed solely to cast doubt on a link between smoking and cancer by highlighting other causes. Testifying under oath in a 1997 trial, a former president of the TIRC could not site a single study it had done on smoking and disease. The vast majority of its studies did not even have anything to do with tobacco. Indeed, one of the federal judges, Judge Lee H. Soroking, who presided over two of the many cases filed against the tobacco industry, declared the TIRC "nothing but a hoax created for public relations purposes with no intention of seeking the truth or publishing it".[6]

---

[6] Janson, D. (1988, April 22). End to suit declared in smoking death. *New York Times*.

Misuse of Third-Party Endorsement Front Groups

The TIRC was not as blatantly misleading as the "National Smokers Alliance," a supposedly grassroots organization created by Burson-Marsteller and funded by the tobacco industry in 1993 to oppose smoking bans in public buildings. But it was on the leading edge of what has become a $1 billion public relations sub-specialty, according to UCLA professor Edward T. Walker who has made tracking these groups a specialty of his own. "In a time when companies are particularly sensitive to protest groups, threats of boycott and accusations of corporate irresponsibility," he wrote, "corporations need grass-roots support, or at the least the appearance of it, to defend their reputations and ability to make profits."[7] Failing to gather authentic support, many companies settle for its appearance, not particularly concerned if it is no more organic than Astroturf, as long as it *looks* like the real thing.

But ethically, third-party endorsers should identify themselves with the party—agency and client—on whose behalf they are acting, especially if they are being paid. When they do not reveal this, such as above, they constitute what has been labeled "front groups." For example, in 2014, the city of San Francisco proposed a two-cents-per-ounce tax on soft drinks to reduce their consumption and to pay for new public health programs. That prompted the American Beverage Association to fund a group called "Californians for Beverage Choice," which fought the proposal as another "nanny state" intrusion into people's personal lives. And the beverage association leaned on another group, the "Coalition for an Affordable City," to argue the soda tax would raise the cost of living for the city's poorer citizens. By hiding its involvement, the association denied voters important information about its self-interested role in the debate. In the end, it drowned out the other side's arguments—the new tax failed to pass.[8] In today's hyper-connected society,

[7] Walker, E.T. (2012, August 10). Grass-roots mobilization, by corporate America. *New York Times.* http://www.nytimes.com/2012/08/11/opinion/grass-roots-mobilization-by-corporate-america.html?_r=0. Accessed July 22, 2015.
[8] Sabatini, J. (2015, November 5). Sugary drink tax measure fails. *San Francisco Examiner.* http://www.sfexaminer.com/sanfrancisco/sugary-drink-tax-measure-fails/Content?oid=2911239. Accessed July 22, 2015.

organizations on both sides of an issue beat the bushes to muster 'expert" support for their position. For example, both the manufacturers of bioengineered food and their competitors in the organic food industry have recruited academics to shore up their public credibility. As one researcher who received financial support from the organic food industry told *the New York Times*, "They could conduct those studies on their own and put this information on their website. But nobody would believe them. There is a friggin' war going on around this stuff. And everyone is looking to gain as much leverage as they can."[9]

Over time, John Hill (1993) condemned the use of "paper groups" established to promote a cause under the guise of being independent. "In a free country, any interest with a cause has the right to present its case to the public, to inform and, if possible, to persuade to its heart's content," he wrote. "But that right of free speech also carries the obligation that the source of it will be in the open for all to see. Attempts to fool the public by making it believe an 'organization' existing only on paper is really a vociferous group favoring this or that cause have cast a shadow upon the business of public relations" (p. 140). Even "Poison" Ivy Lee (1925, p. 23) argued, "The essential evil of propaganda is a failure to disclose the source of information."

Contemporary Examples

It is an evil that bedevils many public relations practitioners, desperate to give their clients the veneer of third-party endorsement or defense. In 2011, Burson-Marsteller encouraged a number of reporters and bloggers to investigate Google's use of customer data.[10] But the agency went to such lengths to hide its client's involvement the writers it approached became less interested in the privacy issue it was flogging than in the secret client it represented. The whole scheme came apart when one of the bloggers Burson approached posted copies of their email exchanges online, and *USA Today* ran a story about the agency's "whisper

---

[9] Lipton, E. (2015, September 6), Emails Reveal Academic Ties In A Food War, *New York Times*, http://nyti.ms/1KRWOiu
[10] Acohido, B., & Swartz, J. (2011, May 10). Google deflects PR firm's attack of Gmail privacy. *USA Today*. http://usatoday30.usatoday.com/money/media/2011-05-06-google_n.htm. Accessed July 22, 2015.

campaign." Within 24 hours, The Daily Beast website had identified Facebook as the Burson client behind the "clumsy smear," a "Keystone Kops" "caper" that had "blown up in their faces."[11]

The Edelman public relations agency courted similar embarrassment when it hired a journalist and a photographer to pose as a couple, touring the country in a recreational vehicle, staying overnight in client Walmart's parking lots and blogging about what a blast they were having. Not surprisingly, every Walmart employee they ran into raved about how much they liked working there and how caring the company is. Critics rolled their eyes and *BusinessWeek* quickly revealed the couple was being paid by "Working Families for Walmart," an Edelman front group, showing, the magazine said, "how hungry Walmart is to find people who have anything positive to say about the company."[12]

Ironically, Edelman was one of the driving forces behind the Word of Mouth Association's Code of Ethics, which at the time stated in part, "Honesty of Identity: You never obscure your identity."[13] The agency's CEO, Richard Edelman, quickly canceled the program and apologized for "failing to be transparent about the identity of the two bloggers from the outset."[14] But, as Edelman told us, "I immediately realized it was no one's fault but my own. I had been blogging since 2004. I had written about the power of social media and the importance of transparency. But I had never instituted an effective training program. So it all happened in an *ad hoc* fashion, with no discussion or rigor around it."[15]

Edelman vowed to change that, setting up a central clearing house for social media programs, spelling out the agency's standards for ethical

---

[11] Lyons, D. (2011, May 10). Facebook busted in clumsy smear on Google. *The Daily Beast.* http://www.thedailybeast.com/articles/2011/05/12/facebook-busted-in-clumsy-smear-attempt-on-google.html. Accessed July 22, 2015.

[12] Gogoi, P. (2006, October 9). Walmart's Jim and Laura: The real story. *Business Week.* http://www.businessweek.com/stories/2006-10-09/Walmarts-jim-and-laura-the-real-storybusinessweek-business-news-stock-market-and-financial-advice. Accessed July 22, 2015.

[13] The Word of Mouth Marketing Association ethical standards were updated in September 2009, in part to better reflect regulations established by the Federal Trade Commission. "Transparency" is still an important standard, but now comes under the heading of "Integrity." You can find the complete up-to-date standards at the organization's website—http://www.womma.org/ethics/womma-code-of-ethics.

[14] Some of the specific steps Edelman took to ensure compliance with its ethical standards for social media were described in an October 20, 2006, entry on Richard's blog. See http://www.edelman.com/p/6-a-m/what-is-edelman-doing/.

[15] *Source:* Conversation with Richard Edelman, April 30, 2015.

behavior online, requiring all employees to take interactive desktop training on the typical situations they might encounter online, and appointing an agency-wide Chief Compliance Officer. All of this ultimately led to the adoption of a broad Code of Conduct, which is reviewed and revised as necessary every year. All employees sign it when they join the firm and as part of their annual performance appraisal.

Ghost-bloggers are not the only shadowy characters prowling the Internet. Organizations ranging from the Vatican and the Central Intelligence Agency to Microsoft and the Church of Scientology have been accused of covertly editing Wikipedia entries they did not like.[16] In most cases, such organizations used a "sockpuppet" or bogus online persona pretending to be an unaffiliated and neutral party. The most famous sockpuppet of all time is probably John Mackey, CEO of Whole Foods, who used a phony screen name to promote the company's stock on Yahoo Finance message boards for nearly 8 years.[17] The practice is a blatant "conflict of interest," but so widespread on Wikipedia, it poisoned the well for reputable agencies that had legitimate issues with the accuracy of some entries about clients. As a result, a number of major agencies signed a joint pledge to comply with the online encyclopedia's policies, starting with crystal-clear transparency.[18]

Sockpuppets are not confined to the online world. Some companies use trade associations to hide their political and social initiatives. In fact, according to the Center for Public Integrity, trade associations now spend more on public relations than lobbying.[19] And many of the agencies they hire seem to specialize in cloudy transparency. For example, "Count on

---

[16] Naturally, Wikipedia has an entry on what it terms "conflict of interest editing." See http://en.wikipedia.org/wiki/Conflict-of-interest_editing_on_Wikipedia. Accessed July 22, 2015.

[17] Richards, K. (2014, April 11). Confirmed: Companies have been editing Wikipedia pages to make themselves look better. *Business Insider*. http://www.businessinsider .com/pr-agencies-agree-to-stop-wikipedia-edits-2014-6. Accessed July 22, 2015.

[18] Wikipedia. (2014, February 7). Statement on Wikipedia from participating communications firms. http://en.wikipedia.org/wiki/Wikipedia:Statement_on_Wikipedia _from_participating_communications_firms. Accessed July 22, 2015.

[19] Quinn, E. (2015, January 10). Who needs lobbyists? *The Center for Public Integrity*. http://www.publicintegrity.org/2015/01/15/16596/who-needs-lobbyists-see-what-big-business-spends-win-american-minds. Accessed July 22, 2015.

Coal" is a front group created by Washington, DC, public relations firm Weber Merritt, under a $4 million per year contract with the National Mining Association. But the only mention of industry sponsorship on the "Count on Coal" website is: "Founded by organizations and companies that recognize the value of coal in our power generation supply chain, the organization is growing to include community, business and political leaders from throughout the US."[20] And that disclaimer does not appear at all in the online petitions it posts, criticizing government proposals to cut carbon emissions.

Native Advertising/Brand Journalism

With spending projected to quadruple to $21 billion by 2018,[21] sponsored content, also called "brand journalism" or "native advertising," is an even faster-growing ethical challenge. Rather than "renting" audiences by advertising alongside someone else's content, brands can "own" a consumer relationship by producing content that is useful in its own right. It is the latest shiny new thing in marketing. And it is ripe for abuse. Some early experiments simply integrated brand-produced content into the run of a publication, labeling it "sponsored" in type the size of the last line on an ophthalmologist's eye chart. All of which prompted New Yorker writer Ken Auletta to observe, "Native advertising is basically saying to corporations that want to advertise, 'We will camouflage your ads to make them look like news stories'."[22] Wall Street Journal editor Gerard Baker called the practice "a Faustian bargain"[23]

---

[20] The Count on Coal. http://www.countoncoal.org/about-us/. Accessed September 6, 2015.

[21] Hoelzel, M. (2014, December 8). Native advertising is soaring. Business Insider. http://www.businessinsider.com/spending-on-native-ads-will-soar-as-publishers-and-advertisers-take-notice-2014-11. Accessed July 22, 2015.

[22] Auletta made this somment on the May 16, 2014, installment of Charlie Rose on PBS. See: http://r2plive.org/conversation-on-the-new-york-times-conversation-with-thierry-de-montbrial/. Accessed July 22, 2015.

[23] Coffee, P. (2013, September 25). Wall Street Journal Editor says native advertising is a deal with the devil. PR Newser. http://www.mediabistro.com/prnewser/the-wall-street-journal-editor-says-native-advertising-is-a-deal-with-the-devil_b73529. Accessed July 22, 2015.

before his own paper jumped headfirst into the trend by launching its own in-house native ad studio.[24]

Baker's turnaround may either reflect a belated and begrudging accommodation to the financial realities of publishing a daily newspaper in a declining advertising environment. Or it may reflect an improvement in labeling practices. It may even recognize that advertiser-created content does not have to be self-serving; it can be interesting, entertaining, even enlightening, and valuable. For example, to promote the second season of "Orange Is the New Black," Netflix ran a multi-media native ad in the *New York Times* that explored the issue of women in prison in the same depth as the best investigative journalism. The ad didn't say a word about the TV series, but it was clearly marked "a paid post" with a prominent Netflix logo.[25]

Still, a study commissioned by Edelman and the Internet Advertising Bureau showed that people do not always know whether or not the content they encounter online has been paid for by a brand. On news sites, as many as 59 percent of respondents said it was either "not very clear," or "not at all clear" that the content they were shown was sponsored.[26] And according to Reuters' 2015 Digital News Report, one-third of the public feels "disappointed or deceived" by native ads.[27]

To its credit, Edelman was early in setting guidelines for the use of sponsored content, requiring that "editorial-style content" be clearly

[24] Moses, L. (2014, March 10). *Wall Street Journal* launches native advertising studio. *AdWeek*. http://www.adweek.com/news/press/wall-street-journal-launches-native-ad-studio-156212. Accessed July 22, 2015.
[25] The Netflix "native ad" was prepared by *the New York Times'* "Brand Studio" and not only carried the notice it was "a paid post" but it also declared at the end that "The news and editorial staffs of *The New York Times* had no role in this post's preparation." See: Deziel, M. (June 2015). Women in prison: Why the male model doesn't work. *The New York Times*. http://paidpost.nytimes.com/netflix/women-inmates-separate-but-not-equal.html?_r=0#.VS50zxPF9Zk. Accessed July 22, 2015.
[26] Marshall, J. (2014, July 22). Sponsored content isn't always clearly labeled research suggests. *Wall Street Journal*. http://blogs.wsj.com/cmo/2014/07/22/sponsored-content-isnt-always-clearly-labelled-research-suggests/?mod=djemCMOTodaysponsored. Accessed July 22, 2015.
[27] Newman, N. (2015). Executive summary and key findings of 2015. *Digital News Report*. Reuters Institute for the Study of Journalism. http://www.digitalnewsreport.org/survey/2015/executive-summary-and-key-findings-2015/

delineated from the rest of the publication or website. And it separated *pitching stories* from the *purchase of paid content*, helping ensure that one was not used to leverage the other. "We will not have any quid pro quo discussions," CEO Richard Edelman declared, "and will not tolerate pay-for-play in any market."[28]

Meanwhile, others are stretching the limits of brand placements. Sweet'N Low artificial sweetener makes several appearances in an e-book and web series aimed at young adults.[29] In one scene, a coworker teases the story's heroine about putting Sweet'N Low in her coffee. "Hellooo, isn't it bad for you?" the friend asks. "They fed lab rats twenty-five hundred packets of Sweet'N Low a day," our heroine replies, "And still the FDA or EPA, or whatever agency, couldn't connect the dots from any kind of cancer in humans to my party in a packet." Cumberland Packing Corporation, the Brooklyn-based company that makes Sweet'N Low paid about $1.3 million for that bit of persuasion. Readers or viewers should know who is behind a safety claim so they can decide whether or not to accept it at face value.

Ghostwriting

Add **visibility** to the list of virtues Aristotle would require of a public relations practitioner. Visibility does not mean public relations people need call attention to themselves. For example, hardly anyone expects busy CEOs or politicians to write their own speeches or printed opinion pieces, even if they have the necessary time and rhetorical skills. They need not credit their ghostwriter every time they get up to speak. It is ethically sufficient for them to provide the content, edit the finished product, and accept responsibility for it. Most ethicists agree the ethics of ghostwriting hinges on the audience's expectations. And, in fact, surveys

---

[28] Richard Edelman announced the principles on his blog. Edelman, R. (2013, July 15). Sponsored content: An ethical framework. *6 AM Blog*. http://www.edelman.com/p/6-a-m/sponsored-content-an-ethical-framework/. Accessed July 22, 2015.

[29] The Sweet 'n Low product placement was described by Alexandra Alter (2014, November 2). "E-Book Mingles Love and Product Placement," *The New York Times*, http://www.nytimes.com/2014/11/03/business/media/e-book-mingles-love-and-product-placement.html. Accessed September 6, 2015.

show most people expect speeches to be written by someone other than the person delivering them, and few have a problem with it (Riley and Brown, 1996).

Other research (Gallicano et al., 2013), however, suggests this principle may not apply to *social media*. For example, a recent study indicates people expect corporate executives and politicians to have someone else write blog posts under their name, including responses to comments on their own blog and comments to postings on others' blogs. However, the researchers did not consider "the permissibility ... high enough to endorse 'ghost-blogging' as long-term relationship strategies" (p. 22). Consequently, they recommended that ghostwritten blogs should include a disclosure statement. We are not so sure that's necessary.

Asking members of the public to assess the "permissibility" of ghostwriting is essentially asking them to act as ethicists. The more apt question is whether knowing who actually wrote the blog or comments would materially change their attitudes or behavior. That is much more relevant to the issue at hand. Judging the ethics of ghostwriting and ghost-blogging hinges on assessing that likelihood. And it is the question ethical practitioners need to answer for themselves.

For most corporate or political speeches, the existence or nonexistence of a ghostwriter—much less his or her actual identity—would make no material difference in the audience's reaction. Who thinks President Obama writes his own Tweets and fund-raising e-mails?[30] However, whether Kim Kardashian was *paid* to Tweet about Carl Jr.'s salads is probably even more relevant than if she thumbed all 140 characters of the message herself. (For the record, she denies being paid.[31]) And publications like medical or academic journals may be a special case. Their readers have a much higher expectation of authors' direct involvement in researching and writing its articles. And any funding or writing assistance authors receive should be acknowledged, along with any other potential conflicts of interest.

---

[30] President Obama announced a new Twitter handle in early May 2015, one he supposedly is managing on his own. Time will tell.

[31] Ms. Kardashian denied the accusation. See: Kim Kardashian Takes on False Twitter Tales. (2009, December 31). *OK!* http://okmagazine.com/get-scoop/kim-kardashian-takes-false-twitter-tales/. Accessed July 22, 2015.

Validity

In addition to veracity and visibility, ethical advocacy is characterized by **validity**—it is based on clear, relevant, rational evidence. The first element of validity is *clarity*—whether information is easily understandable or so cleverly worded to be misleading. As this was written, for example, Sprint offered a new wireless calling plan that promised to cut user's monthly rates in half. But according to a *Wall Street Journal* analysis, "the fine print means many switching subscribers won't see that big a discount" because they will have to buy new phones, a fact that did not make it into the company's ads.[32]

Sprint is not the worse—and certainly not the only—marketer with selective pricing disclosures. Electronic and physical mailboxes fill with offers and appeals that seem attractive on the surface but dissolve into scams on close reading. The fine print that was originally intended to protect consumers has become safe harbor for unscrupulous marketers who are afraid to fully describe their offer in type consumers can read and in language they can understand.

Whether a message is valid also depends on the intended recipient's ability to understand and rationally evaluate it. Promotions directed at children or the elderly, for example, are especially problematic. Google came under fire from consumer groups who believe its YouTube Kids app blurs the line between programming and advertising. While the app might shield tykes from sexy videos, according to the consumer groups, it exposes them to branded channels from the likes of McDonalds, Barbie, and Fischer Price "which are little more than program-length commercials."[33]

Similarly, a Senate Special Committee on Aging raised troubling questions about Publishers Clearing House solicitors who pressured el-

---

[32] Knutson, R. (2014, December 2). Sprint escalates wireless price war with half-off bills. *Wall Street Journal.* http://www.wsj.com/articles/sprint-escalates-wireless-price-war-with-half-off-bills-1417533378. Accessed July 22, 2015.

[33] Consumer group complaints were spelled out in a filing with the Federal Trade Commission. See Georgetown Law Institute for Public Representation. (2015, April 7). *Request for Investigation into Google's Unfair and Deceptive Practices in Connection with its YouTube kids App.* http://www.centerfordigitaldemocracy.org/sites/default/files/4-7-15%20YouTube%20Kids%20Request%20for%20Investigation%20FINAL.pdf. Accessed July 22, 2015.

derly people into buying magazine subscriptions to improve their chances of winning its famous sweepstakes. The committee concluded the company solicitations "appear to 'push the limits' of federal law and settlement agreements.... reached with dozens of Attorney Generals [sic] over two decades."[34]

The second element of validity is *relevance*—do the facts being presented have material bearing on the matter at hand? Two exercises in opposition research within the same week of November 2014 demonstrate the importance of recognizing the difference. In one, the Edelman public relations agency proposed to research a client's opponents; in the other, a senior executive of the Uber car service proposed to research a reporter who had been critical of the company.

Edelman's client had proposed to construct an oil pipeline across Canada. The environmental group Greenpeace, which opposed the pipeline's construction, somehow got its hands on a copy of Edelman's public relations strategy, which called for developing "detailed background research on key opposition groups."[35] That prompted *the New York Times* to characterize the whole affair as an attempt "to spread any unflattering findings about the opposition," noting that the plan documents proposed enlisting third party allies to "put pressure" on the pipeline's opponents "when TransCanada can't."[36]

As described by a BuzzFeed editor, a senior Uber executive attending an industry dinner "outlined the notion of spending 'a million dollars' ... to dig up dirt on its critics in the media—and specifically to spread details of the personal life of a female journalist who has criticized the

---

[34] Senate Special Committee on Aging. (2014, April 15). *Publishers Clearing House Sweepstakes Under Scrutiny.* http://www.aging.senate.gov/publishers-clearing-house-sweepstakes-solicitations-under-scrutiny. Accessed July 22, 2015.

[35] Once Greenpeace got its hands on Edelman's plan, they posted it online. See Greenpeace. (2014). *The Edelman strategy, "Energy East Campaign Organization: Promote, Respond, Pressure."* http://www.greenpeace.org/canada/Global/canada/file/2014/11/eNERGY%20eAST%20CAMPAIGN%20ORG%20PROMOTE%20RESPONSE%20PRESSURE.PDF. Accessed July 22, 2015.

[36] Austen, I. (2014, November 17). PR firm urges TransCanada to target opponents of its energy east pipeline. *New York Times.* http://www.nytimes.com/2014/11/18/business/pr-firm-urges-transcanada-to-target-opponents-of-its-energy-east-pipeline.html. Accessed July 22, 2015.

company."[37] The executive who made the suggestion later explained he thought he was speaking "off the record." He said he "regretted [the remarks] and that they didn't reflect his or the company's views."

There is nothing unethical about analyzing what reporters have previously written to better understand what they think of your company and its industry. There is also nothing wrong with tracking public details about a reporter's private life or information he or she is willing to share, such as a spouse's name, children, alma mater, and hobbies. Such information can help build a stronger personal relationship with the reporter. But digging for embarrassing information is clearly unethical. It is a violation of the reporter's privacy. It muddies the waters of public discussion and deprives people of information about the company by casting irrelevant aspersions on the person reporting it. It is not responsible advocacy by any measure.

The key word here is "relevance" and that could be the safe harbor for Edelman. If its background research was intended to reveal *relevant* information about the pipeline's opponents, such as conflicts of interest or extreme positions they have taken in the past on similar projects, it could be ethical. As Edelman's own plan suggested, "To make an informed decision on this project, Canadians need to have a true picture of the motivations not only of the project proponents, but of its opponents as well." Ethical or not, the publicity embarrassed TransCanada and it parted ways with the agency within a matter of weeks.

Smear campaigns are more common than you might think. Public Relations counselor Bob Dilenschneider told us he is frequently asked to place negative information about competitors in the media.[38] Some executives have even asked him to spread embarrassing information about colleagues to eliminate personal competition. Dilenschneider says he turns down such work. Others are not so picky.

Indeed, raising troubling questions about an acquiring company has foiled many corporate acquisitions. One agency, Kekst & Company,

---

[37] Smith, B. (2014, November 17). Uber executive suggests digging up dirt on journalists. *BuzzFeed*. http://www.buzzfeed.com/bensmith/uber-executive-suggests-digging-up-dirt-on-journalists#.ruW8NwP5m. Accessed July 22, 2015.

[38] *Source:* conversation with Robert Dilenschneider on March 10, 2015/

turned this into a specialty of sorts in the merger-crazed 1970s and 1980s. It foiled the 1975 hostile takeover of the Sterndent dental equipment company by characterizing the prospective acquirers as "the Arab group," even though it included Americans, and suggesting Jewish dentists would boycott the company if they succeeded in buying it. Three years later, Kekst foiled American Express' takeover of publisher McGraw-Hill by suggesting the financial services company would meddle with the editorial integrity of its publications, including *Business Week*. In both cases, the agency's CEO, Gershon Kekst explained, "That's what I thought was happening, and I wanted to be damned sure everyone else thought so too."[39] One could argue the ethics of this approach, but Kekst himself probably put it best in a 1998 interview. "You couldn't get away with that these days," he said.[40]

That assessment may, in fact, be too optimistic. These days, institutions of all kinds hire armies of so-called Internet "trolls" to promote themselves through phony "reviews" or to spread malicious information about their opponents and competitors. Trolls originally amused themselves by hijacking chat room conversations with a steady stream of vitriolic, often nonsensical comments. Today, according to one study, they are increasingly organized into "crowdturfing" campaigns, operating out of China, India, and the United States, "to spread defamatory rumors, false advertising, or suspect political messages." The study found "surprising evidence" not only that such campaigns exist, but "are growing rapidly" (Wang et al., 2011).

The third element of validity is *rationality*. Is information presented in a way that leaves room for the application of reason or does it cloud logic by manipulating emotions? Hill would argue that is precisely the principle he was serving in trying to counter the machinations of crackpot alarmists who had stoked people's fears without any real proof that cigarette smoking harms people's health.

[39] Salmans, S. (1983, July 11). Molder of merger perceptions. *New York Times*. http://www.nytimes.com/1983/07/11/business/molder-of-merger-perceptions.html. Accessed July 22, 2015.

[40] Hoffer, K. (1999, March 12). Gershon Kekst: Master of the 'Saykhl' business. *Directors and Boards*. http://www.thefreelibrary.com/Gershon+Kekst%3a+master+of +the+%27saykhl%27+business.-a054350184. Accessed July 22, 2015.

It is certainly true that media reports about the dangers of smoking alarmed many people. And it is also true that a scientific consensus had not yet developed on the issue in the early 1950s. It is harder to make that claim after the Surgeon General of the United States issued his first in 1964.[41] But by then Hill had retired, and his agency was no longer involved in the TIRC, which adopted a new name—the Council for Tobacco Research—to appear even less connected to the industry that funded its work. The Council focused on finding alternative explanations for the high incidence of lung cancer among smokers, other than the obvious. It was dissolved in 1998 in the historic settlement between U.S. state attorneys general and the tobacco industry.[42]

Hill's situation raises an important question about the role of emotional appeals in advocacy. In the case of tobacco, the opponents of smoking had all the emotional ammunition. They could exploit people's fears—and, in fact, their ideological descendants do so in even more graphic terms today. Ads and posters in the United States feature smoking victims with horrible disfigurements. In Europe, cigarette packages bear photos of diseased lungs and autopsies; the tobacco companies have only succeeded in delaying such pictorial warnings in the United States through suits and regulatory appeals. In this case, the manipulation of people's emotions arguably makes it more difficult for them to make a voluntary decision to smoke. Does this make it unethical? Or does the cause justify any tactic that works?

There is nothing inherently wrong with appealing to people's emotions. Aristotle recognized that emotion is necessary to motivate people even though reason is what distinguishes us from animals. And Ivy Lee (1925, pp. 47–48) thought it of great practical use:

> *The people are not moved by mind, they are moved by sentiment.*
> *The fundamental purpose, therefore, which must underlie any policy*
> *of publicity, must be to induce the people to believe in the sincerity*

---

[41] According to the Centers for Disease Control (2009, July 6), Surgeon General Luther Terry issued his first warning in 1964 based on information from more than 7,000 articles in the biomedical literature. See http://www.cdc.gov/tobacco/Data _statistics/sgr/history/index.htm.

[42] For a full copy of the Master Settlement Agreement with the tobacco industry, see http://publichealthlawcenter.org/sites/default/files/resources/master-settlement-agreement.pdf

and honesty of purpose of the management of the company which is asking for their confidence. If the men in charge of a particular company enjoy the complete confidence of that community, fifty percent of that company's troubles are over.

But Ivy Lee may not be the best guide on matters such as this. Knowing what we do of him, we can be forgiven for thinking his real point is the importance of faking sincerity.

Summary

We have further defined the elements of truthfulness. To veracity—the idea that the information we share should conform to reality and be suitable for the use to which it is put—we added visibility and validity.

Visibility—or transparency—means being clear about the source of communications, whether we issue it ourselves or through third parties. People have the right to know the source of the information they use in making a decision, so they can gauge its credibility and decide how much weight to give it.

Validity refers to the clarity, relevance, and rationality of our communication. Clarity is necessarily a relative judgment—what might be perfectly clear to one audience, might make no sense to another. Indeed, directing persuasive communications to some audiences, such as young children, could be inappropriate in any case. Relevance means information is material to the decision people anticipate making. And rationality means communication is logical and reasonable, that is something supported by evidence or arguments that can be analyzed and evaluated.

That does not mean emotion has no place in the practice of public relations. On the contrary, it plays an important role in capturing people's attention and in motivating them to action. In fact, as philosopher Roderick Long (2013, February 19) notes, "For Aristotle, emotions are part of reason." Appealing to intellect *and* emotions is really addressing the whole person.

Of course, ethical thinking has developed quite a bit since the time of Aristotle, especially in the period of intellectual growth known as the Enlightenment or the Age of Reason. And that is where we will find the principles that build on our developing notions of ethics—a fuller understanding of what it means to be human.

CHAPTER 6

Respect for Reason

The explosion of scientific advancement that began with Copernicus's 16th-century discovery the earth was not the center of the universe and culminated with Isaac Newton's formulation of the laws of gravity in the 17th century gave birth to a period of intellectual fervor we now call "the Enlightenment" or the "Age of Reason."

Western European thinkers began to realize the world we see is only part of reality—much of what we experience is the product of invisible forces that can only be inferred through the exercise of reason. And a lot of what appears obvious to us, like the sun circling the earth, is actually an illusion. Whereas ethical norms in the past were shaped by superstition, tradition, and slavish obedience to authority, the thinkers of the Enlightenment, offered a new engine—the power of human reason.

One of the foremost figures of this period was a German college professor who never married and never wandered more than 10 miles from his hometown of Konigsberg, Germany, now Kalingrad, Russia. But his impact on philosophical thought reverberated far from his hometown and across the centuries.

Immanuel Kant's Approach to Pure Reason

Immanuel Kant (1724–1804) was brought up in a pious Lutheran household and instilled with great self-discipline as a child. He lived such a strict and predictable life, his neighbors could set their watches by the time of his daily walks. He was a prolific writer, turning out more than 20 books and hundreds of essays in both German and Latin, but he was a relatively late bloomer. His most influential book, *Critique of Pure Reason* (Kant, 1781/1787, tr, Meiklejohn, 2014), which is widely considered one of the greatest works in the history of philosophy, did not appear until he was 57. And the book that sealed his reputation as one of the age's greatest ethical thinkers, *Grounding of the Metaphysics of Morals* (Kant, 1785, tr, Ellington, 1993), was published 4 years after that. Neither book makes good bedtime reading, unless one's goal is to nod off quickly. Both are written in a convoluted, abstract, repetitive style.

But Kant succeeded in doing for philosophy what Copernicus did for astronomy—he put human reason at the center of the action.[1] Where others accepted the precepts of morality on faith or despaired of finding any firm grounding for them at all, Kant insisted that moral principles could be discovered through careful reasoning. In fact, the human capacity for reasoning was the foundation of his whole system of ethical thought.

Human Dignity

As philosophy professor James Otteson (2006, p. 5) explains, Kant believed the world could be divided roughly into two categories: *things* and *persons*. "A *thing* is something that we may use to serve our purposes, without bothering to worry about its own interests—generally because a thing *has* no interests," Otteson writes. "A human being, on the other hand, is a *person*, which means, approximately, that it is something that has its own deliberate purposes and exercises its judgment with respect to them." The ability to reason is what sets human beings apart from the rest of creation.

It follows, to Kant's way of thinking, that you do not need a hammer's permission to use it in pounding a nail, but you cannot use other people to serve your own purposes without their permission. "Rational beings," Kant wrote, "are called 'persons' inasmuch as their nature already marks them out as ends in themselves, i.e., as something which is not to be used merely as a means and hence there is imposed thereby a limit on all arbitrary use of such beings, which are thus the objects of respect" (1785/1993, p. 36).

In other words, because people can reason, they can set their own goals, make their own decisions, and guide their conduct by reason. No one has the right to interfere with that without their agreement. Contemporary philosopher Erroll Harris (1908–2009) put the concept of respect in more

---

[1] Kant himself seems to make this claim in the Preface to the second, heavily revised edition of his *Critique of Pure Reason* (1781, 1787). See http://www.gutenberg.org /files/4280/4280-h/4280-h.htm. Accessed July 22, 2015.

contemporary terms, no doubt influenced by his experience with apartheid in his native South Africa. To him, respect is:

> *First, that each and every person should be regarded as worthy of sym-*
> *pathetic considerations, and should be so treated; secondly, that no per-*
> *son should be regarded by another as a mere possession, or used as a*
> *mere instrument, or treated as a mere obstacle, to another's satisfac-*
> *tion; and thirdly, that persons are not and ought never to be treated in*
> *any undertaking as mere expendables* (Harris, 1969).

In other words, respect is more than politeness or tolerance. It is seeing value in others and in their ideas; it is giving them the same considera-tion we would like to be given.

The age of apartheid may have passed in South Africa, but it lives on in parts of corporate America, where employees are often treated as fun-gible *commodities*, easily cast away to goose the company stock price. In our experience, public relations practitioners are usually on the forefront of those calling for a more enlightened approach to employee relations. Where they are responsible for internal communications, they define their role not as placating and distracting employees but as giving them the information they need to do their jobs intelligently, which includes a deeper understanding of the company's purpose, goals and strategies, an assessment of where it is winning and where it is losing, and what it all means for them. This requires more than a publication-centric ap-proach, whether printed or electronic. It means creating an environment of meaningful two-way communication between supervisors and subor-dinates and amongst team members. It means treating employees as ends in themselves, not simply as means to accomplish some goal in which they have little stake.

Autonomy

Kant's system of ethics rests on his belief that **autonomy** is an essential el-ement of being a *person* as opposed to a *thing*. But to Kant "autonomy" is more than "the freedom to do what you want." Rather, in his conception, autonomy's meaning is much closer to its Greek etymology—αὐτο (*auto)* or "self," and νόμος (*nomos*) or "law." Autonomy in Kantian ethics means "one who gives oneself one's own law." In other words, figuring out right from wrong is also an essential element of being human.

Kant was not of the "let a thousand flowers bloom" school of ethics. He reasoned that all human beings have natural obligations, or duties, simply because they're human. Using his own formidable intellectual powers, he reasoned that the most basic rule of morality—the principle that underlies all other ethical precepts—should be obvious to any rational person: "Act only according to that maxim whereby you can, at the same time, will that it should become a universal law" (1785/1993, p. 30). James Ellington, who produced one of the most readable translations of Kant's works, put it in more colloquial terms, "If something is right for me to do, it must be so for everyone else" (Kant, 1785, tr. Ellington, 1993, p. vi). And vice versa. In other words, reason should lead us to rules of behavior—duties—that apply to everyone, including ourselves.

Categorical Imperative

This is the single supreme moral law from which all other moral principles flow. Kant called it a *categorical imperative* because he considered it an absolute, unconditional rule of behavior, or "duty," that must be followed in all circumstances for its own sake and not simply because it will lead to some other good. "Don't speed if you don't want a ticket" is not categorical because following it depends on whether or not you care about getting tickets. A categorical imperative must also be logically consistent and free from internal contradiction. So, for example, "We should keep our promises unless it's inconvenient" would not fly as an absolute moral truth because it's self-contradictory. If everyone broke promises whenever it suited them, promises would not mean anything.

Kant expressed his categorical imperative in many ways, but when properly understood they all amount to the same thing. The formulation most relevant to the practice of public relations is: "Act in such a way that you treat humanity, whether in your own person or in the person of another, never merely as a means to an end, but always at the same time as an end" (Kant, 1785, tr. Ellington, 1993, p. 43). Kant considered this the flip side of his *universal law* formulation and it highlights our natural duty to respect other people's inherent dignity and autonomy.

Privacy

One obvious implication of this duty is to respect people's privacy—what Justice Brandeis called the "right to be let alone" (Warren and Brandeis, 1890, p. 193). Privacy is not mentioned in the Constitution, but the concept is so wrapped up in the notion of freedom and liberty, it has been implied as one of our fundamental rights. In 1890, Brandeis was so offended by media intrusion into the wedding of a friend's daughter that he wrote an article for the *Harvard Law Review* proposing the formal establishment of a right to privacy. Privacy law evolved in fits and starts ever since, responding to social and technological change. Currently, the law holds an individual's privacy can be invaded in four major ways, all highly relevant to the practice of public relations.

1. Unreasonable intrusion on someone's physical solitude;
2. Unreasonably placing someone in a false light before the public;
3. Unjustified publication of embarrassing facts about someone;
4. Commercial appropriation of someone's name, identity, or likeness.

Sadly, despite progress in legislating privacy laws, Brandeis's description of the media behavior that prompted his attention back in 1890 could be written today: "The press is overstepping in every direction the obvious bounds of propriety and decency. Gossip is no longer the resource of the idle and of the vicious, but has become a trade, which is pursued with industry as well as effrontery" (p. 196). And, magnifying the issue is the ocean of consumer data accumulating in corporate databases.

Data and "Big Data"

Big Data increasingly shapes the targeting, content, and performance of public relations, just as it is transforming every other corporate function. Senior public relations practitioners need to work with senior management in thinking through the ethical implications of gathering and using all this data across the entire enterprise. One of us worked at AT&T back when the Internet was just leaving the lab. The economic value of the user data it would produce was already obvious. Less obvious were the boundaries and procedures for storing, accessing, and using all that personal information. That ignited a debate every company needs to have. And however that debate is resolved, companies and practitioners must be transparent about the data they collect, and why they collect it. Tiny-type legal mumbo jumbo that no one reads will not cut it. And when a company suffers a data breach, exposing its customers' personal information, it has an ethical obligation to notify them as soon as possible. To do otherwise, in Kant's language, would be a fundamental violation of people's inherent autonomy and dignity.

This idea that we have a fundamental duty to respect people's dignity and autonomy—to never treat them as means, but always also as ends in themselves—underscores what we have already said about the values of *truth* and *transparency* in the practice of public relations. Respect means recognizing people's inherent right to make decisions for themselves, free from coercion, and based on the best available information. University of Oregon professor Thomas Bivins (2004, p.21) shows how our obligation to tell the truth hangs off this fundamental duty. "To lie to someone," he writes, "is to lead them to act in a manner in which they would not have acted had you told them the truth." Clearly, public relations must be truthful. But Kant's categorical imperative adds an important dimension to our understanding of ethical practice.

Hill & Knowlton's Tobacco Strategy

Consider, for example, John Hill's public relations strategy to defend the tobacco industry.

While conceding that the Tobacco Industry Research Committee (TIRC) could have been more transparent about its activities, John Hill certainly believed Hill & Knowlton's (H&K) overall strategy was ethical. In fact, he saw it as an expression of his duty as a public relations practitioner. In one of his few published comments on his role in establishing the Tobacco Research Committee, Hill wrote, "When an industry is, in effect, accused of mass murder, it is naturally agonizing to it when few voices are lifted in its defense before the bar of public opinion."[2]

---

[2] This and the following two quotes were attributed to John Hill, without citing a source, by John Hill II in a 1992 memo to Philip Morris lawyer Murray Bring, p. 16. See: http://legacy.library.ucsf.edu/tid/eso87e00.

Hill believed every individual and institution in a free society has the right to be heard in the public forum. Otherwise, it would abandon itself to the uncertain currents of the public mood. "The mind of the college professor as well as the unschooled crop picker is inclined to select and retain the facts it wants to retain—those facts that confirm established prejudices or leanings," he reportedly said. Hill believed a few publicity-seeking quacks, amplified by sensationalized headlines, were feeding those prejudices and stirring people into a fever of hysteria.

On the other hand, Hill believed, if the TIRC could "draw some public attention to other sides of the question," the normal American sense of fair play would lead people to decide that, "despite sensational charges, the truth is not yet known and the industry itself is doing what it can to speed the availability of true and reliable answers." In any case, by presenting the "facts" of independent studies, neither he nor his agency was responsible for whatever decisions people made.

But did H&K respect people's right to make intelligent decisions about the health implications of smoking? As we have already discussed, the agency arguably never lied in the classic sense of spreading facts it knew to be false. And Hill himself conceded the "independent research committee" he created was an unacceptable "paper" or "front" group. But H&K's ethical breach was even more serious.

Its core strategy was to cast doubt on research its clients did not like. For example, the TIRC complained that painting nicotine on the skin of mice is not the same as inhaling smoke into human lungs. It pointed out that statistical studies do not take all relevant factors into account. It suggested that lung cancer has many causes, from air pollution to genetic predispositions. And it studiously ignored studies that did not serve its cause. For example, the tobacco companies had known since 1946 that nicotine is addictive and potentially carcinogenic. And Hill himself had stopped smoking for health reasons.

Many have accused Hill of a strategy of obfuscation. Rather than giving people the information they needed to make an intelligent decision about the health risks of smoking, his team seemed intent on freezing people into a permanent state of doubt by raising nagging questions about methodology whenever new medical findings were published. As far as the American Cancer Society was concerned, Hill was "fighting a delaying action to mislead the public into believing that no change in smoking habits is indicated from existing statistical and pathological evidence nor will be until 'direct experimental evidence' is at hand."[3] Indeed, from the 1950s well into the 1990s, the industry's mantra was simple—"More research is needed." According to the *Wall Street Journal* it was "the longest-running disinformation campaign in U.S. business history."[4]

Disinformation

Authors Naomi Oreskes and Erik Conway (2010) call organizations that engage in such disinformation campaigns "merchants of doubt." Their sole goal is to discredit widely accepted scientific data inconvenient to their business interests. Using techniques pioneered by the tobacco industry, companies threatened by regulation have contracted with ideologically like-minded think tanks and academics to churn out studies contradicting data on everything from second-hand smoke and acid rain to ozone depletion and climate change. Even the soft-drink industry has been accused of funding research to cast doubt on the contribution its products make to obesity.[5] Sadly, some public relations firms have developed specialties in such doubt mongering.

One can argue John Hill and his agency were in a difficult position—their clients withheld information from them, the media were in a feeding frenzy over inconclusive data, and a good portion of the public was in a panic. Still, from a Kantian perspective, Hill did not respect people's right to make decisions with the best available information. If anything, under Hill's direction, the TIRC did its best to surround what information was available in a cloud of doubt and unanswerable questions. It is easy to conclude such activities were, on the whole, unethical.

---

[3] Quoted by John Hill II in a 1992 memo to Philip Morris lawyer Murray Bring, p. 11. See: http://legacy.library.ucsf.edu/tid/eso87e00

[4] Freeman, A.M., & Cohen, L.P. (1993, February 11). How cigarette makers keep health questions 'open' year after year. *Wall Street Journal.*

[5] O'Connor, A. (2015, August 9). Coca-Cola Funds Scientists Who Shift Blame for Obesity Away from Bad Diets, *The New York Times. http://well.blogs.nytimes.com /2015/08/09/coca-cola-funds-scientists-who-shift-blame-for-obesity-away-from-bad-diets/*

The more difficult question is, "Ethically, what public relations counsel *should* John Hill have given his clients?"

Ironically, the answer is precisely what the TIRC promised to do and never did—to fund honest research into the possible impact of smoking on people's health, to report the findings promptly, and to take action on whatever the findings indicated.

Public Relations as a Clarifier of Data

In 1990, when cell phones were still a relatively new innovation, several studies suggested the radiation emitted from their antennas could cause brain cancer. As day follows night, personal injury suits were filed against manufacturers and wireless service providers, which prompted more news stories and more suits. One of us was responsible for public relations at AT&T where it is probably fair to say some of the executive offices were as shaken as the tobacco company suites had been 40 years earlier.

Like the tobacco companies, we called in outside public relations counsel. But unlike the tobacco industry, we also had the benefit of Bell Labs scientists who were honest brokers in assessing the available data. And AT&T was already part of an industry association prepared to fund *real* research into the issue. Meanwhile, we did our best to ensure people understood the available research was far from conclusive and, out of an abundance of caution, we made earpieces widely available so our customers could keep the phone antennas as far from their heads as possible. To this day, no independent studies have clearly linked cell phones to cancer. And as health columnist Jane Brody noted in *the New York Times*, "While the incidence of brain tumors has risen slightly in recent years, there has been no disproportionate increase in tumors near the ears, despite a meteoric rise in cell phone use."[6] But one thing is certain: it is impossible to prove a negative.

So the communications industry continues to deal with scare mongering headlines. "Your cellphone is killing you," read one. "What people

---

[6] Brody, J. (1998, August 18). Personal health: Health scares that weren't so scary. *New York Times*. http://www.nytimes.com/1998/08/18/science/personal-health-health-scares-that-weren-t-so-scary.html. Accessed July 22, 2015.

don't want you to know about electromagnetic fields."[7] The irony, of course, is that directing attention to a possible problem distracts people from a more serious hazard—using cell phones while driving. A study in *The New England Journal of Medicine* showed that drivers who use cell phones are four times as likely as nonusers to have an accident (Redelmerier and Tibsgirani, 1997). And texting while driving is even more dangerous.

From a Kantian perspective, an ethical approach to communication about cell phones would give people the information they need to make intelligent decisions about their use. That would certainly include putting cancer concerns into perspective and providing options for avoiding even the unlikely danger of excessive electromagnetic radiation from the phone's antenna. But it would also draw people's attention to the clear dangers of texting while driving.

Ethical considerations do not require companies to adopt a vow of silence when their interests are at stake. Herb Schmertz, who led Mobil public affairs in the 1970s and 1980s when the oil business was being attacked on multiple fronts, said he would not have been doing his job if the company had not participated in debates on public policies affecting his industry. And in 1971, when he came to believe that his company's views were not being reliably reported, he invented the "paid op ed"—short essays that ran opposite the editorial page of newspapers such as *the New York Times* and the *Washington Post*. "If we didn't participate, the debate would be skewed against us because our views were not included," Schmertz said. "And we would have deserved what we got."[8] What readers got were lively and well-reasoned expressions of Mobil's position on issues of the day. And according to a 1976 Harris survey, the public credited Mobil with being "the industry pacesetter on 19 of 21 issues" (Schmertz, 1986, p. 143). People even felt better about its gasoline, though it was never mentioned in the op eds and the company did no other advertising.

---

[7] Blank, M. (2014, April 12). Your cellphone is killing you: What people don't want you to know about electromagnetic fields. *Salon*. http://www.salon.com/2014/04/12/your_cellphone_is_killing_you_what_people_dont_want_you_to_know_about_electromagnetic_fields/. Accessed July 22, 2015.

[8] Schmertz quote is courtesy of the The Museum of Public Relations, which interviewed him for its oral history. See http://www.prmuseum.org/videos/?rq=schmertz.

Emotional Appeals

With all that, we are still left with the other half of the "validity" principle and the question we put in John Hill's mouth: is it ever ethical to manipulate people's emotions?

Public relations practitioners have used emotional appeals from the earliest days of the practice. As we have seen, Bernays exploited women's understandable desire for independence to persuade them to smoke (see, for example, Christensen, 2012, February 27). Others have exploited people's fears, appetites, and desires in the interests of promoting every imaginable product and cause. After all, people's feelings are involved in virtually every decision we make.

Buying generic cereal may seem like a largely rational decision while reaching for one of the higher-priced brands seems more emotionally based. But in reality *both* are driven by emotions. In the one case, thrift; in the other, feelings of athleticism (Wheaties), nostalgia (Quaker Oats), fun (Fruit Loops), or any of dozens of emotional associations marketers have linked to their brand. In fact, neuroscientists have discovered that people who suffered damage to their center of emotions have difficulty making the most insignificant decision, like whether to have coffee or tea for breakfast (Damasio, 1994).

Some observers believe the practice of public relations has been a few jumps ahead of neuroscientists since the 1920s when it adopted the manipulative, emotion-laden techniques used by propaganda specialists in the First World War. In *PR! A Social History of Spin*, for example, Stewart Ewen (1996, p. 401) maintains that public relations abandoned appeals to reason in the 1920s to concentrate on manipulating people's emotions through imagery and the construction of superficial "impressions." In Ewen's view, "inspired by the propaganda successes of the wartime Committee on Public Information and fortified by theories of social psychology, corporate PR ... increasingly sought to stroke and cajole the public psyche."

We are not sure precisely what Ewen meant by "stroking and cajoling" the public psyche. But appealing to people's emotions is not necessarily unethical. It can help draw attention to a basically rational message; it can make it more appealing, easier to understand, and more memorable.

Emotion can move people to action without being coercive or clouding their thinking. For example, charities such as Save the Children and Doctors Without Borders use blatantly emotional appeals to raise money for their causes. Wireless companies around the world have used fear to convince people not to text while driving. And, as we have seen, even public health officials are using our natural instincts of revulsion to make people think twice before smoking a cigarette.

We have long considered emotion disruptive of rational thinking and thoughtful relationships. But scientists now believe emotion helps organize our thinking and structure our social interactions. For example, studies find that when we are angry we are acutely attuned to what is unfair, which helps animate actions that remedy injustice.[9] From a Kantian perspective, emotion in the service of reason respects people's autonomy and dignity. Emotion used to attract attention, to make information more meaningful, or even to motivate action can be ethical as long as the recipient retains the ability to make a reasoned, reflective, voluntary judgment. But it cannot be an illusory ability. Taking advantage of someone in an emotional state that inhibits his or her exercise of reason is no more ethical than exploiting someone under the influence of drugs or alcohol. Whether communicating through words, images, or music, respecting people's dignity means keeping rational and emotional appeals in balance, being careful not to overwhelm people's capacity to reason.

There is also a fine line between attracting attention and offending the very people one is trying to persuade. People for the Ethical Treatment of Animals, for example, gained lots of attention for the cause of vegetarianism with a 2004 campaign equating the slaughter of farm animals to the Holocaust (Freeman, 2007, May 23). But the campaign's premise and its side-by-side use of concentration camp and slaughterhouse images also demonstrated a lack of respect for its audience's feelings, severely undermining its credibility.

---

[9] Dacher, K., & Ekman, P. (2015, July 5). The science of 'Inside Out.' *The New York Times*. http://nyti.ms/1LN9sQG.

Good Will

Kant believed the capacity to reason set human beings apart from other sentient beings. But he also thought reason was matched with another uniquely human quality—the *good will* to follow the ethical precepts reason reveals to us. That second part is an important aspect of autonomy. Kant did not think behavior could be considered ethical unless it stemmed from good will. People cannot be forced to act ethically. They should want to do their duty simply because it *is* their duty. Intention matters.

In fact, for Kant, intention—or good will—is *all* that matters. When we set out to do something, whether or not we achieve the goal we had in mind is often beyond our control. But if we do something because it is our correctly understood duty, according to the categorical imperative, we are acting ethically. Conversely, when we do something right, if we do it for any other reason than simply because it is right, we are not acting ethically. The example Kant (tr, Ellington 1785/1993, p. 10) gives is of a shopkeeper who does not overcharge a child, even though he knows he could get away with it. If his motivation is that he is afraid another customer will see him, he is *not* acting ethically. He would only be acting ethically if he did it because it is his duty to be honest.

Kant kicked up quite a storm in philosophical circles because of the emphasis he put on duty to the exclusion of consequences. We will look into that more deeply in the next chapter, but for now the lesson for us as public relations practitioners is that *intention matters*. In fact, as we will see, it may be what keeps us from joining the ranks of Nazi propagandists like Joseph Goebbels.

The Ethics of Advocacy

Not everyone believes that advocacy—or its more genteel cousin, persuasion—is an ethically appropriate and valid public relations function. In fact, it has been the subject of some confusion, especially between academicians and practitioners. Academics prefer to focus on public relations' function of "building understanding" or "fostering dialogue," while practitioners see their job more pragmatically. No less a figure than Harold Burson, the legendary founder of Burson-Marsteller, has told us, "Fundamentally, PR is about persuasion."[10] Yet the whole idea of persuading people feels a little dirty and unseemly to many scholars.

For example, public relations scholar James Grunig led a team of public relations researchers in a groundbreaking study for the International Association of Business Communicators in the 1980s and 1990s that happily seemed to confirm a theory of public relations he had been developing. According to the study (1991, p. 2):

> *CEOs believe that public relations departments should be characterized by participation in strategic management, symmetrical communication, combined judiciously with two-way asymmetrical communication, and leadership by communication managers rather than technicians.*

Building upon role research by Glen Broom and David Dozier (1986) and others, Jim Grunig distinguished between public relations "managers" (i.e., those who plan and direct public relations) and "technicians" (i.e., those who actually perform public relations activities, such as media relations, employee communications, and speechwriting). He was delighted to find that many CEOs welcomed the participation of senior public relations "managers" in the company's "dominant coalition" (i.e., its most senior policy-making ranks). By definition, he considered this a "strategic" role.

The references to "asymmetrical" and "symmetrical" communication went to the heart of a theory Grunig had developed with a colleague, Todd Hunt, and described in a 1984 book, *Managing Public Relations.* Grunig believed the practice of public relations was going in two incompatible directions. On the one hand, in many places, public relations departments continued to implement what he termed the "interpretive strategies" laid down by people like Ivy Lee, Edward Bernays, and even P.T. Barnum. Those strategies focus on publicity, information, persuasion, and advocacy. He termed the alternative approach "strategic." This kind of public relations is integrated into an institution's operations, focuses more on what the institution *does* than on what it says, and is primarily concerned with engaging in genuine dialog with stakeholders.

---

[10] *Source:* conversations and email exchanges with Harold Burson on April 3, 2014, and March 10, 2015.

Interpretive public relations is "asymmetrical," that is, information travels primarily in one direction, from client to public. Publicity, for example, is strictly one-way. Persuasive communications might seek data about the public in the design of its arguments, making it more two-way, but a lot more information flows toward the customer about the *company* than *to* the company about the customer. But "strategic" public relations is two-way and *symmetrical*. It relies on mutual give-and-take rather than on one-way persuasion, emphasizing negotiation and a willingness to adapt and make compromises.

The report that resulted from Grunig's research, *Excellence in Public Relations and Communications Management*, made a huge impression on academics, many of whom had been searching for a "theory of public relations." Grunig himself thought two-way symmetrical public relations was the wave of the future and considered it inherently more ethical than the old, *a*symmetrical model. There is little evidence the "excellence theory" has had much of an impact on practitioners.[11] Curiously, it seems to be used more by nonprofit organizations, government agencies, and heavily regulated businesses such as public utilities than by competitive, profit-driven companies. But academic journals and conferences have been abuzz about it ever since it was introduced. The theory has figured in hundreds of published articles; Grunig alone has published more than 250. Part of the theory's popularity is undoubtedly due to its strong historical and theoretical underpinnings. But some think its real attraction is that it provides an escape from the dominant criticism of public relations—that it is essentially propaganda, not much different than what Joseph Goebbels did for Hitler and the Nazis. In fact, many journalists and even some in the general public think if Goebbels were alive today, he would feel right at home advising corporations and political candidates.

After all, according to Grunig, old-style public relations' emphasis on "messages, publicity, and media relations is designed to put up a smoke screen around the organization so publics cannot see the organi-

---

[11] A study of IABC members in 1987 revealed little evidence that the symmetrical model of public relations was being used by many practitioners. See David M. Dozier, "Importance of the concept of symmetry and its presence in public relations practice," Paper presented to the Public Relations Interest Group, International Communications Association, San Francisco, May, 1989.

zation's behavior as it truly is."[12] Indeed, Grunig once opined that "the asymmetrical worldview steers public relations practitioners toward actions that are unethical, socially irresponsible, and ineffective.... In spite of the good intentions of practitioners, it is difficult, if not impossible, to practice public relations in a way that is ethical and socially responsible using an asymmetrical model" (Grunig and White, 1992, p. 40).

In contrast, the two-way symmetrical model puts public relations executives in the middle of strategic decision making so they can help manage the behavior of organizations. It facilitates dialogue between management and its publics both before and after decisions are made, resolving conflicts and promoting understanding.

Many practitioners consider this a utopian ideal that has little practical application in the business world. Rather than leading to a joint discovery of the "truth," they suggest symmetrical communications inevitably leads to a blind alley of endless debate in which an organization negotiates with multiple publics that have mutually exclusive goals or unrealistic demands. Rather than leading to understanding, such an exercise can result in resentment and feelings of betrayal.

In fact, Grunig never said public relations *only* role was two-way symmetrical dialog. Even back in 1991, he left room for the "judicious" use of asymmetrical communication. And later, he wrote, "In practice, professional public relations involves both asymmetrical (compliance-gaining) and symmetrical (problem-solving) tactics." But then he could not resist hypothesizing, "the most effective public relations will fall toward the symmetrical end of the continuum" (Grunig and White, 1992, p. 12). So the debate continues, sometimes devolving into a forced march up semantic hill as people talk past each other, sometimes sinking into the hoary depths of systems theory.

But the bigger point here may be the original notion from which the symmetrical principle sprung—Grunig's belief that "companies needed

---

[12] Grunig made these remarks during an online interview with a number of public relations people from around the world in late 2008. Toni Muzi Falconi moderated the interview and published excerpts on his blog, *PR Conversations*. Falconi, T.M. (2008, October 15). See Engaging (and grilling) the social side of James Grunig. http://www.prconversations.com/index.php/2008/10/engaging-and-grilling-the-social-side-of-james-grunig/. Accessed July 22, 2015.

to be concerned about the welfare and the interest of their stakeholders as well as the organization's interest itself."[13] In our experience, that is precisely what distinguishes excellent public relations practitioners from tiresome flacks. As Grunig pointed out from the very beginning, the value of public relations comes from the relationships it forms and nurtures with stakeholders.

Seeking to harmonize the policies and practices of an organization with the needs and interests of its stakeholders is the essence of public relation's role in any organization. Sometimes that requires the organization to change attitudes and behavior; sometimes it means stakeholders change theirs. But it always requires dialog between the two parties. Persuasion based on argument is part of the dialog on both sides. The key difference is that both parties—organization and stakeholders—are open to the possibility of change or compromise and that their arguments are reasoned, not manipulative. (As a practical matter, this often requires public relations practitioners to direct their persuasive efforts to top management, as well as to the organization's stakeholders.)

In this sense, persuasion is not always totally asymmetrical. When one of us was at AT&T, he directed on-going dialogs between senior executives and groups that represented stakeholders ranging from consumers and people with disabilities to small businesses and global enterprises. The goal was to consult with these groups as the company was developing products, services, and policies that would affect them in some way. We discussed everything from new service concepts and product introductions to pricing changes and regulatory filings. Input from those groups sometimes caused us to change our plans; the discussions almost always led to greater understanding of what the company was trying to do, even when the parties ultimately could not agree on some aspects of our plans. That may not have been the idealized model

---

[13] Grunig devotes many of his public appearances to explaining and answering questions about his "excellence theory." This and the next quote were taken from an October 17, 2010, joint presentation by Jim Grunig and his wife Larissa who is a widely published public relations theorist in her own right. See *Public Relations Excellence 2010*. Speech delivered at PRSA International Conference, Washington, DC. http://www.instituteforpr.org/wp-content/uploads/Third-Grunig-Lecture-October-17-2010-Transcript.pdf. Accessed July 22, 2015.

of symmetrical communication envisioned by the excellence model, but it gave stakeholders input into the company's decision making to the benefit of both.

Today, of course, the publics affected by an organization's policies and practices are not waiting for someone to muster them for dialog. They are already talking amongst themselves through social media and sharing information they themselves create. As Grunig points out, "it's not so much a matter of controlling information going to publics but participating in their conversations." Yet even in those instances, public relations practitioners unequivocally engage in persuasive communication.

Can persuasion, which by definition seeks to influence people's attitudes or behavior, be ethical? Our answer is that *it depends*. As we have seen, truthfulness—including the principles of veracity, visibility, and validity—is a pivotal element of ethical communication. Ethical communication does not mislead, misinform, or deceive in action or intention. Ethical communication also respects reason. It allows people to make voluntary, informed, rational, and reflective judgments. And, yes, it is open to dialog because that is the essence of trusting relationships, which as Grunig correctly points out, is public relations' ultimate goal.

The notion of *intent*, so critical to Kant's thinking, deserves special attention. While persuasion and propaganda may share some techniques, their respective intents are decidedly different. Propaganda is self-interested and focused on its own goals even at the expense of its audience. In their classic study of propaganda, Garth Jowett and Victoria O'Donnell (1999, p. 14) identify the conceit at the heart of most propaganda—to make an audience think the propagandist has their interests at heart, while hiding their selfish motives. Ethical persuasion, on the other hand, genuinely considers the interests of the publics it addresses, which more often than not are revealed in two-way symmetrical communication somewhere in the process.

Summary

Under the conditions we have explored in this chapter, one could argue it is perfectly ethical to attempt to persuade or advocate people to change their minds, alter their behavior, or lend their support to a client's cause. The key is to respect people's right to reason. That capability, after all, is what separates human beings from all other creatures and enables us to set our own goals, giving us unique autonomy.

In fact, Kant believed reason reveals the ultimate principle of right and wrong—to act according to rules you would be willing to make universal. One such universal rule—or what Kant called a "categorical imperative"—is to never treat other people as a means to achieving your own goals, but to respect their inherent right to set their own. For public relations practitioners, that means balancing the interests of our clients and the people we're trying to persuade or advocate.

That is the issue we'll explore in the next chapter as we take up the next great ethical theory, utilitarianism, and one of its implications for the practice of public relations—serving the public interest.

CHAPTER 7

The Public Interest

Around the time John Hill was helping the tobacco companies calm waters stirred up by research into the health dangers of smoking, a young public relations guy in Chicago named Dan Edelman was flying multiple sets of identical twin sisters around the country.

Freshly coifed and made up, the twins were smiling embodiments of a long-running ad campaign challenging readers to determine "Which twin had the Toni?" One twin had had a "permanent" wave set in her hair by a professional hairdresser; the other did it at home, using only the sponsor's $2 "Toni Home Permanent" kit. Few could tell the difference.

Dan Edelman (1920–2013) was the Toni Home Permanent company's public relations director when he came up with the idea of taking the twins off the pages of the company's ads and sending them on a cross-country road show to 72 cities. Broadcast and print media ate it up. And when an overly enthusiastic local health official in Tulsa, Oklahoma, tried to jail one of the twins for practicing cosmetology without a license, Edelman doubled down and made sure the Associated Press had the story. The twins were news across the country.

The Toni Twins road show, which many consider the first modern "media tour," was such a successful stunt that within just a few years, Edelman moved down the hall from the company's headquarters in the Chicago Merchandise Mart and opened his own shop, with Toni as his first client. In short order, he was running media tours and otherwise ginning up publicity on behalf of brands like Sara Lee, Morris the Cat, and the Butterball Turkey Hot Line, as well as for causes such as seatbelt laws and the Vietnam Veterans Memorial Wall.[1] "Mr. Edelman didn't invent the publicity stunt but cultivated all sorts of new possibili-

---

[1] Miller, S. (2013, June 15). Public relations pioneer began with 'Toni Twins' stunt. *Wall Street Journal.* http://online.wsj.com/articles/SB10001424127887324235104 578244253082298248. Accessed July 22, 2015.

ties for it at the dawn of the TV age," one trade publication wrote. Plus, "He was a pioneer of integrating public relations into marketing campaigns to sell products."[2]

Richard Edelman, CEO

Edelman expanded his firm in the 1960s and 1970s, opening offices across the United States and in major international cities. He turned the CEO position over to his son, Richard, in 1996, but stayed active in the firm until his death at the age of 93 in 2013. By then, the company had developed expertise in every facet of public relations, from product publicity, which was its original bread and butter, to the relatively new fields of crisis management, litigation public relations, and public affairs.

With his father's support, Richard steadily expanded the company's capabilities even further, attracting new talent and developing deep social media and research capabilities. Today, Edelman is the world's largest public relations firm, with 66 offices and more than 5,000 employees worldwide. Its clients number some of the largest and most prominent companies in the world, including Microsoft, Walmart, Pepsico, General Electric, Unilever, Samsung, and dozens of others.

Of course, running such a far-flung enterprise with so many clients and with fingers in so many specialties is fraught with challenges, sometimes bumping up against ethical boundaries. Just such as issue popped up in an Edelman inbox in late 2014.

A Washington, DC, public interest group called "Investigating Climate Change" partnered with the UK's *Guardian* newspaper to survey large public relations firms on their views regarding climate change. When Edelman's U.S. region president received the survey, he forwarded copies to his staff, adding, "I don't believe we are obligated in any way to respond. There are only wrong answers for this guy."[3]

---

[2] Strahler, S. (2013, January 15). Public relations pioneer Daniel Edelman has died. *Crain's Chicago Business.* http://www.chicagobusiness.com/article/20130115/NEWS06/120919857/public-relations-pioneer-daniel-edelman-has-died. Accessed July 22, 2015.

[3] Goldenberg, S., & Karim, N. (2014, August 4). World's top PR companies rule out working with climate deniers. *The Guardian.* http://www.theguardian.com

Calmer heads prevailed but Edelman's response was long on links to its website and short on specifics. The other five agency responses were equally perfunctory and devoid of news, so the *Guardian* followed up by asking all the firms originally surveyed if they would work for clients that deny the existence of man-made climate change. Not surprisingly, the resulting *Guardian* story focused on its own mini-survey and news that 10 of the world's largest public relations companies "rule out working with climate deniers." Edelman, which replied that it "takes on clients on a case-by-case basis," was not among them. And the *Guardian* gleefully reprinted the agency's internal e-mail about the survey, pointing out that Edelman represented the American Petroleum Institute, which it called "the main energy lobby."

The *Guardian* story was picked up widely, but the report that got under Richard Edelman's skin most ran in the online publication *Motherboard*. Headlined "How the world's biggest PR firm helps promote climate denial," the article said it was not surprised by Edelman's equivocating response to the *Guardian's* survey because it already "helps polluting companies use TV ads, Astroturf groups, and slick websites to promote climate change denial around the globe."[4]

Richard Edelman was so upset he ignored the advice he would give his own clients, and called Brian Merchant, the editor responsible for the *Motherboard* piece, at home. "I just want you to know we're not bad people, that's all," Edelman told Merchant. Asked if he felt his firm's position on climate change had been misrepresented, Edelman said, "Yes. Deeply. Deeply. I don't blame the *Guardian* reporter any more than I blame you—I blame the ham-head who filled out the questionnaire to be a little, uh, slick.... We fired [him] in part because of that stupid note he wrote, about, you know, how we don't answer these kinds of things." Merchant, of course, reported the entire exchange. For his part, Edelman also set the record straight on his blog the very next day.

/environment/2014/aug/04/worlds-top-pr-companies-rule-out-working-with-climate-deniers. Accessed July 22, 2015.

[4] Merchant, B. (2014, August 5). PR firm helps promote climate change denial. *Motherboard.* http://motherboard.vice.com/read/how-the-largest-pr-firm-in-the-world-promotes-climate-change-denial. Accessed July 22, 2015.

Edelman fully recognizes the reality of, and science behind, climate change, and believes it represents one of the most important global challenges facing society, business and government today. To be clear, we do not accept client assignments that aim to deny climate change.

We believe that business, government and society must work together to address climate change by balancing the interdependent priorities of human development, the environment, and the global economy. As such we support our clients' efforts to reduce emissions from their operations, improve energy efficiency, advance alternative fuels and sustainable energy solutions and lead in the transition to sustainable and socially responsible business models. We also work with clients to constructively participate in the dialogue around climate change and contribute to policy discussions, with the goal of making progress on this shared global challenge.[5]

Unlike John Hill, who apparently did not see anything unethical in sowing doubt about the health impacts of smoking, Edelman declared that he and his agency believed in the reality of climate change, and they would not accept client assignments that sought to deny it. What was behind that decision?

The uncharitable will say Edelman was considering the reputational consequences of continuing to work for climate deniers. And that certainly played a role. After all, the agency's response to the *Guardian* survey had already subjected it to heavy criticism, and even ridicule in some quarters. But in the end, Edelman may have been listening to his own father, who back in 1992 had warned his peers, "Let's not allow greed to blur our vision and our commitment to do the right thing, to work for the right kind of people, and to counsel them in the right direction."[6]

Richard Edelman is not coy about being "in the business of advocacy." But he claims his agency is selective about the clients it accepts, limiting its representation to those "committed to fact-based, truthful, and transparent

---

[5] Edelman, R. (2014, August 7). Edelman's position on climate change. *6 AM blog.* http://www.edelman.com/p/6-a-m/edelmans-position-climate-change/. Accessed July 22, 2015.

[6] Edelman, D. (1992, November). Ethical behavior is key to field's future. *PR Journal,* Vol. 48, No. 11, p. 32.

communications." Edelman does not pretend to agree with every position a client may adopt or condone every action it may take. It even reserves the right to take positions that differ from those of its clients. And it supports each employee's right not to work on accounts that do not align with his or her personal beliefs. But it believes vigorous debate is the fuel of the democratic process and makes no apologies for helping its clients present their perspective. On the other hand, it is not simply a gun for hire. Before taking on a client, it considers "the potential ethical, commercial, reputational, and legal implications."[7]

"It helps to be an independent, family-owned company," Edelman says. "I don't have to obsess about this quarter's financial results, or even the year's. I'm focused on the firm's reputation, long-term health, and doing what's right." So it's entirely possible that Richard Edelman was looking at the broader implications of accepting such an assignment, that he in fact was considering something that Kant did not pay much attention to—the consequences of his agency's actions on the public interest.

Consequences

Kant was notorious for his stiff-necked absolutism. To him, whether something is right or wrong depends entirely on whether or not it violates his categorical imperative. And if something is wrong, it is wrong—no exceptions. So when asked if it would be wrong to tell a lie to save someone's life, he quickly replied, "yes," explaining the consequences have no bearing on the rightness or wrongness of someone's actions. This has created a serious conundrum for many. As Australian scholar Alex Messina (2007, p. 39) has noted, "Public relations practitioners—like most people in daily life—are actors not debaters. They need a guide to ethical action consistent with the community of daily life, rather than an idealistic community of absolutes."

Luckily, ethicist James Rachels (1991, p. 131) built an escape hatch from Kant's absolutism. He pointed out that "reversibility" (would I be willing to have it apply to me?), was important in establishing a principle's

---

[7] This and the following quotes are from a conversation with Richard Edelman on May 30, 2015.

universality, but it did not really forbid exceptions. A principle that "it's permissible to lie to save innocent lives" can be both reversible and universal. "All that Kant's basic idea requires is that if we violate a rule, we do so for a reason that we would be willing for anyone to accept, were they in our position." Of course, exceptions must be based on some idea of consequences and Kant did not care about those.

As it happens, while Kant was laying down his theory, a developing school of ethical thought took exactly the opposite perspective—whether an act is right or wrong depends *solely* on its consequences. As we will see, that approach broadens the scope of ethics from what practitioners do to how it affects others. And even to what clients they accept.

Utilitarianism

Some form of consequence-focused ethics has been around since Aristotle's day. But philosophers differed about just what consequences mattered and to whom. Some thought all that mattered were consequences to the person taking action. That resulted in a kind of egoism that was hard to justify socially. Others believed the goal of any action should be the maximization of pleasure. That raw appeal to hedonism seemed rather shortsighted, if not unseemly. Eventually, many philosophers settled on a form of results-based ethics that considers the right choice in any situation to be the one that produces the most *useful* consequences for the greatest number of people. In practical terms, "useful consequences" are those that can satisfy people's needs or wants (i.e., make them happy). The theory is called **utilitarianism**, and its greatest proponent was a British philosopher and civil servant named John Stuart Mill (1806–1873).

John Mill

Mill was to the 19th century what Kant was to the 18th—one of the time's most critical thinkers. Mill did not invent utilitarianism—that honor probably belongs to his godfather, Jeremy Bentham (1748–1832). But Mill's father, James, a philosopher in his own right, was so taken by Bentham's "utilitarian" theory, he set out to raise a "genius" who would promulgate it after he and Bentham were gone.

Luckily, Mill was a precocious child. He learned Greek by the time he was three and Latin by eight. In his teens, he was studying philosophy and economics essentially on his own and under his father's tutelage. A non-conformist and atheist, he refused to join the Church of England so he was barred from attending Oxford or Cambridge. Nevertheless, he eventually became rector of Scotland's University of St. Andrews and a Member of Parliament. He wrote broadly on issues of social justice and economics. For example, he was opposed to slavery and a proponent of women's rights, including the right to vote. But he is probably best known for his contribution to ethics.

Mill developed and refined Bentham's theory in a series of essays gathered together in a book under the title *Utilitarianism* in 1863. In it, Mill formulated a single ethical principle, which he said formed the basis of the utilitarian theory:

> *The Greatest-Happiness Principle holds that actions are right in proportion as they tend to promote happiness, wrong as they tend to produce the reverse of happiness* (Mill, 1863/2001, p. 10).

Most importantly, as Mill made clear, what is at stake here is not the agent's own happiness "but the greatest amount of happiness altogether" (p. 10). In other words, we should always try to produce the greatest balance of good over bad for "all concerned" (p. 19). And we should draw the circle of those concerned as broadly as possible to include society as a whole, making the common good an ethical consideration.

There are obvious complications to this approach. To start, utilitarianism tends to favor the majority over any minority. If something has good consequences for most of the people in a community, but is unalterably bad for a small number, utilitarianism would seem to favor the majority. More recently, philosophers like John Rawls (1921–2002) jumped to utilitarianism's rescue by suggesting it include considerations of justice. According to Rawls the greatest good for the greatest number should not be used to trample the rights of the few. Fairness counts, too. The problem, of course, is defining fairness. Rawls suggested a thought experiment called "the veil of ignorance" that cleverly did the trick: design a society fair enough that you would agree to be born into it without knowing what position you would occupy within it. Such a society, he suggested (1985, p. 227), would conform to two principles, paraphrased as:

First, basic liberties such as freedom of speech, conscience, and assembly would be unlimited until they began to infringe on other people's liberties.

Secondly, no one would be allowed to gain more power or wealth than others unless (a) everyone else had the same opportunity and (b) in the long run, it worked to the advantage of the worse-off.

Rawls' ethical arguments are more complex than that, of course, but for our purposes, he rounds out the theory of utilitarianism in a way that protects the rights of the few from the tyranny of the many.

With that, utilitarianism seems like a practical approach to resolving ethical problems and, at least initially, it looks relatively easy to use. But, in fact, it is sometimes difficult to predict all the consequences of our actions, which can roll out in a long cascading chain. Many are unknowable until they happen, which could be far off in the future. And it could take forever to measure the potential consequences of our actions on *everyone* affected. Furthermore, some consequences—like anger, fear, and despair—are hard to quantify at all, leading to the conclusion that if something cannot be counted, it does not count. For those reasons, among others, most utilitarians today encourage us to use *rules of thumb* in ordinary circumstances. Mill himself suggested it is not hard to figure out what typically makes people happy or unhappy.

Bentham and Mill spoke in terms of "happiness" and "pleasure." Bentham, in fact, had developed a complicated "hedonic system" for evaluating pleasure and pain by such factors as their intensity and duration. Mill had a more elevated notion of happiness, giving greater weight to intellectual satisfaction than physical pleasure. But both men were essentially hedonists. Many modern ethicists, wary of trying to compare one person's happiness to another's, focus instead on people's general welfare.[8]

---

[8] This is, of course, somewhat of a simplification. There are many versions of utilitarianism. Contemporary philosophers have defined the ultimate good in many

And that, in fact, is what may have motivated Richard Edelman's decision to ban work on behalf of climate deniers. He believes the science on climate change is sufficiently settled to make muddying those waters contrary to the public interest and ethically wrong.

Public Interest

The public interest is one of those concepts that everyone bandies about without a clear notion of what it means. Practically everyone who has given public relations' social obligations a moment's thought has invoked its duty to *act in the public interest*. In a 1939 speech to railroad executives, Arthur W. Page of AT&T said that any large enterprise's success depended on "conducting itself in the public interest."[9]

But what exactly do we mean by "the public interest"? In its "Code of Ethics," the Public Relations Society of America (PRSA) suggests responsible advocacy serves the public interest essentially by definition. "We serve the public interest by acting as responsible advocates for those we represent." Furthermore, it uses public interest as a kind of corral around the obligation of client loyalty: "We are faithful to those we represent, while honoring our obligation to serve the public interest."[10] But PRSA members would have to search wide and far to get an explanation of just what constitutes the "public interest" and how to balance it with a client's.

We are not picking on the PRSA. The International Association of Business Communicators (IABC) takes somewhat the same tack in its very first principle: "Professional communicators uphold the credibility and dignity of their profession by practicing honest, candid and timely communication and by fostering the free flow of essential information in accord with the public interest."[11] The International Public Relations

---

ways, ranging from George Moore's ideals of beauty and friendship (*Principia Ethica*, Chapter 6) to Peter Singer's rational preferences (Mautner, 1997, pp. 521–522).

[9] Page addressed executives of the Chesapeake and Ohio Railway Company on "Industrial Statesmanship" in White Sulfur Springs, VA, on October 27, 1939. See http://comm.psu.edu/page-center/speech/industrial-statesmanship

[10] The full text of the PRSA Code of Ethics can be found at http://www.prsa .org/aboutprsa/ethics/codeenglish/#.VFASUpPF_Io.

[11] The full text of all these association codes is online. The IABC Code of Ethics can be found at http://www.iabc.com/about/code.htm. of the IPRA Code of Ethics can be found

Association (IPRA) takes the same approach, noting, "Public relations, by fostering the free flow of information, contributes to the interests of all stakeholders." The Global Alliance for Public Relations and Communications Management (GAPR) prefaces its "guiding principles for ethical practice" by cautioning, "In making decisions, we should be guided by a higher sense of serving the public as a whole as opposed to specific constituencies on an exclusive basis." The Chartered Institute of Public Relations (CIPR) only mentions the public interest in connection with resolving complaints against members, to wit, "Members of the Institute have a duty to bring a complaint against a Member, where it is in the public interest to do so." So we are left with the impression that this public interest thing is pretty important while scratching our heads to define it. If serving the public interest is the linchpin on which the ethical practice of public relations hangs, we have to get a better handle on it.

In legal terms, the public interest is "the well-being of the general public," and it appears in the codes of professionals from architects to zoologists.[12] But how is this "general well-being" to be measured? Do we take a utilitarian approach, invoking the principle of the greatest good for the greatest number? Or do we get all Kantian and try to find a universal interest to which no reasonable person could object? Is the public interest a matter of counting noses or plumbing the public psyche? Some public relations scholars have pondered these questions only to throw up their hands in frustration. Alex Messina (2007, p. 38), for example, concluded, "there is no definable role for the 'public interest' as a standard to measure ethical persuasion."

But the term's very imprecision may be what makes it most useful. To start with, the *public* interest clearly connotes interests that are broader than "private," suggesting that, public relations practitioners have an obligation to look beyond their own and their client's narrow,

---

at http://www.ipra.org/about/ipra-codes the GAPR Code of Ethics can be found at http://www.globalalliancepr.org/website/sites/default/files/nolie/Governance/Code%20of%20ethics/GA-Code%20of%20Ethics.pdf.   the CIPR Code can be found at http://www.cipr.co.uk/sites/default/files/Code%20of%20Conduct%20-%20agreed%20changes%20November%202013.pdf. Accessed September 7, 2015.

[12] See, for example, West's Online Encyclopedia of American Law. (n.d.). http://www.thefreedictionary.com/public+interest. Accessed July 22, 2015.

selfish interests to the public's well-being. And one need not wait for 100 percent certainty on that score. Outside of logic and mathematics, such levels of certainty are impossible. Science, for example, is all about narrowing uncertainty. "Settled science" is a provisional conclusion shared by a broad consensus of experts, based on the preponderance of evidence. Where such consensus exists, as in the advisability of childhood vaccinations and the validity of evolution and climate change, the public interest compels us to recognize and honor it. Where no consensus exists, it obligates us to open and respectful dialog.

Similarly, how public relations initiatives affect the general welfare cannot be calculated with mathematical precision. Available evidence is often ambiguous, conflicting, and even contradictory. But that is true of every major business decision practitioners make. Here too, they are obligated to examine the issue from all sides to arrive at a reasonable judgment of what is in the general welfare, at minimum ensuring they do no harm.

In most cases, this calculation will be the responsibility of the most senior public relations executive in an agency or a corporation, in close consultation with clients. But that does not absolve the individual practitioners who report to them from making their own personal assessment. In some cases, that may cause some practitioners to ask to be reassigned. In very rare cases, if they conclude they cannot in good conscience work for an organization dedicated to a purpose they believe will seriously harm the general public, it may even require them to resign.

The concept of "the public interest" may be as imprecise as many ideals, but it can be just as powerful. As one scholar put it, "The rule of law, due process, a free press, a loyal opposition, and the public interest are all value-laden concepts the limits and substance of which are difficult to define with precision, but all are significant in the maintenance of democratic government."[13] By adhering to the standard of serving the public interest, the practice of public relations could ennoble itself and rise to the level of a profession, rather than a simple trade.

---

[13] Herring, H. (1968). *International Encyclopedia of the Social Sciences*. Encyclopedia.com. http://www.encyclopedia.com/topic/Public_interest.aspx. Accessed July 22, 2015.

"Court of Public Opinion"

Of course, decisions like Edelman's raise an old question—whether or not everyone is entitled to public relations representation. John Hill would have taken issue with the very question. "Every man has a right to a hearing," Hill (1993, p. 138) wrote, "and if he is under public attack, the right to defend himself publicly." He considered his job similar to a lawyer's. He was simply arguing the tobacco industry's case in what he called "the court of public opinion," representing his client as best he could. As Hill put it, in public relations, American business has "a shield and a spear. It can defend or attack, as the case may be" (p. 259). Why should any business lay down its shield or blunt its spear in the face of an existential assault such as that besieging the tobacco industry? Let the litigants present their cases and let the public decide whose arguments carry the day, just as in a court of law.

It is a compelling argument. But the courtroom may be a false analogy. Indeed, scholars like Scott Cutlip (1981) suggest the "court of public opinion" is more like an arena with gladiators than a courtroom full of lawyers.

In a courtroom, both sides have an equal voice in the proceedings, with a judge serving as impartial referee to rule on evidence and to ensure that both sides follow the rules. If one side submits evidence the judge believes will unduly prejudice the jury, he or she can exclude it, even if it is relevant. But in the arena of public opinion, one side can swamp the other simply by spending more. Short of outright fraud, there is no one to rule on what they claim. Courts of law are designed to decide cases based on the facts without regard to the feelings of those involved. In fact, juries are frequently instructed to ignore any emotional appeals one of the litigants might have made. But as noted in earlier chapters, public opinion is often ruled by emotion, with both sides trying to exploit people's prejudices and fears. Furthermore, the legal arena is not as time-bound. While the Constitution promises everyone a "speedy trial," in practice both sides can often stretch the time to trial out as it suits their purpose. In civil and appelate trials, judges can take all the time they need to render a decision. Lawyers are under no obligation to speak to the media. In fact, in some cases, they are forbidden to discuss the trial out of court. But public relations people almost always are asked for comments within hours, sometimes minutes. Journalists (and other members of the general public) appear to respect attorneys who ask for a continuance or refuse to comment on a legal matter. But public relations people (understandably) are not granted that luxury.

Perhaps most importantly, in a court of law, the stakes are much higher than in the arena of public opinion. No one goes to jail simply because bad press hurts their reputation. As ethicist Patricia Parsons (2004, p. 16) points out, lawyers who represent notorious criminals are not displaying belief in their client, but rather in an elaborate legal system and everyone's right to due process. "No such infrastructure exists for public relations, she notes." All of which helps explain why lawyers are expected to represent people accused of the most reprehensible crimes, while a public relations practitioner's choice of clients can also redound on its own reputation.

For example, Ketchum long counted Russia among its clients, managing the country's English-language website, setting up foreign visits for its ministers, and lining up businessmen, lawyers, and academics to write pro-Russian op eds for U.S. and European media.[14] On September 11, 2013, it placed an op ed by Russian president Vladimir Putin in the *New York Times* urging President Obama to reconsider airstrikes against Syria for chemical weapons violations.[15] That raised a few eyebrows, but to Ketchum it was just another account and a profitable one at that, with more than $25 million in billings between 2006 and 2013.[16] Still, following the Russian invasion of Ukraine in March 2014, the agency felt compelled to announce it was "not advising the Russian Federation on foreign policy, including the current situation in Ukraine."[17] By

[14] Lake, E. (2014, March 11). Confessions of a Putin spin-doctor. *The Daily Beast.* http://www.thedailybeast.com/articles/2014/03/11/confessions-of-a-putin-spin-doctor .html. Accessed July 22, 2015.

[15] Putin, V. (2013, September 11). A Plea for Caution from Russia, *New York Times,* http://www.nytimes.com/2013/09/12/opinion/putin-plea-for-caution-from-russia-on-syria.html

[16] Elliott, J. (2013, September 12). From Russia with PR. *ProPublica.* http://www .propublica.org/article/from-russia-with-pr-ketchum-cnbc. Accessed July 22, 2015.

[17] Sullivan, A. (2014, March 6) "Russia's U.S. PR Firm Distances Itself From Ukraine Dispute," Reuters. See: http://www.reuters.com/article/2014/03/06/ukraine-crisis-ketchum-idUSL1N0M22BB20140306

2015, as the Ukrainian crisis dragged on despite Western sanctions, Ketchum no longer represented the Russian Federation, though it is unclear whether it had quit or been fired.[18] Not to worry though. As D.C. reporter Tess VandenDolder put it, "there are a number of firms here in Washington willing to work with unsavory foreign characters."[19]

In fact, a number of U.S. public relations agencies work for regimes with questionable human rights records, including Qorvis (Equatorial Guinea), APCO Worldwide (Azerbaijan), Racepoint Group (Rwanda), Levick (Nigeria), Glover Park Group (Egyptian strongman General Sisi), and the Rogich Communications Group (China).[20] Some argue that, except for a small number of countries under U.S. economic sanctions, such as Syria and North Korea, there is nothing illegal about it. Such representation can even help improve relations by giving foreign leaders a better view of how their actions are being perceived. The Page Society's Roger Bolton pointed out other benefits. "When public relations firms advise clients, they invariably advocate for the importance of listening to and accommodating others' views," he wrote. "The fact that this hasn't worked [in Ketchum's work for Russia] says more about President Putin's political views and ambitions than it does about the value of engagement."[21] Ketchum got bad press, but was its representation of Russia really unethical?

Ethics of Representation

As founder of Burson-Marsteller, Harold Burson has on more than one occasion had to weigh whether or not to represent a company. Now in his mid-90s, he can still rattle off the clients he has turned down and why he passed on the assignments. Sometimes, it was simply because it

[18] Wollstonecraft, M. (1792). *A Vindication of the Rights of Woman*. http://www .gutenberg.org/ebooks/27083. Accessed July 22, 2015.

[19] VandenDolder, T. (2014, December 3). Why Russia may cancel its contract with DC PR firm Ketchum. *DCInno*. http://dcinno.streetwise.co/2014/09/03/why-russia-might-cancel-its-contract-with-dc-pr-firm-ketchum/. Accessed July 22, 2015.

[20] Ainger, K. (2015, January). Spin doctors to the autocrats. *Corporate Europe Observatory*. http://corporateeurope.org/pressreleases/2015/01/european-pr-firms-whitewashing-brutal-regimes-report. Accessed July 22, 2015.

[21] Bolton, R. (2015, March 13). Ketchum and Russia. *PageTurner Blog*. http://www .awpagesociety.com/2015/03/ketchum-and-russia/.

conflicted with an existing account. But sometimes it was a matter of principle. And he can still articulate his philosophy in a soft voice that commands attention. "I believe that every institution, every person is entitled to have public relations representation," Burson told us. "I do *not* believe that I am compelled in any way or manner to be the one who provides that representation." That does not mean he has to agree with every client on every issue. "I think that [in regards to] unpopular causes which are legitimate [and with] which I may not agree, I do not think it's unethical for me to represent that client as long as I can do so in a way that my client is not compromised by my disagreement."[22]

But in the end Burson believes public relations practitioners need to believe in what they are being asked to do. "I am engaged to motivate individuals or groups to take a position or take an action that my client seeks to have taken," Burson says.

> *I think I should ... make the judgment on whether I represent such a client by asking myself the question, "Is what this client wants to do in the public interest?" I believe that no action can be sustained or successful if, in the long run, it is not in the public interest despite the wide disparity in its definition. As a former Supreme Court justice said of pornography, "you know it when you see it."*

Existing codes of conduct published by the various professional associations may dance around the issue, but Burson puts the public interest at the center of ethical decisions in the practice of public relations. And that points up the dual nature of public relations ethics. Ethical behavior depends on a client's goals, as well as to the way practitioners try to achieve them. If a client's purpose is unethical, nothing a practitioner does can compensate.

Sometimes the ethics of a client's cause are not so obvious, except in hindsight. And guilt by association is always a danger. Prior to World War II, Ivy Lee worked for I. G. Farben Industrie, a German company closely aligned with the Nazi party. Although he never advised the German government, a 1934 Congressional Committee accused him of

---

[22] Source for this and the following quotes: conversations and email exchanges with Harold Burson on April 03, 2014, and March 10, 2015.

being anti-Semitic and of doing propaganda work for the Nazi government. He died of a brain tumor before the details of his work could be established (Cutlip, 1994). Carl Byoir, whose agency promoted tourism to Germany in the 1930s, at least had the satisfaction of being cleared by the FBI when a U.S. Congressman accused him of un-American activities.[23]

In some cases, the law makes ethical determinations for us. But what are we to make of legal, but unsavory products such as pornography, gambling, or marijuana? When one of us worked for AT&T, its cable television division began carrying hard-core pornography. When it became public, the Board of Directors questioned how it would affect the company's brand, but ultimately gave in to the financial arguments in favor of carrying channels with 90 percent profit margins. Was that an ethical decision?

Burson-Marsteller was once asked to help the U.S. Council of Catholic Bishops explain its anti-abortion stance. The agency turned the job down because its executives did not want to put employees in the position of possibly working on an account with which they disagreed and because they did not want to attract media coverage that might embarrass other clients. Meanwhile, Hill & Knowlton accepted the work and shrugged off the criticism. Which agency was acting ethically?

One could argue that Hill & Knowlton's decision was ethical because (1) there is no clear consensus on the issue of abortion and (2) representing the American bishops could lead to better understanding amongst the parties on both sides. In fact, the agency's CEO at the time, Robert Dilenschneider, put it in precisely those terms. "In my view, everybody—whether it's Jack the Ripper or the Catholic Church—has the right to be heard," he told us.[24] To him, that is clearly in the public interest. (Of course, in practice, much would depend on how the agency—and its client—comported themselves. But in theory if they respected their opponents' autonomous dignity, it would be ethical.) At the same time, Burson-

---

[23] FBI Clears Carl Byoir of 'Nazi Propaganda' Charge. (1940, July 18). *JTA*. http://www.jta.org/1940/07/18/archive/fbi-clears-carl-byoir-of-nazi-propaganda-charge. Accessed July 22, 2015.

[24] *Source:* conversation with Robert Dilenschneider on March 10, 2015.

Marsteller had no ethical obligation to take on a client that made it uncomfortable, whatever the reason. On the other hand, accepting an account and then dumping it simply because it turns out to be unpopular could be unethical because it would be unfair to the client.

Another Ethical Conundrum

For example, consider the following ethical conundrum: AT&T was once caught in the crossfire between the forces of the pro-choice and pro-life movements. The AT&T Foundation had long made an annual contribution to Planned Parenthood to support programs preventing teen pregnancy. But by 1990, the organization had become a leading advocate of abortion rights and some executives worried the company's contribution made it look like it was taking sides in the debate on abortion. So after some debate, the Foundation decided to quietly stop its contributions to Planned Parenthood.

When the *Washington Times* included AT&T in a roundup story on "Right to Life Victories," Planned Parenthood was outraged and issued a news release accusing AT&T of "corporate cowardice." It also ran full-page newspaper ads vilifying the company for caving in to the religious right and asking people who believed in "The Right to Choose" to "Hang Up on AT&T." The ads had two coupons: one to send as a protest to AT&T, the other to send money to Planned Parenthood. Editorial writers and columnists jumped on the bandwagon. A *Boston Globe* columnist wrote that "AT&T" now stood for "Abortion, Timidity and Teeming millions more unplanned babies."[25] Within just a few weeks AT&T received 40,000 coupons from those Planned Parenthood ads, along with 90,000 phone calls and 53,000 letters. Ironically, AT&T never intended to take a position on abortion. But by allowing itself to be cowed into submitting to the demands of one side in the abortion debate, it arguably *did* make a choice.

The president of the AT&T Foundation—who was personally pro-choice—insisted he was not "caving in to outside pressure," but listen-

---

[25] AT&T's Scarlet Letter. (1990, March 29). *Boston Globe.* http://www.highbeam.com/doc/1P2-8166855.html. Accessed July 22, 2015.

ing to the views of the foundation's stakeholders and trustees, not to mention the CEO of the company that funded it. He insisted he had an obligation to "disentangle the company from identification with what had become highly political, hyperactive, single-issue advocacy." It was, he argued, "a matter of principle." After all, money is fungible and support for Planned Parenthood's clinical work, which constitutes more than 95 percent of its budget, can easily slide over into its advocacy work. Besides, he pointed out, "only a handful of customers lodged protests by leaving AT&T" (Levy, 1999, pp. 103–105).

But from a consequentialist perspective, AT&T threw fuel on the fires of a raging debate, casting plenty of heat, without contributing a single ray of enlightened discourse. With the benefit of 20/20 hindsight, AT&T should have stood its ground, explaining its Planned Parenthood contributions were to prevent teen pregnancy, and taking whatever heat came its way. Instead, it tried to find a middle path only to discover it no longer had any ground to stand on.

On the other hand, when its self-interest was more obvious, the company was steadfast. For example, the religious right had also attacked AT&T for its inclusive employment policies. It was the first major American corporation to include sexual orientation in its formal diversity policy, back in 1975. The company sought to create a productive and supportive working environment for gay, lesbian, bisexual, and transgender employees. Many of its employees celebrate Gay Pride Month, just as they do Hispanic Heritage Month or other cultural and ethnic commemorations.

All this infuriated some on the religious right, who accused the company of everything from "indoctrinating" its employees in "aberrant lifestyles" to "encouraging immorality." Nevertheless, the company never wavered on its diversity policy. To compete in an industry whose principal engine is human creativity, AT&T simply must attract and keep the best talent available, without regard to race, gender, disability, religion, sexual orientation, or any other irrelevant circumstance The issue is so fundamental to its own self-interest there is no room for compromise.

Bringing It Full Circle

On some controversial issues the lines between right and wrong—good and bad—are pretty thin. On hot button issues ranging from abortion and genetically modified food to gun control and gender identity, there are intelligent people of good will on both sides and still little chance of consensus. To come full circle, even though Edelman declared it would not support climate change denial, its critics ask how it can provide *other* services to fossil fuel companies, such as promoting their environmental programs or their carbon-based products. Some environmental groups have even asked museums to "cut all ties" with fossil fuel companies and philanthropists who made their money in oil.[26] For its part, late in 2015. Edelman announced it would no longer work "with clients in the coal production industry" because "coal emits the most CO_2 of any fossil fuel per unit of energy obtained."[27]

Summary

As we have noted, the concept of the public interest is imprecise and at best a general guide in ethical decision making. That is not to say it is futile to ask the question; only that two different people, each striving to do what is right, could come up with diametrically opposed answers. What is critical is that they be able to justify their reasoning on ethical grounds.

What we can say is this: where personal and professional values are at odds, one owes it to a client to reveal the conflict. And whenever practitioners have reason to doubt that a client's purpose is in the public interest, they are obligated to resolve the issue to their personal satisfaction, either by resigning the account or by satisfying themselves that the arguments in its favor are sufficiently persuasive to warrant their support.

---

[26] See An Open Letter to Museums from Members of the Scientific Community. (2015, March 24). http://thenaturalhistorymuseum.org/open-letter-to-museums-from-scientists/. Accessed July 22, 2015.

[27] Ironically enough, the policy change was first reported in *The Guardian* newspaper. See Goldenberg, S. (2015, Sept, 15). Edelman ends work with coal producers. *The Guardian.* http://www.theguardian.com/environment/2015/sep/15/edelman-ends-work-with-coal-and-climate-change-deniers. Accessed October 13, 2015.

In all these considerations, practitioners need to guard against personal arrogance, the certainty that they are inalterably right and others are absolutely wrong. They should remain open to the possibility that what seems certain today might, under different circumstances or with new information, appear less categorical. And they should recognize the importance of free speech and vigorous debate in a democracy. But in the end, one must live with integrity, with no space between beliefs and behavior.

Meanwhile, as we will see in the next chapter, the background music to this discussion, sometimes lifting it along, sometimes drowning it out, is a debate that has been raging for more than four decades—what is the fundamental responsibility of business?

CHAPTER 8

Corporate Responsibility

Every October, National Football League (NFL) stadiums across the country are awash in pink. The cheerleaders' little outfits and pompoms, the penalty flags, the players' cleats, gloves, and wristbands, quarterback towels, referee whistles and caps, sometimes even portions of the field itself—all pink. It is the NFL's annual campaign to "help fight breast cancer." The league even donates a portion of proceeds from sales in the NFL Shop to the American Cancer Society's programs to increase awareness, education, and screenings for women over 40.

Since the program began in 2009, the league has raised more than $8 million by selling pink NFL merchandise and auctioning off pink apparel worn in the game.[1] According to Nielsen research, an NFL commercial promoting the importance of annual breast cancer screenings was the most memorable ad run during the games among the core 18- to 34-year-old audience.[2] The NFL estimates that every October its campaign brings the message of early detection to more than 150 million viewers, including more than 58 million women age 18 and older.[3]

Many would call this an exercise in corporate social responsibility (CSR). Some are not so sure.

Critics point out that the league's annual donation to the American Cancer Society amounts to less than 0.01 percent of annual revenue in excess of $13 billon. Others suggest the very idea of annual mammography screenings is expensive and ineffective, pointing to research showing

---

[1] See the NFL's "A Crucial Catch" http://www.nfl.com/pink.

[2] Poogi, J. (2014, November 4). NFL's breast cancer ad most memorable commercial among millenials. *Ad Age*. http://adage.com/article/media/top-10-commercials-millennials-october/295711/. Accessed July 22, 2015.

[3] According to the latest NFL news release on the program issued on October 1, 2012. See http://www.nfl.com/news/story/0ap1000000068474/article/nfl-supports-breast-cancer-awareness-month

it has no impact on survival rates of women with the disease.[4] And political cartoonist Jeff Darcy suggested the NFL choose the wrong color: "All the pink [on] Sunday couldn't hide the fact that the NFL is black and blue over its stunning lack of domestic violence awareness."[5]

As it happens, October is also Domestic Violence Awareness Month and, in 2014, the league had to deal with criticism it was not policing its own players' behavior off the field. For example, the League suspended Baltimore Ravens running back Ray Rice for two games when he knocked his then fiancée unconscious in an Atlantic City hotel elevator. But when a video emerged showing Rice actually throwing the punch and then dragging her out of the elevator, that penalty seemed woefully insignificant and the League, totally out of touch.

In response to a rising wave of criticism, the League suspended Rice indefinitely,[6] pledged to develop more effective domestic abuse programs for its players, promised to donate "multiple millions" to victim support groups, and ran a commercial to raise awareness of the issue during that year's SuperBowl.[7] Still, to many, the league's notion of corporate responsibility seemed largely an exercise in window dressing.

Nobel-winning economist Milton Friedman would have had an even harsher view. He tried to end all this misguided do-gooding in a *New York Times* Sunday magazine article way back in 1970, calling it "fundamentally subversive … in a free society."[8] And that gets us into a

---

[4] Sinha, S. (20143, October 8). The NFL's pink October does not raise money for cancer research. *Vice Sports*. https://sports.vice.com/article/the-nfls-pink-october-does-not-raise-money-for-cancer-research. Accessed July 22, 2015.

[5] Darcy, J. (2014, October 7). *Northeast Ohio Media Group Editorial Cartoonist*. http://www.cleveland.com/darcy/index.ssf/2014/10/nfl_domestic_violence_awarene s.html. Accessed July 22, 2015.

[6] Rice was also fired by the Ravens. He challenged both his firing and suspension. The Ravens settled his suit against them, paying him a reported $3.5 million for the time left on his contract. A mediator reversed his indefinite suspension, making him eligible to play for another team. As of this writing, no team has picked him up.

[7] Leaders of the NFL's Domestic Violence Response Pledge 'Multiple Millions. (2014, October 2). *Chronicle of Philanthropy*. http://philanthropy.com/article /Leaders-of-the-NFL-s/149185/. Accessed July 22, 2015.

[8] This and later quotes are from Friedman, M. (1970, September 13). The social responsibility of business is to increase its profits. *The New York Times Sunday Magazine*. http://www.colorado.edu/studentgroups/libertarians/issues/friedman-soc-resp-business.html. Accessed July 22, 2015.

debate that has been raging since the creation of limited liability, joint-stock enterprises in 1856[9]—what is the purpose of a business corporation? There are two principle schools of thought on the subject, each serving different masters—shareowners on the one hand and stakeholders on the other.

Shareowner Value

The shareowner value school of corporate purpose was perhaps most clearly enunciated by Milton Friedman in his 1970 article. In a free society, he claimed, business has "one and only one social responsibility—to use its resources and engage in activities designed to increase its profits so long as it stays within the rules of the game, which is to say, engages in open and free competition without deception or fraud." This sounds selfish, but Friedman believed the greatest good for society results from people pursing their own self-interest. In accord with Adam Smith's (1759/1976, p. 184) proverbial "invisible hand," while business people focus on making money, they are simultaneously creating jobs, raising the general public's standard of living, and helping to create a more stable, growing economy.

As far as Friedman is concerned,

in the free-enterprise, private-property system, a corporate executive is an employee of the owners of the business. He has direct responsibility to his employers. That responsibility is to conduct the business in accordance with their desires, which generally will be to make as much money as possible while conforming to the basic rules of the society, both those embodied in law and those embodied in ethical custom.

Friedman suggests that corporate executives who spend their company's resources for any other purpose than making money are stealing

---

[9] England's Joint Stock Companies Act of 1856 made it possible for private investors to organize themselves as a company with limited legal liability. An 1896 court decision in *Salomon v. A Salomon & Co. Ltd.* found that a business incorporated under that statute has a distinct legal personality, separate from that of its individual shareholders.

from its owners. And he does not leave much wiggle room in the apparent loophole of "ethical custom." CSR and "the nonsense spoken in its name" may "be in the long-term interests of a corporation," "make it easier to attract desirable employees or have other desirable effects," and may even "generate good will," he maintained. But it is still "hypocritical window-dressing" "approaching fraud" and "clearly harms the foundations of a free society."

Friedman's thesis was based on several closely related beliefs. First, that corporate share ownership is a form of private property that no one can use without permission and fair compensation. Second, that a corporation is "an artificial person" with "artificial responsibilities" limited to the purpose for which it was established, that is, to make money for its owners. And third, that it is government's job to see to the public welfare. If voters cannot elect public officials who will tend to social problems such as controlling pollution or training the hardcore unemployed, they should not be allowed to pressure corporations to do it, which he characterized as "seeking to attain by undemocratic procedures what they cannot attain by democratic procedures."

Capitalism

Capitalism, the economic system most closely associated with the shareowner value theory, seems to work. In 2014, the *Wall Street Journal* reported that, according to the World Bank, the share of the world population living in extreme poverty had fallen by more than 50 percent since 1990.[10] "The credit goes to the spread of capitalism," the *Journal* declared. "Over the past few decades, developing countries have embraced economic-policy reforms that have cleared the way for private enterprise." Indeed, the newspaper anointed capitalism as "the ultimate global anti-poverty program." Adam Smith's invisible hand seems to have been tending to the world's poor.

The shareowner value theory also seems to have a solid legal foundation. At the turn of the 20th century, Henry Ford envisioned a "horseless

---

[10] Irwin, D. (2014, November 3). The ultimate global anti-poverty program. *Wall Street Journal.* http://online.wsj.com/articles/douglas-irwin-the-ultimate-global-antipoverty-program-1414972491. Accessed July 22, 2015.

carriage" in every driveway, and he poured every cent he made into manufacturing them. Instead of paying higher dividends, he used the company's profits to build better, cheaper cars and to pay higher wages. Some of his shareowners disagreed with this strategy, especially the two Dodge brothers who had dreams of their own and had already started a competing car company. When Ford refused to pay a higher dividend, the Dodge brothers hauled him into court.

In 1919, the Michigan Supreme Court sided with the Dodge brothers and ordered Ford to pay a special dividend.[11] While the justices said they would not interfere with Ford's judgment on things like pricing and building new plants, they made clear he was mistaken in his belief that his company could pursue any altruistic end he wanted:

> *There should be no confusion . . . . A business corporation is organized and carried on primarily for the profit of the stockholders. The powers of the directors are to be employed for that end. The discretion of the directors is to be exercised in the choice of means to attain that end, and does not extend to . . . other purposes.*

That decision became the go-to argument in defense of the shareowner value theory. It is widely cited as proof the law requires corporations to have a "profit maximizing purpose" (Clark, 1986, p. 6768) and "managers and directors have a legal duty to put shareholders' interests above all others and [have] no legal authority to serve any other interests ..." (Bakan, 2004, p. 36).

But while other courts have confirmed the priority of shareowner interests, none have declared it a company's exclusive or sole purpose. In fact, Leo Strine, Chief Justice of the Delaware Supreme Court, which has the broadest influence on corporate law, offered what he called a "clear-eyed look" at the issue:

> *When the corporation is not engaging in a sale of control transaction, the directors have wide leeway to pursue the best interests of stockholders as they perceive them, and need not put any specific weight on maximizing current share value. As a means to the end of*

---

[11] *Dodge v. Ford Motor Co.*, 170 N.W. 668 (Mich. 1919) at 684. http://www.law.illinois.edu/aviram/Dodge.pdf. Accessed September 7, 2015.

increasing stockholder welfare, directors may consider the interests of other constituencies (2015, March 20, p. 16).

Long Term vs. Short Term

In other words, a company's directors may pass up a higher short-term profit if they believe it will best advance the interests of stockholders in the long run. Employee health insurance, for example, costs money in the short run, but in the long run healthy employees may have higher morale and be more productive. And the U.S. Supreme Court recently noted that "While it is certainly true that a central objective of for-profit corporations is to make money, modern corporate law does not require for-profit corporations to pursue profit at the expense of everything else."[12]

Finally, when Friedman began his career, stock ownership was relatively concentrated. Today, it is widely dispersed and volatile. The average mutual fund turns over nearly its entire portfolio every 12 months. So shareholder value has really become a euphemism for this quarter's profits. But Justice Strine (2015, March 20, p. 4) drew a clear distinction between "the current stock price" and what he termed "shareowner welfare." Company directors must focus on the latter, not the former. Still, the debate continues. And since Friedman's 1970 manifesto, other business thinkers have offered alternative views.

Stakeholder Theory

Philosopher and management theorist R. Edward Freeman developed one of the most influential alternate theories in his 1984 book *Strategic Management: A Stakeholder Approach*. Freeman maintains that, in addition to the people who invest in a company, businesses need to serve the interests of a broad array of other parties, including employees, customers, suppliers, and the communities in which they operate. Freeman called these people "stakeholders" and defined them as "groups and individuals

---

[12] *Burwell, Secretary of Health and Human Services et. al. v. Hobby Lobby Stores, Inc. et al.* (June 30, 2014). U.S., Nos. 13–354. http://caselaw.lp.findlaw.com/scripts/getcase.pl?court=US&vol=000&invol=13-354#opinion1. Accessed July 22, 2015.

that can affect, or are affected by, the accomplishment of organizational purpose" (p. 41). And he argued that in today's globalized economy, a corporation's long-run success depends on taking their interests into account.

To do this, Freeman suggested the theory of the firm must be reconceptualized "along essentially Kantian lines, meaning each stakeholder group has a right to be treated as an end in itself, and not as means to some other end," and therefore must "participate in determining the future direction of the firm in which [it has] a stake" (Evan and Freeman, 2012, pp. 97, 105).

In a sense, Freeman believed the shareowner theory that businesses exist to create wealth was correct, but defined the recipients of that wealth too narrowly. "The very purpose of the firm is, in our view, to serve as a vehicle for coordinating stakeholder interests," Evan and Freeman (2012, p. 103) wrote. "It is through the firm that each stakeholder group makes itself better off." On Kantian grounds, corporations have an ethical duty to respect the rights of the people they deal with. On consequentialist grounds, they are responsible for the effects of their actions. And for those who claim that corporations are only obligated to follow the law, proponents of stakeholder theory would quote Supreme Court Justice Stewart Potter who reputedly observed, "Ethics is knowing the difference between what you have a right to do and what is right to do."

A Theory with Many Advocates

Perhaps, reflecting concern that shareowner theory had been used to justify short-term financial engineering with disastrous social consequences, many scholars and even some business people rushed to embrace the stakeholder theory. In the first decade after publication, it was the subject of more than a dozen books and hundreds of articles, each giving it a slightly different twist. Out of this thicket of theorizing, ethicist Thomas Donaldson and business professor Lee Preston (1995) developed a thesis that has, in turn, been cited more than 1,000 times, serving as a firm foundation for our ethical inquiry. It starts with a two-part definition of stakeholders:

*(a) Stakeholders are persons or groups with legitimate interests in pro-
cedural and/or substantive aspects of corporate activity. Stakeholders
are identified by their interests in the corporation, whether the corporation has any corresponding functional interest in them.*

*(b) The interests of all stakeholders are of intrinsic value. That is,
each group of stakeholders merits consideration for its own sake and
not merely because of its ability to further the interests of some other
group, such as the shareowners* (pp. 65–81).

In ethical circles, these are known as "normative" statements. That
is, they do not merely describe things as they are, but as they ought to
be. In Davidson and Preston's view, stakeholders are ethically entitled to
certain rights. As it happens, it is also descriptive because surveys show
that, despite the apparent popularity of the shareowner theory of the
corporation, most managers say they consider more than shareowner
interests in making decisions.

A 2006 survey of global business executives by the consulting firm
McKinsey & Company found only a minority wholeheartedly embraced
Friedman's view. Sixteen percent of respondents agreed that business
should "focus solely on providing the highest possible returns to investors while obeying all laws and regulations." But 84 percent said the role
of large corporations should be to "generate high returns to investors but
balance [that] with contributions to the broader public good."[13]

"Managers may not make explicit reference to 'stakeholder theory',"
Donaldson and Preston (1995. p.75) admit, "but the vast majority of
them apparently adhere in practice to one of (its) central tenets, namely,
that their role is to satisfy a wider set of stakeholders, not simply the
shareowners."

Popularity aside, Donaldson and Preston justify the stakeholder theory
using the very principle of property rights that underlay Friedman's arguments in favor of his shareowner theory. They point out that property

---

[13] McKinsey & Company. (2011, October). How companies manage sustainability:
McKinsey Global Survey results. *McKinsey Quarterly*. http://www.mckinsey
.com/insights/energy_resources_materials/the_business_of_sustainability_mckinsey_
global_survey_results. Accessed July 22, 2015.

rights have never been considered absolute and therefore do not "support the claim that the responsibility of managers is to act solely as agents for the shareowners" (p. 84). Legal scholars agree that what we call "property" is actually a bundle of many rights, some of which may be limited. In fact, Donaldson and Preston quote conservative economist Svetozar Pejovich (1990, pp. 27–28), who wrote that, "Property rights are relations between individuals," "not an unrestricted right," and thus "it is wrong to separate human rights from property rights."

Of course, that leaves open the question of which "individuals" have a valid stake or claim in the "property" represented by a corporation. Donaldson and Preston (1995, pp. 85–86) maintain that, as a matter of justice, stakeholders include all those who experience actual or potential harms and benefits as a result of the firm's actions or inactions. In practice, they write, "the appraisal of the legitimacy of such expectations is an important function of management, often in concert with other already recognized stakeholders."

If anything, Donaldson and Preston accuse earlier proponents of the stakeholder theory of harboring an overly expansive view of stakeholders as "anything influencing or influenced by the firm" (p. 86). Such a definition swept competitors, as well as the media, into the ranks of stakeholders. It even allowed some to suggest that "the natural environment" is a stakeholder. But while both the media and competitors might affect the firm, neither could reasonably expect to benefit from the firm's success, nor do they bear the risks of its failure except in the broadest sense. And while a healthy environment is obviously important to a firm's success, it is not a human being. And denying it the ethical status of "stakeholder" in no way lessens a company's obligation to treat it with care as a "public good." Nor does denying "stakeholder" status to the likes of the media, social activists, and competitors mean companies can safely ignore them. On the contrary, as intermediaries who can influence genuine stakeholders, corporations will want to manage relationships with them carefully, but without any sense of ethical obligation beyond those owed other human beings.

However, we believe all those parties who genuinely contributed to the firm's success or bore the risks of its failures, and whose support the company voluntarily accepted, have a moral interest in its affairs.

Corporations have an ethical obligation—as a matter of fairness—to recognize and respond to those interests, over and above the respect and care due stakeholders as human beings and in addition to any narrow contractual obligations they may have.

The principal criticism of stakeholder theory is that it divides management's attention, forcing a business's leadership to balance the interests of multiple, often competing, constituencies. As Freeman *himself* once observed: "Owners want higher financial returns, while customers want more money spent on research and development. Employees want higher wages and better benefits, while the local community wants better parks and day-care facilities" (2001, p. 44). But rather than seeing this as a distraction from a company's primary task of making money, Freeman considered it the essence of corporate management.

"Stakeholder theory is the idea that each one of these groups is important to the success of a business, and figuring out where their interests go in the same direction is what the managerial task and the entrepreneurial task is all about," he wrote. "Stakeholder theory says if you just focus on financiers, you miss what makes capitalism tick ... that shareholders and financiers, customers, suppliers, employees, communities can together create something that no one of them can create alone" (Freeman, 2009, October 1).

Freeman went so far as to claim his theories and Friedman's may seem opposed, but really are not. He wrote,

> *I actually think if Milton Friedman were alive today ..., he would be a stakeholder theorist. He would understand that the only way to create value for shareholders in today's world is to pay attention to customers, suppliers, employees, communities and shareholders at the same time. What Friedman was against was the idea of social responsibility that does not have anything to do with business. I'm against that too* (2009, October 1).

Kantian and Consequentialist Roots

Whether Freeman or Friedman, both or neither, is right about the purpose and responsibilities of the corporation is a question that each of us needs to answer for ourselves. Senior public relations counselors especially need to understand their client's views on the subject because it will inform their counsel and work. In extreme cases of fundamental disagreement, it could even prompt a parting of the ways. Because what is actually at stake here is an ethical principle with both Kantian and consequentialist roots—*a company's ethical obligation to respect the autonomy of the human beings it deals with, to avoid causing them harm and, whenever possible, to do good.*

More companies than the average person might suspect are exercising that ethical principle. For example, some of the United State's largest food and beverage companies have pledged to remove billions of calories from their products to help combat the nation's obesity epidemic. Brands from Bumble Bee, Campbell, and Coke to Kellogg's, Kraft, and Pepsi are re-engineering products, reducing portion size, and shifting advertising to lower calorie offerings to help reduce obesity.[14] And a growing number of firms realize their ethical obligations do not stop at the edge of their parking lots. Companies from Apple to Xerox have taken steps to ensure their suppliers conform to a global code of conduct on labor, health, safety and environmental activity. To be sure, at least some of these companies are motivated by enlightened self-interest. Consumers increasingly favor healthier food and expect companies to act responsibly. In fact, the term of art for such initiatives is "corporate *social* responsibility" (CSR) to emphasize a company's impacts on society in general.

Corporate Social Responsibility

CSR need not be in conflict with a company's obligation to its share-owners to operate at a profit. In fact, legendary management consultant Peter Drucker (1993, pp. 343–344) referred to this as "Bounded Goodness." A company's "specific mission is also society's first need and interest," he wrote. And it has a responsibility to make a profit on that mission. "The first 'social responsibility' of business is to make enough profit to cover the costs of the future," Drucker (1984, p. 62) wrote.

---

[14] Begley, S. (2014, January 9). Food, beverage companies slash calories in obesity fight. *Reuters.* http://www.reuters.com/article/2014/01/09/us-calories-idUSBRE A0805F20140109. Accessed July 22, 2015.

"Decaying businesses in a decaying economy are unlikely to be good neighbors, good employers or 'socially responsible' in any way."

But Drucker was clear that business is accountable for more than its economic performance. It is also accountable for minimizing any negative impacts it might have on society. And he urged companies to take action on social problems, subject to the limits of their competence and authority. "To take on tasks for which one lacks competence is irresponsible," he wrote, "It is also cruel. It raises expectations which will then be disappointed" (1993, pp. 343–344). And, of course, no business should seek to put itself in the place of government or try to impose its values on a community.

In the decades since Drucker set "the bounds of goodness," many executives have concluded that CSR is not something a company does in addition to its real business; it is the *way* it does business. A 2010 McKinsey global survey shows that 76 percent of executives believe CSR contributes positively to long-term shareholder value.[15] If that is not a practical enough justification, consider business strategist Michael Porter's perspective that CSR should be a high priority for business leaders because governments, activists, and the media "have become adept at holding companies to account for the social consequences of their activities" (Porter and Kramer, 2006, December, p. 1).

Shared Value

But perhaps even more important than those coldly pragmatic reasons, Porter sees another more fundamental rationale—CSR "can be a source of opportunity, innovation, and competitive advantage." But first companies need to look at CSR as more than a cost, a constraint, or a nice thing to do.

Business professors Mark Schwartz and Archie Carroll (2003) studied the different motives that prompt companies to engage in CSR programs and came up with a theory of three over-lapping domains. Basically, they

---

[15] McKinsey & Company (2010). How Companies Manage Sustainability: Mckinsey Global Survey Results. *McKinsey Quarterly*. See: https://www.mckinseyquarterly .com/.

concluded companies were motivated by economic considerations (to be profitable), legal (to obey the law), or ethical (to sustain their license to operate by responding to society's expectations). Like Schwartz and Carroll, Porter believes the ideal CSR program operates at the intersection of all three domains—economic, legal, and ethical. "The essential test that should guide CSR," he maintains, "is not whether a cause is worthy but whether it represents an opportunity to create shared value—that is, a meaningful benefit for society that is also valuable for the business" (Porter and Kramer, 2006, December, pp. 7–8).

In later papers, Porter elaborated on this notion of "shared value," suggesting that in today's economies, "societal needs, not just conventional economic needs, define markets" and that "social harms or weaknesses frequently create *internal* costs for firms—such as wasted energy or raw materials, costly accidents, and the need for remedial training to compensate for inadequacies in education" (Porter and Kramer, 2011, January, pp. 62–77). He points to companies like General Electric, Google, IBM, Intel, Johnson & Johnson, Nestle, and Walmart, which have "have already embarked on important efforts to create shared value by reconceiving the intersection between society and corporate performance".

In fact, he suggests the key is to focus on the interdependence of corporations and society rather than on the tensions between them. The latter approach, he suggests, has proven impotent. Companies that have built a pool of "good will" to draw on when they get into trouble have discovered it evaporates when the least heat is applied. "A firm that views CSR as a way to placate pressure groups," he writes, "often finds that its approach devolves into a series of short-term defensive reactions … with minimal value to society and no strategic benefit to the business" (Porter and Kramer, 2006, December, p. 4).

Strategic CSR

A strategic—and we submit ethical—approach to CSR takes an *inside-out/outside-in approach,* first examining how a company impinges on society in the normal course of business (inside-out) and then considering how society impacts the underlying drivers of a company's competitiveness wherever it operates (outside-in). This will produce different results for different companies. For example, the social consequences of operating a factory are different in China than in Europe. What might be nice-to-do for one company might be of strategic importance for another. For example, supporting a dance company might be of little strategic value to a local utility, but important to a credit card company that depends on tourism and entertainment.

In Porter's view, CSR operates at three levels:

1. exercising good citizenship that meets community expectations,
2. mitigating harm from a firm's activities, and
3. "mounting a small number of initiatives whose social and business benefits are large and distinctive" (pp. 9–10).

Creating economic value and social value simultaneously is not impossible. For example, working in partnership with nongovernmental organizations, Pepsico's Sustainable Farm Initiative teaches local farmers from China to Mexico new agricultural techniques. The farmers improve their productivity; Pepsico gets a more reliable source of supply and helps preserve the environment.[16] In the high-tech world, Cisco has partnered with educational institutions around the world to establish "networking academies" to train young men and women in information technologies. So far the academies have graduated more than 5.5 million students in 170 countries, building the skilled workforce Cisco's customers need while improving people's lives.[17] Southwire, a cable manufacturer in rural Georgia, partnered with the local school system to hire high school students at risk of dropping out. The company paid more than minimum wage, but to keep their jobs, the students had to stay in school. Graduation rates jumped 10 percent and Southwire's earnings increased by $1.7 million.[18]

---

[16] See Pepsico's website: http://www.pepsico.com/Purpose/Environmental-Sustainability/Agriculture. Accessed July 22, 2015.

[17] See Cisco's website: https://www.netacad.com/web/about-us/about-net working-academy;jsessionid=8EEA987D2A1CAD9F73E89A887F7CEE44. node2. Accessed July 22, 2015.

[18] See Porter, E. (2015, September 9). Corporate Action on Social Problems Has Its Limits, *The New York Times.* http://nyti.ms/1KZPbH2 Accessed September. 9, 2015.

However, there have also been instances of social responsibility done out of so much self-interest that it sucks any sense of responsibility to society out of it. We are thinking of programs that spend orders of magnitude more on promoting a company's good works than on the good works themselves. Or philanthropy directed less at serving a real social need than at extorting political support from an influential charity. Both AT&T[19] and Comcast[20] have been accused of making large donations to community groups and then twisting their arms to support mergers unrelated to their charitable mission.

Moral Purpose

Porter has no illusions about the moral purpose of business. "The most important thing a corporation can do for society," he says, "is contribute to a prosperous economy." But in the accomplishment of that purpose, they cannot "shirk the social and environmental consequences of their actions." And in a small number of well-defined instances, every company can and should address social issues that intersect with its business. "When a well-run business applies its vast resources, expertise, and management talent to problems that it understands and which it has a stake," he writes, "it can have a greater impact on social good than any other institution or philanthropic organization" (Porter and Kramer, 2006, December, p. 15). That is being responsible. It has also become so popular *Fortune* magazine has launched yet another list: the 50 companies it believes have "made significant progress in addressing major social problems as a part of their core business strategy."[21]

Unfortunately, the literature is littered with stories of companies that said all the right things about one cause or another, but in the final analysis

[19] Krigman, E. (2011, June 10). AT&T gave cash to Merger Backers. *Politico.* http://www.politico.com/news/stories/0611/56660.html. Accessed July 22, 2015.
[20] Lipton, E. (2015, April 5). Comcast recruits its beneficiaries to lobby for Time Warner deal. *New York Times.* http://www.nytimes.com/2015/04/06/business /media/comcast-recruits-its-beneficiaries-to-lobby-for-time-warner-deal.html. Accessed July 22, 2015.
[21] Murray, A. (2015, September. 1). Doing Well by Doing Good. Fortune, pp. 57–74. http://fortune.com/change-the-world/. Accessed September 10, 2015.

accomplished little. For example, after a decade of futilely trying to counter fears ignited by the publication of Rachel Carson's *Silent Spring* in 1962, many chemical companies realized they could more easily delay, modify, or even avoid significant government regulation if they at least *appeared* to be cooperating with the environmental movement rather than opposing it on every front. Some companies were sincere and partnered with environmental groups to dramatically improve their operations. Others decided they could take action on the edges of their business where the cost was low and the results easily measurable and highly promotable. Recycling, for example, was easy to explain internally and externally. It could potentially reduce costs. And it came with a handsome logo to splash on promotional material. Thus was born the practice of *greenwashing*, the spray tan of corporate responsibility. Today, the environmental consultancy of Underwriters Laboratories estimates 95 percent of eco-friendly claims are based on irrelevant, weak, or non-existent data. [22]

All of which leaves us with the question that started this chapter—what to make of the NFL's "partnership" with the American Cancer Society? Is it an exercise of CSR or an attempt at "pink washing," that is, associating itself with a popular cause to distract the public from its own failings?

Summary

Any discussion of corporate responsibility leads inevitably to the question Aristotle considered the foundation of any ethical practice: What is its fundamental purpose? By definition, the ethical practice of business must serve the purpose for which it was established.

So far, so good, but as we have seen, some people have diametrically opposite views of a business's purpose. Adherents of the so-called "shareholder theory" of the corporation believe a business exists solely to create wealth for its owners. They acknowledge that businesses are obligated to follow rules of the road, such as laws and regulations. But they also maintain that they bear no responsibility for dealing with any

---

[22] TerraChoice (2010). "The Sins of Greenwashing," http://sinsofgreenwashing.com/index35c6.pdf Accessed Oct. 15, 2015.

"externalities," such as pollution, that are not specifically mandated by those rules. Indeed, many of them believe using corporate resources to alleviate societal problems is essentially stealing from the shareowners. While using those resources to beat back further regulation serves their owners' interests.

Meanwhile, followers of the "stakeholder theory" maintain that a business exists to create wealth (or value) for everyone who contributes to its success or bears the risks of its failures. They acknowledge that some of a corporation's responsibilities to these stakeholders are covered by legal agreements and contracts. But they maintain businesses also have an ethical obligation to their stakeholders over and above what the law requires. Indeed, they suggest that maintaining a proper balance between all stakeholders' interests is management's prime responsibility.

Business thinkers from Peter Drucker to Michael Porter have tried to build bridges between these seemingly opposing views by suggesting that defining business's purpose broadly may not only be in a company's enlightened self-interest, but also could be the source of competitive advantage. They believe every company needs to address three sets of interest—*economic* (to be profitable), *legal* (to obey the law), and *ethical* (to respond to society's expectations). Drucker suggests companies should be bound by the limits of their competencies in addressing social problems. Porter suggests undertaking such work should be strategic, focusing on a small number of issues that intersect with the business and where a company can create value shared by itself and society.

With all that, the debate about corporate purpose continues. And, as Aristotle suggested thousands of years ago, where you come out on the question will determine how you think about corporate responsibility and ethics. It will require a careful balancing of interests, obligations, and rights—all of which are the topic of our next chapter.

CHAPTER 9

Duties and Rights

British philosopher Philippa Foot (1920–2010) was living in an attic flat in Central London when the Nazis began raining V1 missiles down on the city. At night, sirens and the sounds of nearby explosions would send her rushing into the bathtub for protection from breaking glass; on her way to work in the morning, she would walk by the ruins of still-smoldering buildings hit the night before. Then, as suddenly as they had started, the missiles stopped.

It was only after the war that Foot discovered British double agents had fed the Nazi war machine misleading information about their missile targeting, redirecting them to fall short of the core of the city into South London. The government claimed the ruse had saved thousands of lives. It also prompted one of the most famous thought experiments in ethics.

Foot wondered about the ethics of redirecting missiles that were certain to kill people no matter where they landed. And she recast the dilemma in a homely little riddle. As she originally framed it, a runaway tram will kill five track workers unless the engineer switches it to a siding where it will only kill one hapless victim. There will inevitably be a death, but whether it is one or five is up to the engineer. Should he flip the switch?

Studies show most people reluctantly say "yes." Indeed, the consequentialist theory of ethics seems to demand it. After all, by flipping the switch the engineer would save five lives, even at the cost of one. The rub, as Foot pointed out, is that few people would make the same decision under situations with exactly the same cost-benefit ratio, say killing one person in order to harvest organs that could save five lives. Why do people react so differently to situations that, at least mathematically, seem so similar? Foot explained the difference by drawing moral distinctions between intended and unintended consequences, between doing and allowing.[1]

---

[1] The full ethical implications of Foot's thought experiments are vividly described in David Edmond's *Would You Kill The Fat Man*, Princeton University Press, 2013.

Ethicists ever since have had a field day designing situations with slightly different variations on the trolley riddle to unmask exactly what is going through people's minds as they ponder their choices. In the process, they gave birth to a whole new field of applied ethics dubbed "Trolleyology." Ironically, they might have lowered their aim a bit. What is going through people's minds seems less important than what's going on in their guts.

Jonathan Haidt

Social psychologist Jonathan Haidt has been studying people's moral intuitions ever since he wrote his PhD thesis at the University of Pennsylvania—"Moral Judgment, Affect and Culture, Or Is It Wrong to Eat Your Dog?" (1992). Using an ingenious mix of experiments and online surveys in the United States, Europe, Brazil, and India, Haidt discovered we all share a fairly consistent set of moral values, the largely unconscious norms that cause us to think something is good or bad, right or wrong, worthwhile or worthless. Haidt (pronounced "height") speculates evolution hardwired these moral intuitions into us starting about 10,000 years ago, before the invention of language, when the only thing standing between our ancestors and a dinner of mastodon was an inclination to selfishness. Hunters who were inclined to work in groups survived and had offspring who learned the same cooperative behavior. The loners and the free riders did not do so well.[2]

Of course, working in groups was not the only behavior that benefited from those gut feelings. Hunter-gatherers who bit into rotten meat did not live as long as those who were disgusted by it, a feeling passed down to future generations. In all, Haidt came up with at least six psychological mechanisms that "comprise the universal foundations of the world's many moral matrices" (Haidt, 2012, p. 181). Briefly, expressed as opposite ends of a spectrum, they are care/harm, fairness/cheating, loyalty/betrayal, authenticity/subversion, liberty/oppression, and sanctity/degradation. Haidt

---

[2] Don Stacks put forth a similar proposition in his notion of preverbal areas of the brain set at birth as compared with others that are only partially set and culturally adaptive. See Stacks (1983) and Stacks and Anderson (1989).

left plenty of room for the discovery of additional psychological mechanisms, but the point is less their number than their innate universality.

Haidt believes moral feelings are as much a part of our DNA as opposable thumbs. We use reason to explain and systematize our moral feelings or to convince others of our beliefs. Societies give different weights to these individual feelings. That is why moral standards vary so widely from culture to culture. But all people make their initial moral choices on a mix of these universal gut feelings. In fact, neuroscientists claim they can see it happening using functional magnetic resonance imaging scans.[3]

W. D. Ross

William David Ross (1877–1971) died before Haidt and others set forth their evolutionary-based theories of moral sentiments. But he would not have been terribly surprised by them. W. D. Ross, as he is known in ethical literature, was an *intuitionist*. That is, he believed that certain fundamental ethical rules—like keeping promises or telling the truth—are so obvious as to be self-evident, requiring no lengthy explanation or reasoning. "The moral order ... is just as much part of the fundamental nature of the universe," he wrote, "as is the spatial or numerical structure expressed in the axioms of geometry or arithmetic" (Ross, 1930/2002, pp. 29–30). In fact, Ross believed all human beings have at least seven axiomatic duties or obligations toward others:

1. **Fidelity.** To keep promises and to be honest and truthful.
2. **Reparation.** To make amends when we have wronged someone else.
3. **Gratitude.** To be grateful to others when they perform actions that benefit us and to try to return the favor.
4. **Harm-prevention** (or non-maleficence). To prevent harm to others either physically or psychologically.

---

[3] Haidt takes special note of studies by philosopher and neuroscientist Joshua Greene, especially a paper he co-wrote with R. B. Sommerville, L. E. Nystrom, J.M. Darley, and J.D. Cohen. (2001). An fMRI Study of Emotional Engagement in Moral Judgment. *Science,* Vol. 293, pp, 2105–2108.

5. **Beneficence**. To do good to others, to foster their health, wisdom, security, happiness, and well-being.
6. **Self-improvement**. To improve our own health, wisdom, security, happiness, and well-being.
7. **Justice**. To be fair, distributing benefits and burdens equitably and evenly.

Ross was open to the idea of adding duties, but critics have usually found a way to squeeze them into the canonical list.[4] For example, some suggested "respect for freedom: to avoid coercing people in any way," only to conclude it is included in beneficence. Others, suggested "non-parasitism: to abide by the rules of an institution from which we derive benefits," but that seemed to be included in the duty of justice. There was a groundswell for the duty of "care: to attend to the needs of those with whom we have a special relationship, such as within families or among close friends," but it already seems part of beneficence. (Nevertheless, a whole ethical theory has been built around the concept of care and we will devote some attention to it in Chapter 10.)

Whatever their number, Ross termed these duties *prima facie*. That is Latin for "at first sight," but he did not mean they were simply *apparent* duties; he considered them very real. Unlike Kant, he believed human beings had multiple ethical duties rather than a single categorical imperative. And he realized that in real life, these obligations would often conflict, with one duty having greater urgency than the others, depending on the circumstances.

Ross did not prioritize these duties in the abstract; he believed every situation must be evaluated separately. However, he did offer some "rules of thumb." For example, he suggested duties of non-malfeasance, fidelity, reparation, justice, and gratitude are usually weightier than the duty of beneficence (1930/2002, pp. 75–77). And he would probably

---

[4] There is also some controversy about the precise number of duties Ross prescribed. His initial list counted five—fidelity, gratitude, reparation, beneficence, and non-maleficence. But he later added justice and self-improvement, even while arguing that they could also be included in beneficence. In the end, he thought people might want to add to the list, but he was confident the seven he enumerated represented a person's core duties.

agree that, unless a great deal is at stake, it is wrong to harm others in order to keep a promise, correct a previous wrong, or express gratitude.

Ross (1930/2002, p. 27) was also quick to point out that in actual experience these various duties are "compounded together in highly complex ways." For example, our duty to obey our country's laws arises partly from gratitude for the benefits of living there, partly from an implicit promise to obey them, and partly because they prevent harm and do good.

Ross was a very practical philosopher, and the two things he disliked most about Kant's approach to ethics were its level of abstraction and its absolutism. To Ross's mind, ethics is a nonexact, practical science that deals in probabilities not certainties. Its fundamental precepts may be self-evident, requiring no further proof, but their application is messy, and people frequently disagree about what is right and wrong in a given case. That does not make right and wrong relative; it simply recognizes that, in practical terms, it is often difficult to get everyone on the same page (Ross, 1930/2002, p. 31).

Right and Good

That is why Ross distinguished between the *right* and the *good*. The "good" refers to an objective standard that is sometimes difficult to determine with certainty. It is there, but we do not always see it. The "right," on the other hand, refers to actions. And Ross agreed with Kant's conception of "good will," that for an act to be ethical, we must do it *because* we believe it is the right thing to do. A right action is one motivated by good will. Not all right actions, however, produce results that are "good" in a moral sense. Rather, Ross said, even the most careful, reflective actions necessarily involve, moral risk. That is what makes dilemmas such as the trolley problem so stressful (Ross, 1930/2002, p. 30).

Interestingly, many of Ross's *prima facie* duties seem to be consequentialist. Beneficence, non-malfeasance, self-improvement, reparation, and justice all address the consequences of our actions in one way or another. Because of that, some ethicists consider Ross a bridge between Kant and Mill (i.e., between deontologists and utilitarians). But Ross himself cautioned that we should never make moral judgments solely on the basis of their consequences, but rather on the relative weight our intuition tells us to give our conflicting duties in a given situation (pp. 21–27). And he did not claim our moral intuitions are infallible. On the contrary, he said they required deep reflection and consideration, especially in the context of our human relationships.

Ross believed the particular roles we play in the lives of others give rise to specific ethical obligations that might not be so obvious. For example, in the everyday practice of public relations, we have specific duties to at least six categories of people: ourselves, our employer, our clients, client stakeholders, our fellow practitioners, and society in general. For example,

- Duties to *ourselves*. To preserve our personal integrity, to avoid violating our own values and beliefs, to maintain our professional competence.
- Duties to our *employer*. To follow the employment practices and policies of whoever is paying our salary, to be loyal and protect their confidences.
- Duties to our *clients*. To give our clients competent service and to respect their confidences.
- Duties to our *clients' stakeholders*. To communicate openly and truthfully, respecting their rights, including the right to reason.
- Duties to *fellow practitioners*. To adhere to professional standards and to do nothing that casts the practice of public relations into disrepute.
- Duties to *society*. To serve the common good.

Note that these duties are *interrelated*. For example, providing competent service is something we owe our employer and our clients as well as ourselves. It includes ensuring we have the skills to handle the assignments we take on, recognizing our own limitations, and never overpromising. How we relate to our clients and to our clients' stakeholders will reflect on fellow practitioners and should be in keeping with best practice. Similarly, our duty to serve the common good arises not only from our own *prima facie* duty of beneficence, but also from our duty to serve our client faithfully. As we have seen, our clients themselves have a duty to serve the common good, and helping them do so is part of our role as public relations practitioners.

Complicating matters, as previously noted, the duty of beneficence, which Ross considered the basis for serving the common good, has traditionally taken a back seat to all the other *prima facie* duties. Benevolence is what Ross and Kant termed an "imperfect duty," something we are only obliged to do when we can. As business ethicist William Shaw (2005, p. 61) points out, "Most non-utilitarian philosophers, like Ross, believe we have some obligation to promote the general welfare, but they typically view this obligation as less stringent than, for example, the obligation not to injure people." Under that theory, in a world of practical constraints, it would be perfectly ethical for a factory owner to spend money reducing pollution (non-malfeasance) rather than opening an on-site day care center (beneficence).

But Shaw suggests there is another way to look at these dilemmas. In some ways, it is the flipside of Ross's theory of duties—the concept of rights. Duties are obligations we have to others; rights are legitimate claims others can place on us. The legitimacy of some rights comes from the law, as in the right to vote. But people are also entitled to many rights simply because they are human beings. These human rights are natural; they do not depend on social institutions as legal rights do. They apply to everyone equally and cannot be given up or sold to someone else.

Universal Human Rights

Following World War II, the newly established United Nations made one of its first orders of business the declaration of inalienable human rights recognized by all members of the international community. It includes civil and political rights such as life, liberty, free speech, and privacy, as well as social and economic rights such as security, health, and education. The interpretation and implementation of these rights has been uneven across the international community. But some believe the concept of moral rights changes the ethical playing field. As Shaw (2005, p. 63) points out, "Once moral rights are asserted, the locus of moral judgment becomes the individual, not society." The goal is no longer the greatest good for the greatest number, but respecting the rights of the people directly affected. So even though Facebook could run a more reliable experiment by not telling nearly a million users it was manipulating their news feeds, most ethicists—and the company itself—concluded it was ethically wrong.[5]

From an organizational perspective, Ross's theory of *prima facie* duties recognizes the existence of multiple, sometimes conflicting obligations that can pull an organization in different directions as it pursues its legitimate interests. But the concept of human rights puts those obligations within a bounded context, by demanding that an ethically responsible organization carefully consider how its actions will impinge on the legitimate claims of those to whom it owes *prima facie* duties, including its investors, customers, employees, and the communities in which it operates. As Shaw (2013, p. 64) noted, under Ross's ethical theory, "moral rights place distinct and firm constraints on what sorts of things an organization can do to fulfill its own ends."

Occasionally—and perhaps more frequently than we might expect—corporations fail in the exercise of those duties. In late 2014, *the New York Times* revealed that General Motors had compiled a list of 13 people killed as a result of faulty ignitions. Yet, apparently the company had not notified any of the surviving families directly, even though they were entitled to compensation and the deadline for applying was less than two months away. One family did not know until called by a reporter.[6] After *the Times* reported on the issue, GM remembered its *prima facie* duty of reparation and extended the deadline by one month.

---

[5]Facebook's chief technical officer, Mike Schroepfer (2014, October 2), apologized for manipulating newsfeeds to see how people reacted to friends' positive and negative postings. The results published in June 2014 generated such a strong backlash, Schroepfer issued an apology and outlined steps the company had taken to improve its research. The company's guidelines are available at http://newsroom.fb.com/news /2014/10/research-at-facebook/.

[6] Abrams, R. (2014, November 10). 11 years later, woman's death is tied to G.M. ignition defect. *The New York Times*. http://www.nytimes.com/2014/11/11/business/11-years-later-death-is-tied-to-gm-defect.html?ref=business. Accessed July 22, 2015.

In such cases and under certain circumstances, public relations people have an ethical duty to themselves, to their colleagues, and to society at large to intervene. Assuming you are operating on more than suspicions and have concrete evidence of unethical behavior, your responsibility to report it increases depending on the severity of the problem you have observed, the certainty of the harm it will cause, your own degree of involvement, the cost of acting, and the certainty of solving the problem. The closer you are to the problem—for example, if it is in your own organization—the greater your responsibility.

In many cases, your company code of conduct will demand that you report your suspicions and it will provide a confidential channel for doing so. If that avenue does not work, and you are certain that you have uncovered genuine wrongdoing that could lead to serious harm or is against the law, you have an obligation to bring it to the attention of outside authorities. Some people will not like it, and you could be wrong. But research shows bad behavior spreads when good people look the other way.

Duties and Loyalties

An additional complicating factor for public relations practitioners is that our duties quickly translate into loyalties. In fact, ethicist Patricia Parsons (2008, p.25) defines loyalty this way—someone to whom we owe a duty and who in return places trust in us. It is not surprising then that when we have conflicting duties—or loyalties—we gravitate to the party who has placed the most obvious trust in us, often manifest in the form of our paycheck. Furthermore, in practice, public relations people tend to identify with their clients. In many cases, they have bonded in the course of their work, especially if they have weathered a difficult crisis together. But public relations people have to balance their duty to their clients with their duty to operate in the public interest. And that brings us to one of life's challenges—balancing basic values. Recent studies show that considerations of loyalty and fairness influence whether or not people report unethical behavior (Waytz et al., 2013). People who value fairness more than loyalty are more willing to blow the whistle, while people who value loyalty over fairness are more hesitant.

The whole point of ethical reasoning is finding the right balance between values. But our natural inclinations can skew us in one direction or another. Like all of us, you probably give more weight to some ethical values than to others. Try to understand which. Then ask yourself if it is appropriate in the circumstances at hand. If you find that question difficult, consider taking the moral foundations survey at www.yourmorals.org. It will give you some insight into the foundation of your personal ethics.

Summary

Many evolutionary psychologists and anthropologists believe we are all hardwired with moral instincts, gut feelings that make certain behaviors—like harming others, cheating, or acting disloyally—physically uncomfortable. That may be why the Trolley thought experiment dumbfounds so many people. In one case, they will sacrifice one life to save five, justifying it as serving the greater good. But in a similar situation, with the prospect of getting identical results, they will refuse to act. The difference seems to have something to do with one's direct involvement in sacrificing one person for five. When it is only a matter of flipping a switch, we can calculate the greater good; but when we actually have to shove someone in the path of the trolley … oh my.

Although he was less concerned with people's guts than their minds, W. D. Ross believed everyone is instinctually aware of certain fundamental duties—to keep promises, treat people fairly, avoid harming others, make amends when we wrong someone, improve ourselves, express gratitude for favors, and do good for others. He thought these duties were obvious (*prima facie*), but he also realized they would sometimes conflict. What if keeping a promise harms someone? Life is full of such conflicts, especially because we all play multiple roles—employee, parent, child, friend, and so forth—and each role comes with a separate set of duties. As public relations practitioners, we have duties to at least six categories of people: ourselves, our employer, our clients, client stakeholders, our fellow practitioners, and society in general.

Furthermore, other people have rights, legitimate claims they can place on us. Some rights are granted by law; many are rights people possess simply because they are human beings. These natural human rights are universal, nontransferable, and define the boundaries within which a company can legitimately pursue its economic, legal, and ethical interests.

Public relations people operate within the free fire zone of these conflicting loyalties and interests. Finding the right balance between them is messy and not without moral risk. In the next chapter, we will examine an attempt to reconstruct traditional ethical theory along the lines of contemporary feminist values and experiences, with particular emphasis on two of Ross's *prima facie* duties, justice and care (non-malfeasance and beneficence).

CHAPTER 10

Care and Justice

By now, you have probably noticed that all but one of the ethical theorists we have discussed, from Aristotle to W. D. Ross, were men. And that simple fact deeply colored their approach to questions of right and wrong.

In some instances, their male bias was quite obvious. In *Politics*, Aristotle (350 BCE) flatly states, "The male is by nature superior, and the female inferior; the one rules, and the other is ruled; this principle, of necessity, extends to all mankind" (Aristotle, tr. Jowett, 1999, Book 1, Part 5). More than two millenia later, Kant reflected the same conviction, writing, "[Woman's] philosophy is not to reason, but to sense.... Women will avoid the wicked not because it is un-right, but because it is ugly; and virtuous actions mean to them such as are morally beautiful. Nothing of duty, nothing of compulsion, nothing of obligation!" (Kant, 1763, tr. Frierson, 2011, p. 81).

The 18th-century feminist Mary Wollencraft (1759–1797) captured the tenor of the times perfectly in her complaint that, while boys were taught morals, little girls were taught manners. "All the writers who have written on the subject of female education and manners," she wrote, "have contributed to render women more artificial, weaker characters, than they otherwise would have been; and consequently, more useless members of society" (1792, pp. 14–15). Not all philosophers were captive to this patriarchal conceit of course. John Mill, for example, was one of the earliest advocates for women's rights, calling patriarchy a primitive form of society. In his 1869 essay, "The Subjection of Women," Mill wrote that the ethical problem for women was how to claim equal rights. "The legal subjugation of one sex to another is wrong in itself, and now one of the chief hindrances to human improvement," he wrote, "It ought to be replaced by a system of perfect equality, admitting no power or privilege on the one side, nor disability on the other" (1869, p. 2).

Women eventually won a measure of the political equality for which Mill argued. But the patriarchal foundations of ethical theory endured. Feminist thinkers point out, for example, that traditional ethical theories overemphasize culturally masculine traits such as "autonomy" and "will," while ignoring culturally feminine traits such as "community" and "interdependence." They also fail to adequately address issues of particular interest to women—such as equality of opportunity, reproductive technology, militarism, and the environment. And they trivialize some of women's daily concerns, such as sharing housework and childcare. Furthermore, many long-accepted ethical tenets were built on assumptions at odds with women's moral experience.

For example, social contract theory assumes individuals are autonomous, independent, and self-interested, while women are more likely to see people as part of interdependent relationships. Virginia Held, in her 1993 book, *Feminist Morality*, argues that standard social contract theory is constructed around the concept of "economic man," a self-centered, competitive individual who is focused on maximizing his own interests (pp. 71–72). Given this conception of human nature, ethical theory naturally focused on people's rights and obligations.

Indeed, Thomas Bivens, who holds an endowed chair in media ethics at the University of Oregon's School of Journalism and Communications, says this characterized "the major approach to moral philosophy over the past several hundred years" (2009, p. 160). But, as Held points out, it constitutes a particularly "impoverished view" of human relations (1993, p. 194). For example, by ignoring the existence of children and of the women who have historically provided their care, social contract theory fails to account for the totality of people's moral obligations. "Contemporary moral philosophy often conceptualizes humans on a level of abstraction so high that many morally salient differences become invisible," philosopher Alison Jaggar (2000) warns. "Women, perhaps the majority of women, prefer to discuss moral problems in terms of concrete situations," adds ethicist Nel Noddings (1993, p. 23). "They approach moral problems not as intellectual problems to be solved by abstract reasoning but as concrete human problems to be lived and to be solved in living."

That perspective reflected psychologist Carol Gilligan's work in the 1970s and early 1980s purporting to demonstrate empirically that women's moral development follows a different path and arrives at a different destination than men's. For example, a paper she published in 1977 suggested that girls and women see moral dilemmas as conflicts of responsibilities rather than of rights, and try to resolve them by repairing the underlying relationships. Gilligan concluded that while men tend to apply principles of fairness and equality to ethical issues, women adhere to a morality of care, characterized by values of inclusion and protection from harm. The validity of Gilligan's research was criticized by many, and she later softened her position on gender-driven ethical differences, conceding that some men value care as highly as women do, and some women are just as concerned as men with issues of fairness (Gilligan, 1982, p. 2).

Feminist Ethics

But if Gilligan failed to demonstrate that all men and women approach ethical questions from different perspectives, she nevertheless revealed moral concerns requiring greater attention. "Gilligan has discerned the *symbolically* female moral voice, and has disentangled it from the *symbolically* male moral voice," wrote Marilyn Friedman (1995, p. 65). The point of "feminist ethics" is not that women think differently than men, but that the construction of ethical theory over the ages reflected the cultural norms of less than the whole population. It was the product of men who reflected primarily masculine cultural norms. Friedman hypothesized that traditional ethics was therefore based on an age-old division of "moral labor," in which men assumed responsibility for managing "public institutions" (e.g., the social and economic order), while women tended to "private personal relationships" (e.g., the family and raising kids).

Feminist ethics stems from a two-fold insight. First, considerations of care and of justice are nearly always intertwined in the moral judgments of both men and women. Secondly, and to the contrary, traditional ethical theory focuses almost exclusively on justice. But as moral philosopher Annette Baier (1995, p, 51) wrote, "Justice is not enough ... Respect for rights are quite compatible with very great misery, and misery whose causes are not just individual misfortunes and psychic sickness, but social and moral impoverishment."

Feminist ethics seeks to rebalance the scale. First, by eliminating male biases that tend to rationalize women's continuing subordination. And then, by reflecting women's moral experience in ethical theory. Feminist ethics is not "ethics for women," but an approach that offers something of value to *all* human beings. Indeed, because the lives of men and women are so intertwined today, there are fewer "men's issues" and "women's issues." Childcare, for example, is a family issue. It is only considered a woman's issue in households where the male partner has a distorted view of his spouse's status. Similarly, war is usually directed by men, but its impact falls primarily on women and the children in their care, who almost always constitute the majority of its victims.[1]

But if feminist ethics is united in a common destination, it has taken two distinct paths to get there. One focuses on care as a moral value; the other, on women's equality as a matter of justice and a prerequisite to consideration of such values as care. Neither path has been free of potholes, blind alleys, and sniping from all sides. At times, they even seemed to run in opposite directions. But for public relations practitioners, both paths offer lessons of immediate application.

Justice

In feminist history, the fight for equality started as an effort to win some of the rights reserved for men, such as voting. But as small battles were won, it soon became obvious the real problem was not inequality of legal rights, but the *de facto* subordination of women to men in every aspect of life. Male dominance was encoded in the culture, as well as in the psychologies of both genders. Obviously, changing that state of affairs would be a multigenerational effort. Many feminists believe we are still in the early years of that correction.

---

[1] See Women, Peace, and Security. (2002). *New York: United Nations.* http://www.un.org/womenwatch/daw/public/eWPS.pdf. Accessed July 22, 2015.

So even in 2014, retailers like Old Navy could charge $12–$15 more for plus sized women's jeans, but not for men's. The extra cost, according to an Old Navy spokesperson, was due to "curve-enhancing and curve-flattering elements such as four-way stretch materials and contoured waistbands, which most men's garments do not include."[2] But *Time* magazine pointed out that women's and men's clothes in smaller sizes are roughly the same price.[3]

Meanwhile, a Dillard's department store in West Palm Beach, Florida, put a sign in the girls' clothing section that read, "Dear Santa, This year, please give me a big fat bank account and a slim body. Please don't mix those two up like you did last year." According to a company spokesperson, the sign was supposed to be sold in the home merchandise area with other "whimsical" items. When a local TV station called attention to the sign, headquarters banished it from all 298 of the chain's stores.[4]

Equal rights is more than a political battle; it goes to the very heart of public relations' purpose, which one scholar defined as "active participation in the social construction of meaning" (Gordon, 1997, p. 64). Treating people equally regardless of their gender, race, ability, or other incidental characteristics, such as size, means using language free of stereotypes and distortions. For example, calling attention to gender irrelevancies as in "male nurse" or "female lawyer," or using gender-specific language ("chairman") when it could refer to a man or a woman, can reinforce biases and stereotypes. A University of Warsaw study showed that men perceive women with feminine job titles like "chairwoman" to be less warm and competent (Budziszewska et al., 2014). And irrelevant references to people's weight can only lead to body shaming and even contribute to eating disorders such as bulimia and anorexia.

---

[2] Stuart, H. (2014, November 20). Old Navy under fire for charging plus-size women more than plus-size men. *Huffington Post.* http://www.huffingtonpost.com /2014/11/11/old-navy-plus-size-_n_6140478.html. Accessed July 22, 2015.

[3] Stampler, L. (2014, November 12). Old Navy explains why it charges more for women's plus sizes. *Time.* http://time.com/3580891/old-navy-women-plus-size-price/. Accessed July 22, 2015.

[4] Lee, J. (2014, November 11). Dillard's drops "Dear Santa" sign asking for slim body. *USA Today.* http://www.usatoday.com/story/money/business/2014/11/11 /dillards-santa-sign-slim-body/18857955/. Accessed July 22, 2015.

So when Facebook removed "feeling fat" from its list of status updates in 2015, banishing its emoticon's chubby cheeks and double chin to digital purgatory, it struck a small blow against negative body images. On a larger scale, Dove's "Real Beauty" campaign challenged the Photoshopped artificiality of most advertising models and celebrated the natural beauty of real women. Procter and Gamble's "Always" campaign for feminine hygiene products turned the age-old taunt "you (throw, hit, run, etc.) like a girl" on its head. By asking, "When did doing something 'like a girl' become an insult?" it effected positive change in gender identity and attitudes.[5] Both campaigns started as advertising concepts but gained momentum through the power of public relations to turn an idea into a movement. That is what "the social construction of meaning" means.

None of this is an exercise in political correctness. It is simply a matter of according women the same respect as men. And by the same principle, public relations practitioners need to pay greater attention to the governance of their own industry. In 2005, researchers estimated that 69 percent of public relations practitioners were female, the natural result of studies estimating that 70 to 80 percent of students in U.S. college public relations classes are women (Andsagera and Hustb, 2005, p. 85). Yet, by 2011, *PRWeek* could observe, "Women still make up less than half of the executive committee roles at most large PR firms and only four women lead agencies with more than $100 million in global revenue."[6]

Judging from the membership of the Arthur W. Page Society, women seem to be rising to leadership positions in corporate public relations at a faster rate. Whereas only 6 percent of the Society's members were women in 1991, by 2015 44 percent were. Nevertheless, according to a 2015 salary survey, women in public relations make a third less than men, especially at higher levels.[7] And the president of an association of women in public relations ruefully told another trade publication: "One

[5] Neff, J. (2014, June 26). P&G's always aims to change what it means to be "Like a Girl." *Ad Age.* http://adage.com/article/cmo-strategy/p-g-s-change-meaning-a-girl /293895/. Accessed July 22, 2015.

[6] Lee, J. (2011, March 4). Diversity of agency leadership still up for debate. *PRWeek.* http://www.prweek.com/article/1264912/diversity-agency-leadership-remains-debate. Accessed July 22, 2015.

[7] Fidelzeid, G. (2015, March 2). How to close the gender pay gap in PR. *PR Week.* http://www.prweek.com/article/1335944/close-gender-pay-gap-pr. Accessed July 22, 2015.

male director used to say to me quite openly that it was great for the agency image (and I suspect his) to walk into the client's office with a beautiful, young girl at his side. Having at least one attractive girl on the pitch team was also felt to be really important."[8]

On one level, such attitudes are antediluvian, but in an image-obsessed society, they are probably to be expected. However, public relations people have an obligation not to perpetuate demeaning portrayals of others. Objectifying women, whether in the campaigns we mount or on the "qualifications" we expect of them, does precisely that—it robs them of meaning, reducing them to an object that exists only to please men. It violates the most basic principles of justice and demonstrates a lack of empathy or care.

Care

One could argue considerations of care permeated all of W. D. Ross's *prima facie* duties introduced in Chapter 9. Non-malfeasance (to do no harm) and beneficence (doing what we reasonably can to improve the situation of others) obviously addressed it directly. But the duty of self-improvement can also be seen as self-directed care. And the duties of gratitude, fidelity, reparation, and justice likewise have elements of care since their implementation improves someone's lot in life either by reciprocating for prior favors (gratitude), keeping promises (fidelity), repairing harms done in the past (reparation), or respecting their rights to equal treatment (justice). However, if all Ross's *prima facie* duties touched on *care*, it was at best fleeting contact, easily trumped by non-malfeasance. But simply avoiding harm does not constitute an ethic of care. A true ethic of care is *affirmative*—it focuses not simply on avoiding harm, but on doing good. Less on others' rights than on our own responsibility toward them.

That need not be hopelessly Pollyannish. Calling a product to a customer's attention can be a real service if it fills a legitimate need. Helping change damaging attitudes, as in the "Like A Girl" campaign, can make a lasting contribution to society. Even promulgating a client's

---

[8] Parker, D. (2014, October 23). Is there sexism in PR? *PR Moment.* http://www.prmoment.com/2793/is-there-sexism-in-public-relations.aspx. Accessed July 22, 2015.

point of view on a controversial issue contributes to public understanding, if the advocacy is honest and respects the audience's right to reason.

Furthermore, the practice of public relations gains dignity as it moves more into the realm of creating mutual understanding between an organization and diverse publics, inside and outside its walls. And, as scholars have demonstrated, in that context, feminist values of "cooperation, respect, caring, nurturance, interconnection, justice, equity, honesty, sensitivity, perceptiveness, intuition, altruism, fairness, morality, and commitment" gather even greater importance, not only as normative standards but also as productive qualities (Grunig, L.A. et al., 2000).

Unfortunately, according to at least one study female students of public relations appear to be gravitating toward subspecialties they perceive to be more "feminine," such as fashion and beauty, rather than "areas of expertise that have traditionally been within the male purview—technology, finance, sports, and industry" (Andsagera and Hustb, 2005, p. 89). Even though they acknowledged the more masculine specialties paid more, women preferred the more female-oriented specialties because they considered them "more ethical and more caring about people." "Caring about people" may be a tent pole of feminist ethics, but it is not a gender-specific principle. As public relations ethicist Thomas Bivens (2009, p. 165) notes, "In the final analysis, media communicators cannot afford to ignore such characteristics as empathy and caring." In the ethical practice of public relations, empathy and caring rank right up there with integrity, fairness, and respect for others. In fact, all three are an expression of caring. But what does "caring about people" really mean?

People People

There was a time when some thought all you needed to succeed in public relations was to be "a people person." That was such a shallow notion it became a timeworn joke. But feminist theory may be restoring some of the hidden truth in the cliché. "The goal would be to respect the other's dignity and integrity," feminist Linda Steiner suggests (1989). "To make the [communication] process more collaborative and egalitarian, less authoritarian and coercive." That would seem to be a minimal goal, an expression of the ethical principles of truth and respect.

Gaining genuine understanding of publics and more narrowly, audiences, is a necessary step in revealing their needs, aspirations, and values so we can respond to them appropriately. That, in fact, was the foundation on which Always built its "Like A Girl" campaigns. In this sense, feminist ethics raises "beneficence" from something we do when we have the time and inclination, to the essence of ethical public relations. Even so, "doing good" is not a get out of jail card, allowing us to trample on the rights of some to care for others. Justice and care are tightly intertwined principles. And as W.D. Ross maintained, the relative weight we give each will depend on the particular circumstances in which we find ourselves.

Those "circumstances" have developed in ways Ross probably could not have imagined. For example, homosexuality was not decriminalized in his home country of England until the very last years of Ross's life; today, gay marriage is legal there, as it is as of 2015 for the entire American population. And the next battlefield for gay rights will be winning greater respect for transgender people, who have long been a hidden minority. Vice President Joe Biden has called this, "the civil rights issue of our time."[9] Respecting people's right to be different without being marginalized will require the exercise of both justice and care. For example, while some transgender people take steps to correct a mismatch between their bodies and their gender identities, others accept themselves as they are, calling for a third option to traditional categories of "male" and "female." So-called genderqueer people consider themselves a distinct third gender. So Facebook now offers more than 50 options for gender identity, including "pangender," "agender," and "trans person." Many universities give students the option of declaring a Preferred Gender Pronoun at registration so professors will know whether to refer to them by "he/him," "she/her," "they/them" or some other term (e.g., "ze," suggested by the German *sie,* is used in some transgender communities).

Feminist ethics calls for more than a change in language and symbolic behavior, as important as that is. It requires more than curing inequities in women's salaries and career advancement, as overdue as that is. And it demands respect not only for women, but also for all historically marginalized

---

[9] Bendery, J. (2012, October 31). Joe Biden: Transgender discrimination is the civil rights issue of our time. *The Huffington Post.* http://www.huffingtonpost.com/2012/10/30/joe-biden-transgender-rights_n_2047275.html. Accessed July 22, 2015.

groups, including people of color, the elderly, the disabled, the immigrant, and those who are not exclusively heterosexual. But more fundamentally, feminist ethics would move public relations' center of gravity from "messaging" to "relationship building," which can only emerge from embracing diverse perspectives.

But despite a long series of high-profile "diversity programs," public relations staffs on both agency and client sides still don't mirror the diverse marketplace they purport to serve. "Most diversity programs focus on entry level positions," says veteran public relations counselor Mike Paul. "And [it's] like a revolving door, with young people of color only staying 2 to 3 years because they don't see anyone like themselves in senior positions." Paul says what's needed is a real effort to recruit senior executives of color into P&L positions, but "it's like [agency and client] leaders don't think they exist." [10] Yet, he points to senior public relations executives of color in politics and the military and he challenged major agencies and corporations to set recruitment goals within that universe of candidates. That could be the tipping point in addressing both an ethical issue and a fast-growing $2 trillion market. [11]

Summary

"Communication will always be more than the shuttling of mind-stuff," scholar John Durham Peters wrote. "It is the founding of a world" (Peters, 1999, p. 112). In more prosaic terms, it is bringing diverse stakeholders together into a single community, based on considerations of justice and care. As Stocker and Tusinski Berg put it, "The public relations practitioner recognizes the individuality of a particular public and then reconciles, not eliminates, those differences in building a relationship" (2006, p. 13). A patriarchal model seeks to minimize differences through *quid pro quo*

---

[10] *Source:* conversation with Mike Paul, May 3, 2014.

[11] The University of Georgia's Selig Institute estimated that in 2013 people of color (African-American, non-white Hispanic, Asian, and others) purchased more than $2 trillion in goods and services and their purchases are growing faster than the white population's and would total more than $3 trillion by 2018. *Source:* Selig Center for Economic Growth, Terry College of Business, The University of Georgia, June 2013. See: http://www.latinocollaborative.com/wp-content/uploads/2013/10/Multicultural-Economy-2013-SELIG-Center.pdf

negotiations driven by each party's concept of fairness. A feminist model seeks to reconcile differences by building an enduring relationship based on considerations of care and justice that reveal a common ground of agreement. As Stocker and Tusinski-Berg explain, this may sound like abstract theory, but it is as bare-knuckled practical as "when the local bank sponsors an evening budgeting class for newlyweds, a bike manufacturer trains a local Boy Scout troop to assemble and service their own bikes, and a newspaper sponsors the community spelling bee" (p. 13).

In the next chapter, we will explore some of the practical challenges of ethical decision making, from behavioral and situational obstacles to the challenges of working across cultures.

CHAPTER 11

Ethical Decision Making

Multiple studies suggest public relations people have about the same level of ethical development as the average college-educated adult. On the standard tool customarily used to measure ethical development, public relations practitioners score just above business people but below journalists. Not surprisingly, philosophers scored highest of all and prison inmates, lowest.[1]

And yet when one researcher examined the philosophy stacks in 31 leading academic libraries, he discovered the majority of missing books were on the subject of ethics (Schwitzgebel, 2009). In fact, obscure texts of interest only to scholars were about twice as likely to be missing. It is a wonder prison library shelves are not more empty than they are.

---

[1] Psychologist Lawrence Kohlberg divided ethical development into three primary levels of two stages each. The first or "preconventional" level is guided by punishment or reward. The second or "conventional" level is guided by the expectations of a given society as in "doing one's duty." The third or "postconventional" level is guided by universal, shared principles such as justice and care. Another psychologist, James Rest developed the "Defining Issues Test" (DIT) to quantify Kohlberg's model. It presents six ethical dilemmas accompanied by 12 ranked statements that correspond to Kohlberg's six stages. Respondents are instructed to rate these statements according to their perceived levels of importance in making an ethical decision about the dilemma presented. The score obtained from these rankings is considered a reflection of moral development. Since the DIT was developed, it has been taken by thousands of people, providing average scores for a number of professions. Several researchers have applied the DIT to public relations practitioners. For example, Paul Lieber's (1998) Masters' Thesis used it to gauge the ethical decision making patterns of public relations practitioners He expanded on this work in a 2008 paper for *Public Relations Review*. In 2009, Lieber's thesis advisor, Renita Coleman, (2009) did her own analysis of PR practitioners' moral development with colleague Lee Wilkins for *Public Relations Research.*. The DIT scores cited here are drawn from that research, which showed the following "scores": prison inmates, 23.7; business professionals, 38.13; adults in general, 40; graduate students, 44.9; public relations practitioners, 46.2; journalists, 48.68; philosophers, 65.1. Links to all these papers are provided in the References section.

All of which suggests that, contrary to Aristotle's notions of character as a disposition to act in a certain way, our ethical behavior is malleable and dynamic, the product of psychological and social forces operating in the darkest recesses of our mind below all levels of consciousness.

Situational Influences

In a classic series of experiments conducted by Stanley Milgram at Yale University in the 1960s, participants were instructed to inflict electrical shocks on someone they could not see, but could certainly hear (Milgram, 1963). The results were always the same—a majority of the participants continued inflicting shocks at higher and higher voltages, even when the unseen subject was screaming in agony. "Stark authority was pitted against the subjects' strongest moral imperatives against hurting others," Milgram (1973, p. 62) wrote, "and, with the subjects' ears ringing with the screams of the victims, authority won more often than not."

A similar experiment by Philip Zimbardo and colleagues at Stanford University explored the psychological effects of becoming a prison guard or a prisoner (Haney et al., 1973). Volunteer university students were assigned roles as "guards" or "prisoners" in a mock prison in the basement of the psychology building. The "guards" carried wooden batons and wore military style khaki uniforms and mirrored sunglasses. The "prisoners" wore badly fitting smocks, stocking caps, and a chain around one ankle. They were addressed only by the number sewn onto their smocks. Within six days of a planned two-week experiment, the guards were exhibiting sufficiently sadistic behavior, and the prisoners were suffering from such extreme stress, the whole thing was called off.[2]

Both experiments were heavily criticized at the time, but they were also replicated elsewhere with substantially the same results, strongly

---

[2] The Stanford Prison Experiment was conducted on behalf of the U.S. Navy and was documented in a paper by the principal researchers, Craig Haney, Curtis Banks, and Philip Zimbardo (1973). See http://www.zimbardo.com/downloads/1973% 20A%20Study%20of%20Prisoners%20and%20Guards,%20Naval%20Research%2 0Reviews.pdf. There is also a website dedicated to the experiment. See http://www .prisonexp.org/psychology/41. It has even inspired a movie. See http://www.imdb .com/title/tt0420293/

suggesting our ethical behavior is highly influenced by the concrete situations in which we find ourselves.[3]

A long litany of psychological experiments demonstrates those influences can be quite subtle. One study showed that someone standing outside a bakery with the smell of fresh bread in the air is more likely to help a stranger than someone standing outside a "neutral-smelling hardware store" (Baron, 1997). Someone asked to read sentences with words like "honor" and "respect" is more polite, minutes later, than someone who read words like "obnoxious" and "bluntly" (Bargh et al., 1996). People are more likely to litter if there is a lot of trash lying around (Chialdini et. al., 1990). Graffiti leads to more graffiti and even to more theft (Keizer et al., 2008).

Implicit Cognition

And if that is not discouraging enough, it turns out our deepest attitudes are not as pure as we thought. The relatively new field of "implicit social cognition" studies the unconscious associations and impressions we accumulate indiscriminately as we go about our daily life. Unlike explicitly held knowledge, these impressions do not go through fact checking and reconsideration as they are formed. But they become deeply-rooted assumptions about the world and the people around us. And as Harvard social psychologists Brian Nosek and Jeffrey Hansen (2008, p. 554) put it, they operate "without the encumbrance of awareness, intention, and control." But they manifest themselves as positive or negative attitudes that reflect what we like or dislike, favor or disfavor, approach or avoid.

---

[3] For replications of Milgram's experiments, see Burger (2009) More shocking results: New research replicates Milgram's findings. *Monitor on Psychology,* Vol. 40, p. 3. http://www.apa.org/monitor/2009/03/milgram.aspx. For cross-cultural implications, see Shanab and Yahya (1978). A cross-cultural study of obedience. *Bulletin of the Psychosomatic Society,* Vol. 11, pp. 267–269. http://link.springer.com/article/ 10.3758/BF03336827#page-2. Although contemporary ethical concerns have made it difficult to repeat the Stanford prison experiment in later years, it was recreated for a BBC television program with similar results. See Wells (2002, January 24) BBC halts "prison experiment." *The Guardian.* http://www.theguardian.com/uk /2002/jan/24/bbc.socialsciences.

Many people would repudiate those negative attitudes if they were aware of them. Nevertheless, they do affect our behavior. For example, Eugene Caruso, a professor of behavioral science at the University of Chicago, gave participants in a trivia game the option of choosing partners based on certain traits such as IQ or weight. Although participants said weight was "the single least important factor in their choice," a clear preference for thin partners emerged. In fact, participants sacrificed between 10 and 12 IQ points to work with thinner teammates. In another study, participants were willing to accept a 20 percent lower salary to work for a man, instead of a woman (Caruso et al., 2009). Leaving IQ points or money on the table, especially when one explicitly reports that weight and gender do not matter, is hardly rational.

In 2004, behavioral economists at MIT and the University of Chicago sent resumes out to prospective employers in Boston and Chicago. All the resumes listed the same backgrounds, experience, and qualifications, but half were for candidates with names like "Emily" or "Greg," while the others were for people named "Lakisha" or "Jamal." The "white-sounding" names received 50 percent more callbacks (Bertrand and Mullainathan, 2004). Research in Europe with people who had Muslim-sounding names produced similar results (Rooth, 2010).

Other research has demonstrated that the effects of unconscious negative racial attitudes extend into every aspect of life, from the serious to the trivial. Doctors are more likely to prescribe life-saving care to whites (Green et al., 2007), people feel less empathy toward someone in pain if they are of a different race (Avenanti, A. et al., 2010), and basketball referees subtly favor players with whom they share a racial identity (Price, and Wolfers, 2010). As Harvard Law professor Jon Hanson once said, "Our brains, it seems, have a mind of their own."[4] Our brain's "mind" operates at levels far below our awareness, at frightening velocity, with powerful biases. "What we think we know about what is moving us is only a tiny, and often a misleading, part of what is actually going on in those parts of our brains that elude introspection but that can nonetheless manifest in

---

[4] Hanson, J. (2009, February 19). Why race may influence us even when we "know" it doesn't. *The Situationist.* https://thesituationist.wordpress.com/2009/02/19/why-race-may-influence-us-even-when-we-know-it-doesnt/. Accessed July 22, 2015.

our perceptions, emotions, and actions," Hanson says. We may think we are colorblind, but our brain knows differently. We do not choose our unconscious attitudes. We are bombarded every day by cultural messages associating white with good and black with bad. (If you would like to better understand your own implicit biases, take one of the online surveys at http://implicit.harvard.edu).[5]

Compounding matters, a long series of experiments have demonstrated that as soon as humans bunch together we start to copy other members of our group, favor members of own group over others, look for a leader to worship, and eagerly fight anyone not in the group (De Dreu et al., 2010). And it is amazing how little it takes to corral people into herds. Psychologists assigned teenage boys to different groups based solely on their preferences for paintings by Klee and Kandinsky (Tajfel et al., 1971). The boys never met each other and had no idea what significance their group assignment had. But when each boy was asked to distribute money to the members of both groups, they distributed more money to those in their own group than in the other, even though they seemingly had nothing to gain from it, suggesting that people build their own identities from their group memberships. The boys in the experiment were boosting their own identities by rewarding their group. Such is the power of group membership.

Moral Balance

Even when external influences are not at play, our behavior can be surprisingly inconsistent with our values and beliefs. Psychologist Mordecai Nisan suggests we internalize a "sort of moral balance ... of all morally relevant actions within a given time span" (1991, p. 213). We make deposits and withdrawals from that account, but we will not allow ourselves to go below a certain "personal standard." Faced with an ethical choice, we select the option that allows us to maintain a "satisfactory

---

[5] Harvard University is conducting an online study on implicit bias in a wide variety of contexts such as attitudes toward fat people, people of color, or people who are gay. See https://implicit.harvard.edu. Nearly 80 percent of everyone who has taken the test—including Blacks, Non-Blacks, Hispanics, and Asians—have had "pro-white" biases.

balance," taking into account all we have done to the present and what we have committed to do in the future.

Research supports his theory. For example, several experiments show that, if the probability of getting caught is low enough, many people will seize the opportunity to advance their self-interest. Whether participants reported on their ability to add columns of numbers (Gino et al., 2009) or to win simple coin tosses (Batson et al., 2003), a significant proportion would fudge their results to win a small reward if their chance of discovery appeared low. But interestingly, they changed their results just a little, suggesting there is a limit to how much people will cheat. Other experiments (Rosenhan et al., 1981) have shown a rise in altruistic behavior (deposits in the moral balance) following an ethical transgression (withdrawals from the moral balance).

Inconsistencies between behavior and belief can also be the product of moral disengagement. Psychologists have known since the 1950s that behavior inconsistent with beliefs creates psychological tension that can only be relieved by changing one or the other. When the cost of changing behavior is high enough, many people will unconsciously change their beliefs in a process known as cognitive dissonance (Festinger, 1962). And they will find creative excuses to justify their behavior, for example claiming it serves a moral purpose, blaming it on external factors, minimizing its consequences, or dehumanizing its victims (Shu et al., 2009). And in the end, no matter what ethical theory we follow, research shows we are far more likely to condemn behavior that leads to a bad outcome (Gino et al., 2010).

Bounded Rationality

All this has clear implications for the application of ethical theory. Faced with an ethical dilemma, we never have enough time to decide what to do, and how we use the time available depends to a great extent on unconscious influences. We never have enough hard data either, but whatever information we do have goes through the filter of our past experience, our current concerns, and our innate prejudices, biases, and cognitive illusions. That is not to suggest we should ignore our deepest sensations and inclinations, as if they are devoid of meaning. On the contrary, our feelings and passions brim with information. We must strive to understand and articulate their meaning so we can control them and factor what is useful and true into the ethical choices we make. For example, knowing what makes us angry or uncomfortable can help us manage our feelings. Recognizing our unconscious biases and inclinations can be the first step in controlling them. Taking note of the developing field of behavioral science, Nobel prize winning economist Herbert Simon (1916–2001) called this process "bounded rationality" (Simon, 1982).

Relative or Universal

Adding another element of complexity to ethical decision making is an age-old debate over the *universality* of ethical standards. Some people believe ethical rules are relative and apply differently in different cultures. They point out, for example, that in many Western countries, we would consider it unjust to give relatives preferential treatment in hiring and promotion decisions. But in some Asian and Arab countries it would be considered unfair and discourteous to do otherwise.

Others believe ethical rules are universal and apply everywhere, regardless of local norms and customs. A large U.S. computer company discovered how naïve this is when it required its Saudi Arabian engineers to attend the same sexual harassment training as its U.S.-based managers, including a case in which a manager makes sexually explicit remarks to a female employee over drinks in a bar. The Saudi engineers were so baffled and offended by that scenario, they missed the main message about sexual harassment.

We believe the basic problem is confusing "universal" with "absolute." An *absolute approach* allows no exceptions and no room for interpretation or expression that may vary from culture to culture. A *universal approach* recognizes that basic ethical tenets apply to all human beings in like circumstances, but their interpretation and application can vary from society to society. Since ethical decisions are often based on deciding what is best for society, in practice their application is highly influenced by cultural values or what a group believes to be good, right, and desirable as passed on from generation to generation (Herskovitz, 1952, p. 634).

Cultural Differences

The Dutch social psychologist Gert Hofstede (2010) constructed a framework for differentiating cultures by their respective "values," which he defined as "broad tendencies to prefer certain states of affairs over others." Initially, Hofstede's framework had four primary dimensions (here, highly simplified):[6]

> *Whether the culture is individualistic or collective.* Are people and their families essentially on their own? Or do they belong to strong groups from birth onwards?
>
> *How power is distributed within a culture.* Is the culture hierarchical or nonhierarchical? Is unequal distribution of power expected and accepted?
>
> *How a culture handles uncertainty.* Are people comfortable in unstructured or new situations? Or do they like familiar situations and strict rules and standards?
>
> *How "masculine" or "feminine" a culture is.* Are the men assertive and competitive or more modest and caring? Are women modest and caring or competitive and assertive?

While these dimensions can help in understanding a culture, it would be a mistake to assume they work mechanistically. For example, it is generally accepted that the culture of the United States is toward the "individualistic" end of the scale, while Latin and Asian cultures tend to be more "collectivist." But those are broad generalizations. A group of Stanford University researchers (Morris et al., 2001) studied the conditions under which Citibank employees in different countries would agree to help a colleague with a task. They could have had any of a range of reasons for complying with the request—the rank of the employee making it, the requestor's past cooperation, or maybe they just liked him or her. But their

---

[6] We have taken the liberty of slightly changing Hofstede's nomenclature in the interests of clarity and succinctness. The actual names of the six dimensions are: Individualism, Power Distance, Uncertainty Avoidance, Masculinity-Femininity, Long-Term Orientation, and Indulgence versus Restraint. For more, consult Greet Hofstede's web site: www.geerthofstede.nl or his book, *Cultures and Organizations: Software of the Mind*, McGraw-Hill, New York, 2010.

actual reason tended to follow a similar pattern, depending on the country. As expected, in the individualistic culture of the United States, reciprocity was the key motivator. U.S. employees usually asked, "What's this guy or gal done for me before?" In China and Spain, employees reflected the culture's collectivist leanings, but in different ways. The Chinese asked themselves, "Is the person making the request connected to someone of higher authority?" while the Spaniards asked themselves, "Is the requestor connected to any of my friends?" The Germans, also in a collectivist culture, asked, "What do the rules require?" Even though each culture behaved in ways consistent with their position on the individualistic/collective dimension of Hofstede's framework, they approached the request very differently.[7]

So Hofstede's research, as groundbreaking as it was, should only be considered a starting point in understanding other cultures. One nation's culture can only be described relative to another's. And even then, there are no absolutes. Hofstede is dealing with the central tendency within one culture as compared to others. But there is always variation around a central tendency, the "standard deviation" in math-speak. There is also nothing magical about the number of dimensions Hofstede identified—he started with four and, as more data came in, he added two—whether a culture's orientation is toward the future or the past and whether a culture fosters immediate gratification or restraint.[8]

But what of ethical standards themselves? Are they universal or relative? Our own view is that ethical standards are the product of reason informed by local culture. More importantly, as we noted in Chapter Two, we are constantly refining our understanding of good and evil,

---

[7] This brief summary of the Citibank study merely touches the surface. The full study is available at http://www1.gsb.columbia.edu/mygsb/faculty/research/pubfiles /1913/1913.pdf. It's well worth reading for anyone interested in better understanding inter-cultural persuasion.

[8] Hofstede's work has been validated through a number of studies and dozens of books and articles have been written on his theory of national cultures. However, Hofstede's theories have not been free of criticism. Some researchers believe that cultures are too complicated to be measured like the weather trends in different countries. Others argue with the specific dimensions Hofstede identified. And, of course, some argued with his methodology. The International Business Center has a web page that lists the most prominent critiques, along with links to the original publications. See http://geert-hofstede.international-business-center.com/

right and wrong. For example, it is pretty clear our understanding of human equality is more complete today than it was a century ago. And it is probably fair to speculate it will be better a hundred years in the future. But our progress is almost always uneven and halting, especially at the margins of human activity.

Nor should we assume progress in understanding ethical standards is a phenomenon of western civilization. Western ideas about the ethical rights of women may be superior to those in some less developed societies, but we should also be open to the possibility that the reverence some of the least developed societies have for the natural environment is superior to our relative indifference. And who knows? A hundred years from now vegetarianism may be a widely held ethical standard rather than a culinary preference. So we should always approach questions of ethics with some humility and even a dose of uncertainty. Our goal should not necessarily be to find the absolutely right answer that applies everywhere all the time, but the best answer under the circumstances—and to justify it to the best of our abilities.

Ethical Relativism

Respecting differences and recognizing our own limits as human beings do not equate to ethical relativism. As Bill George , the former CEO of Medtronic and now a professor at the Harvard Business School, once wrote in *Business Week*, "To sustain their success, companies must follow the same standards of business conduct in Shanghai, Mumbai, Kiev, and Riyadh as in Chicago."[9] Ethical values are not something we put on and take off like a comfortable overcoat depending on the temperature of the country we are in. And there is a big difference between etiquette and ethics. Respect for people's human dignity is a matter of ethics; whether a woman chooses to wear a veil or not is a matter of etiquette. We can respect the latter without denying the former.

---

[9] George, B. (2008, February 12). Ethics must be global, not local. *Business Week*. http://www.businessweek.com/stories/2008-02-12/ethics-must-be-global-not-local businessweek-business-news-stock-market-and-financial-advice. Accessed July 22, 2015.

It is also important to distinguish between customary behavior in some societies and underlying ethical standards that may or may not be consistent with them. For example, we cannot think of a single culture that does not value honesty. But in some countries reporters expect compensation for covering a news conference or for writing a story based on a company news release. Some public relations practitioners do not consider this very different from tipping a waiter. "Reporters in some countries do not make much money," they have told us. "These payments are considered part of their compensation."

That may be true, as far as the bribe-taking reporters are concerned. But it seems to us paying reporters to run a news release violates a number of ethical principles. In terms of consequences, it harms the reporter's readers. When they read a newspaper, they expect articles free from outside influences. Even on the assumption that a news release contains no misleading information, its very appearance in the paper gives it, more significance than it might otherwise have, which makes it misleading. It also violates a public relations person's duty to engage in fair and open communications. Public relations people are supposed to contribute to the free flow of information. This behavior corrupts one of any democracy's key institutions—a free press. And on the level of virtue, it is clearly dishonest; otherwise, why hide it? Tipping a waiter is done in the open for everyone, including the waiter's employer to see. But the waiter's employer would likely frown on a gratuity quietly slipped to a server prior to the meal to ensure priority service. Such behavior would put other diners at a disadvantage and endanger the employer's reputation. That is more analogous to the situation at hand.

Local Customs

Local customs clearly complicate the situation. It is true that "tipping" journalists is condoned in some circles in some countries. But even in those countries, newspaper readers would likely consider it corrupt and unethical. At minimum, an ethical public relations practitioner would insist on disclosure of the payment so readers can draw their own conclusion about the resulting article's newsworthiness and read it with full knowledge of its sourcing. Bribing reporters is not really an accommodation to cultural differences; it is capitulation to a dishonest practice no culture should accept.

As in many areas of ethical decision making, hard and fast rules in global public relations are rare. But some standards are universal, starting with the most basic principle of the United Nation's Declaration of Human Rights—*everyone is born equal under the law with basic rights and freedoms.* "Cultural relativism is morally blind," writes Thomas Donaldson (1996, September–October), professor of law and business ethics at the Wharton School of the University of Pennsylvania. "There are fundamental values that cross cultures, and companies must uphold them." In Donaldson's view, and ours, all organizations have an ethical duty to respect human dignity, to respect people's basic rights, and to practice good citizenship.

The first of these duties—to respect human dignity—means treating people as ends, not simply means to accomplish corporate purpose. It means respecting their autonomy and right to reason. Giving them a safe place to work and producing safe products and services. Respecting people's basic rights means acting in ways that support their rights under the UN Declaration of Human Rights, including full equality, liberty, and personal security. And practicing good citizenship means supporting social institutions that further these rights, such as the economic system, the educational system, and organizations to protect the environment. And, yes, a free press.

Business ethicist Richard DeGeorge (2000, September 1, p. 50) proposes a very similar set of guidelines to address international business ethics questions:

- Do no direct intentional harm.
- Produce more good than harm for the host country.
- Respect the rights of employees and of all others affected by one's actions or policies.
- To the extent consistent with ethical norms, respect the local culture and work with and not against it.
- Pay your fair share of taxes and cooperate with the local governments in developing equitable laws and other background institutions.

Google's Chinese experience

In practice, even adhering to broad ethical standards such as these will present ethical dilemmas. Google, for example, operates under the standard of "Don't be evil." Yet when the Chinese government instructed the company to censor the results of its search engines based in Mainland China to omit subjects deemed "offensive" or "subversive," the company complied.

There is little question American companies have to obey the laws of their host countries if they want to operate within their borders. The real question is whether or not they want to operate there at all. As in many ethical questions, it all comes down to finding the right balance between benefits and costs. And as Google correctly determined, the relevant cost/benefits were not only those the company itself would endure or enjoy—lost market opportunity if it left, revenue and criticism if it stayed—but the effect *on the people of China*. Google's ethical calculus had to include the effects of its decision on the Chinese people.

On that basis, Google decided that censored search capabilities, which was its only option since it needed Chinese government approval to locate its servers in the country, would be better than nothing. Google cofounder Sergey Brin explained his reasoning to *Fortune* magazine. "We felt that by participating there, and making our services more available, even if not to the 100 percent that we ideally would like, that it will be better for Chinese Web users, because ultimately they would get more information, though not quite all of it."[10]

Importantly, Google made all the limitations of its China service known. If a computer user typed something like "Tiananmen Square" into the Google China search engine, the results pages would not show the protestors and government tanks that show up on the same search from any other country, but it would include a small disclaimer at the bottom of the page—"Local regulations prevent us from showing all the results." Meanwhile, Google did not shut down the existing uncensored search engines located outside China, and it stayed away from e-mail or

---

[10] Kirkpatrick, D. (2006, January 25). Google founder defends China portal. *Fortune.* http://money.cnn.com/2006/01/25/news/international/davos_fortune/. Accessed July 22. 2015.

blogging services based on the mainland to avoid future government demands to cough up user identities.

Nevertheless, Google was criticized for its "surrender" to the Chinese. Amnesty International, for example, said Google's decision showed that "when it comes to the crunch, profits have come before principles."[11] Google lived with that criticism for four years. But in 2010, when the Chinese government increased censorship of search results even further and the offshore Gmail accounts of Chinese dissidents were hacked, the company pulled its Web search engine from Mainland China and explained its reasoning online.[12] Still, as the *Wall Street Journal* observed, "stepping back from these countries is financially risky for Google because they are large economies with growing online populations."[13] And as this was written the company was thinking about dipping its toes back into China through its mobile app store.[14]

Implications for Public Relations Practice

Sometimes—as in South Africa during apartheid—the answer to these ethical questions will be "doing business here will cost the local people more than it will benefit them." There are no general rules of thumb to make these decisions easier. Different companies, operating under different conditions, may even come to different conclusions. But a *global* company needs to know how to make those decisions, drawing on the best available advice, if possible from the people most directly affected, and with clear transparency. Part of the secret to global success is knowing how to be local

---

[11] Amnesty International. (2006, January 26). http://www.amnesty.org.uk/press-releases/china-google-and-others-must-end-complicity-restricting-freedoms.   Accessed July 22, 2015.

[12] A New Approach to China: An Update. (2010, March 22). *Google Blog*. http://googleblog.blogspot.com/2010/03/new-approach-to-china-update.html.   Accessed July 22, 2015.

[13] Sonne, P., & Schechner, S. (2014, December 12). Google to shut engineering office in Russia. *Wall Street Journal*. http://www.wsj.com/articles/google-to-shut-engineering-office-in-russia-1418401852?KEYWORDS=google. Accessed July 22, 2015.

[14] Winkler, R., Barr, A., & Ma, W. (2014, November 20). Google looks to get back into China.   http://www.wsj.com/articles/google-looks-to-get-back-into-china-1416527873. Accessed July 22, 2015.

without sacrificing one's core values ("thinking global, acting local"). And that involves a lot more than knowing what side of the road to drive on.

But it would be a mistake to assume western companies will only encounter ethical conflicts in countries with authoritarian regimes. For example, conceptions of privacy are very different in the United States than in Europe, which has granted its citizens "a right to be forgotten" that extends beyond its borders. Many observers believe the U.S. Constitution would prohibit such a provision in the United States. Nevertheless, American companies doing business in Europe have to find a way to work within those standards because even if they manage to get the rules changed, they will have to deal with the public attitudes that underlie them. And that points up another issue American companies bump up against worldwide—their preference for light regulation conflicts with other countries' political history and reality.

Summary

As this chapter illustrates, public relations operates on the ragged edges of the social and psychological sciences. Whether practicing at home or abroad, we operate in a gray area of ambiguity and uncertainty. Some impediments arise from the particular situation we are in, some from our personal psychological makeup, some from unconscious biases, and some from an unfamiliar cultural context. So what are we to do when facing a thorny ethical dilemma?

- First, we should ensure we have the cognitive and emotional space to think clearly.
- Second, we should recognize any factors in the situation or in ourselves that could influence our decision making, consciously or unconsciously.
- And third, we should question our knee-jerk thinking patterns, carefully adhering to a systematic and organized approach.

That systematic and organized approach—a framework for ethical reasoning—will be the topic of our next chapter.

CHAPTER 12

Frameworks for Ethical Reasoning

One of the nagging questions to emerge from the great corporate scandals at the beginning of the 21st century is "Where were the public relations people at all those companies?"

The two largest companies convicted of accounting fraud—Enron and WorldCom—each had highly paid public relations officers. They managed to get their CEOs—and even their chief financial officers—on the covers of leading publications. Both companies consistently ranked at the top of reputation surveys, lauded for their innovation and reliable earnings growth. Yet, when the music stopped, both companies ended up in bankruptcy, their most senior executives went to jail, and thousands of their employees lost their jobs. Their public relations people were apparently as clueless as the rest of us regarding the financial shenanigans underway deep within their corporate offices.

Maybe they were not part of the "dominant coalition," as sociologists describe an organization's leadership. And, if they were, maybe they were not sufficiently curious or appropriately skeptical when talk of cutting accounting corners came up. More likely, they were not around when the books were actually cooked, which usually happens in darkened backrooms with as few witnesses as possible. After all, even the companies' certified public accountants claim to have been hoodwinked. And they are supposedly expert at ferreting out fraud. So those public relations leaders may not deserve indictment. But they—like we—probably wish they had been more observant and that they had a firmer framework from which to judge the ethics of what was going on around them.

Virtue, Duty, and Consequences

We have now reviewed the major theories of ethical reasoning. Generally, these three approaches differ in their primary focus:

1. Virtue-based ethics is primarily concerned with the character of the *person* making the decision.
2. Duty-based ethics examines the *action* in which the person is engaged or considering.
3. Consequence-based ethics considers the *results* or consequences of an act.

Each of these theories has advantages and limitations. A virtue-based ethic has the advantage of focusing on the specific behavioral characteristics necessary for us to flourish as ethical public relations practitioners. For example, it puts a high premium on truthfulness and honesty, among other virtues. But it also has limitations. It does not provide much guidance on what to do in genuine dilemmas. For example, sometimes ferreting out the truth is not easy, and there can always be good arguments on both sides of what is truly fair. What then? There is no canonical list of virtues and no standard for weighing their relative importance. What if virtues conflict? Is justice more important than loyalty?

A duty-based ethic has the advantage of certainty, identifying the basic obligations we have as rational human beings. For example, Kant reasoned that every rational human being has inherent value. He cautioned us to respect every person's right to reason and to avoid using people simply as means to accomplishing our own goals. People should never be tricked, manipulated, or bullied into doing things. W. D. Ross (1939, 2002) built on Kant's theory by recognizing that everyone has multiple duties that need to be balanced in specific situations. Included among those duties is not only to avoid harming others, but to actually do good.

But a duty-based ethic also has some limitations. In practice, it is hard to reconcile conflicting duties. As public relations professionals and practitioners, for example, we have multiple duties to multiple parties—to our employer, to our client, to our family, to our colleagues, to our client's customers, to our employer's shareowners, to the practice of public relations, and to society as a whole. Those duties can pull us in different directions, and it is not always obvious which duty should prevail.

A consequence-based ethic solves that dilemma by declaring the right choice in any situation is the one that produces the greatest good for the greatest number. Focusing on results is flexible and takes circumstances into account. It considers the consequences for everybody, including society as a whole. And when it is impossible to produce good results, it at least tries to do the least harm. But it also has limitations. It is often difficult to predict the consequences of our decisions. And some consequences are difficult, if not impossible, to quantify. How do you measure and compare fear, anger, despair, joy, and uncertainty, which are all potential consequences of public relations practice? Dealing with those issues can slow decision making, which produces bad consequences in itself.

Focusing only on consequences ignores ethically important factors such as intentions and fairness. So an act with good results done by someone intending harm is as good as if it was done by someone who intended to do good. And a total focus on consequences can be inconsistent with human rights. For example, based solely on the consequences, it might appear ethical to move a billionaire to the top of a heart replacement list if he pays for 1,000 other transplants. That might produce a lot of good, but it could produce disastrous consequences for the person currently at the top of the list, who might die.

No one has come up with the perfect ethical theory, one that would bring certainty to the thorniest dilemma and be easy to apply in every situation. Thousands of years into thinking about ethics, we are still pretty much on our own. That is one of the reasons the major public relations associations have drafted ethical codes for their members. Anticipating the most common situations in which public relations people will find themselves and drawing on these ethical theories, they have drafted some basic principles, or rules of the road, for their members.

Codes of Ethics

The Public Relations Society of America (PRSA), the International Association of Business Communicators (IABC), the International Public Relations Association (IPRA), and the Global Alliance for Public

Relations and Communications Management (GAPR) have all produced thoughtful codes. Copies are easily available online.[1]

All four codes are in general agreement on the basic principles of
ethical behavior, as well as many instances of practical application. For
example, they all strike a blow against Astroturfing, masking the source
of messages so they appear to come from unbiased people at grassroots
of society. The IPRA code, for one, directs members to "be open and
transparent in declaring their name, organization and the interest they
represent" and not to "create or use any organization to serve an announced cause but which actually serves an undisclosed interest."

However, as might be expected, the emphasis of each association's
code differs somewhat, reflecting the nature of its members' work.
IABC, which has many internal communications people among its
members, is unique in emphasizing cultural sensitivity and "good taste"
in its code. PRSA, whose membership skews more toward mid-level
public relations practitioners, puts more emphasis on client loyalty,
keeping confidences, conflicts of interest, and objectivity. GAPR is focused on positioning public relations as a *bona fide* profession so it em-
phasizes continuing education and a practitioner's duties to the broader
society as well as to clients. And appropriate to its global membership,
the IPRA Code of Ethics draws heavily from the ideals of the United
Nations's Charter, focusing significant attention on the obligation to
respect human rights and "the dignity and worth of the human person."

PRSA and GAPR urge their members to perform "responsible advocacy," but leave it to individual practitioners to define what that means in
practice. For its part, IPRA suggests responsible advocacy requires that its
members "seek to establish the moral, cultural and intellectual conditions
for dialog, and [to] recognize the rights of all parties involved to state
their case and express their views." All four codes urge their members to

---

[1] All four association codes are available online. The IABC Code of Ethics for Professional Communicators is at http://news.iabc.com/index.php._s=40&item=10,html.
The International Public Relations Association Code is at www.ipra.org/about/ipra-
codes. The Global Alliance for Public Relations and Communications Management
Code of Ethics is at www.globalalliancepr.org/website/page/code-ethics. The Public
Relations Society of America Member Code of Ethics is at http://www.prsa.org/
aboutprsa/ethics/codeenglish/#.VbAmdehViko. Accessed September. 7, 2015.

be "truthful," but are relatively silent on its practical meaning, leaving the door open to communication that muddies the waters of public debate to delay rather than aid decision making.

But the most serious flaw in these codes is their voluntary nature and lackluster enforcement. The PRSA, in particular, has moved away from even pretending to enforce its code, while reserving the right to expel any member "who has been or is sanctioned by a government agency or convicted in a court of law of an action that fails to comply with the Code."[2]

A Universal Code?

So the "universal, multilaterally honored code of ethics" envisioned by public relations ethics scholar Dean Kruckeberg in 1989 still seems quite remote. The closest we have come to such a code is IPRA's, which claims to be "endorsed and subscribed to by professional communicators in all transnational corporations worldwide." It is unique in throwing cold water on the assertion that bribery is an ethical custom in some countries, warning that members should not "directly nor indirectly offer nor give any financial or other inducement to public representatives or the media, or other stakeholders," nor should they "propose nor undertake any action which would constitute an improper influence on public representatives, the media, or other stakeholders."

IPRA is the granddaddy of public relations associations, tracing its roots to a 1949 meeting in London between two Dutch and four British public relations practitioners. Since then, IPRA has grown into an association of senior-level public relations managers in more than 100 countries. One of the IPRA's most potent contributions has been a decades-long exploration of ethical standards going back to its founding and guided by such leading educators and professionals as Sam Black and Tim Traverse-Healy.

The current version of the IPRA code, ratified in 2011, is a decidedly pragmatic document, warning against "poaching" clients from other members "by deceptive means" and cautioning members "not [to] intentionally

---

[2] From the Preamble of the PRSA Member Code of Ethics. http://www.prsa.org /AboutPRSA/Ethics/CodeEnglish/#.VfMTR51Viko

injure the professional reputation of another practitioner." It tells members to "avoid any professional conflicts of interest and to disclose such conflicts to affected parties when they occur." And it warns that members should "not obtain information by deceptive or dishonest means."

But it is IPRA Code's intellectual and moral underpinnings that really set it apart. The original version of the IPRA Code of Ethics was authored by Lucien Matrat of France, adopted at a membership meeting in Athens in May 1965 (known as the Code of Athens), and slightly modified during a meeting in Teheran in April 1968.[3] That document put the practice of public relations firmly within the framework of the UN Declaration of Human Rights. While acknowledging that public relations practitioners possess a "power that has to be restrained by the observance of a strict moral code," it set a constructive purpose for public relations, starting with a firm declaration that "public relations practitioners can substantially help to meet [people's] intellectual, moral and social needs." Indeed, the code, as originally conceived and amended in 1968 and 2009, gave public relations people a positive and uplifting charge, including:

> To contribute to the achievement of the moral and cultural conditions enabling human beings to reach their full stature and enjoy the indefeasible rights to which they are entitled under the Universal Declaration of Human Rights.

> To establish communications patterns and channels which, by fostering the free flow of essential information, will make each member of the group feel that he/she is being kept informed, and also give him/her an awareness of his/her own personal involvement and responsibility, and of his/her solidarity with other members.

> To establish the moral, psychological and intellectual conditions for dialogue in its true sense, and to recognize the rights of these parties involved to state in their case and express their views.

> To act, in all circumstances, in such a manner as to take account of the respective interests of the parties involved; both the interests of the organization which he/she serves and the interests of the publics concerned.

---

[3] Code of Athens. (1965, amended 1968 and 2009). http://www.ipra.org/pdf/Code_of_Athens.pdf. Accessed July 22, 2015.

Furthermore, in the interests of informed decision making, it instructed public relations professionals to "recognize the right of each individual to judge for himself/herself." And in requiring members to tell "the truth," it banned the distribution of information "not based on established and ascertainable facts," suggesting that information be held to an objective standard of whether it is provably true or false. That is a higher standard than required by many codes, including the current IPRA version. Looking back over his 66-year career, Tim Traverse-Healy, one of the IPRA's founding members, pinpointed what gives public relations societal meaning and community worth. "In almost equal measure," he wrote, "these ingredients are truth, paramount concern for the public good, and genuine dialogue."[4]

We are unabashed fans of the Code of Athens. At the same time, we understand the need to bring greater focus to the few critical rules of the road that should guide public relations people in their day-to-day practice. For all their limitations, such codes are essential in addressing the ethical challenges professionals and practitioners face in the course of a normal day, from identifying and resolving conflicts of interest to developing strategic communications plans. After all, few public relations practitioners want—or have the time—to apply ethical theory to every decision they have to make, especially not under the pressures of time or conflicting demands.

But in unique situations, or when the codes themselves provide ambiguous guidance, we need more. When we are traveling treacherous roads, or even if we are on a familiar road with unusual twists and turns, no ethical code can provide much more than a high-level map. What we need then is a way to analyze a situation at ground level and measure it against the theories that underlie the codes. We need to be able to build ethical decisions on a relatively sturdy and reliable framework.

That is the Holy Grail of ethical study. And as it happens, many public relations ethicists have developed their own versions of such

---

[4] Traverse-Healy, T. (2014, March 3). Public relations credo by Tim Traverse-Healy. *S. Waddington Blog Public Relations, Marketing and Social Media Thinking and Doing.* http://wadds.co.uk/2014/03/03/public-relations-credo-tim-traverse-healy/. Accessed July 22, 2015.

frameworks. We will briefly outline several before tackling the construction of a personal framework tailored to our own unique needs and perspective.

TARSE Test

The most basic of these ethical frameworks is the TARSE test, which is an acronym for its components—Truthfulness, Authenticity, Respect, Social Responsibility, and Equity. Developed by Sherry Baker and David Martinson in 2001, it draws heavily from the concept of virtuous communication. The idea is that in any persuasive or advocacy campaign, a public relations practitioner should consider five interconnected factors (Baker and Martinson, 2011):

- *Truthfulness of the message.* Public relations communication must result in an audience with enough information to make an informed choice on the issue being presented.
- *Authenticity of the persuader.* Public relations practitioners must ask themselves if this message will benefit someone other than their client.
- *Respect for the person being persuaded.* Communicators should see their audience as "human beings," and ensure that their messages are shaped and transmitted with appropriate respect.
- *Social responsibility for the common good.* Public relations campaigns should serve the interests of the public at large. And,
- *Equity of the appeal.* Public relations practitioners should avoid communication that intentionally takes advantage of the vulnerabilities of a specific audience.

A company called Legacy Learning could have saved $250,000 and a major hit to its reputation if it had applied the TARSE test to its marketing plan. Legacy created a set of DVDs and written materials to teach people how to play guitar and it marketed them through bloggers who claimed to have taken the course and endorsed it, both on their sites and elsewhere on the web. Legacy also linked to the endorsements on its own website. But what people did not know was that the company paid each blogger a commission when its endorsement produced a sale. And some of the bloggers—including a professional musician—had never actually taken the course.

The company's marketing was not *truthful* because it withheld a material fact—the bloggers were paid for their endorsements and some of them never took the course. Materiality is defined as a fact that would lead someone to make a different decision had they known it. Knowing that someone is being paid to praise a product would cause most people to question the sincerity of their endorsement. By omitting that information, the company was not giving potential customers the full truth about its product.

This ties in to the second element of the TARSE test—authenticity. *Authenticity* means a message is genuine or real, exactly as it appears. But Legacy's message was inauthentic—the people who claimed to have used it to learn to play guitar only said that because they were paid to. No one who knew that would have bought the course.

The next step is to respect consumers, including their *right* to make a voluntary, intelligent decision. Legacy and its paid bloggers did not respect potential consumers because they withheld relevant information from them.

Equity asks whether a company is treating consumers fairly in its communications. Legacy had a hidden advantage because consumers had no way of knowing its endorsements were not genuine. They were more likely to think the reviews were from regular people like them, not someone being paid off by the company.

The Federal Trade Commission eventually filed a complaint against Legacy for failing to disclose its payments, and the company settled for a $250,000 fine. But the company could have avoided the whole controversy if it had used the TARSE test

Six Questions

Another checklist-like framework teases some broader questions out of the ethical principles we have discussed. These questions potentially apply to more than persuasive communications, and they approach ethical issues from Aristotelian, deontological, and utilitarian perspectives of virtue, duty, and consequences. Each question is relatively simple but carries significant implications.

1. *Does this action represent the kind of person I am or want to be? Does it represent the kind of organization I want to belong to?* Being an ethical person means more than following rules; it means developing habits of acting in a way that we think good people should act.

2. *Am I fulfilling my duties in this situation?* Identify the obligations we have in this situation—to ourselves, our client, our employer, and anyone who might be affected. Do those obligations conflict in any way? How can we resolve those conflicts? Do some obligations trump the others? Why? And what should we do about that?

3. *Are the people affected by my decision able to make their own choices?* We should respect others as individuals who have an innate right to make their own choices free from coercion and interference. We should allow them to make an informed choice. For example, would they choose differently with additional or different information?

4. *Am I respecting the rights of everyone involved in this situation?* Some rights are codified in laws, which can vary from country to country. Others spring from the intrinsic value we all have as human beings. The United Nation's Universal Declaration of Human Rights lists what many consider essential human rights. The acid test of a right is to ask whether you would claim it for yourself.

5. *Will what I propose to do or say produce the best outcomes for everyone affected? Am I maximizing good and minimizing harm for everyone?* Do your best to predict the probable short and long-term outcomes and to determine their relative value to different individuals and groups. Then select the action that produces the greatest benefits over costs for everyone affected.

6. *Am I doing my part to look out for the common good in this situation?*
   We all live in a community, which requires us to pay attention not just to our own welfare, but also to the general welfare, including the social systems, institutions, and environments on which we all depend. Since we all benefit from these common goods, we all have obligations to protect and grow them.

Each of these questions has strengths and weaknesses, and they probably work best in concert. The character and duties tests could benefit from consideration of outcomes. The best outcomes test might benefit from also considering the common good test. And so forth. There is an approach that combines elements of all these tests. It is called the professional responsibility theory.

Professional Responsibility Theory

Many public relations practitioners straddle two worlds, often uncomfortably. On the one hand, they are advocates for clients, accountable for representing their interests in the marketplace of products and ideas. On the other hand, clients also expect them to be their social conscience, helping them meet their responsibilities to the public at large.

To reconcile the seemingly contradictory roles of professional advocate and social conscience, ethics professors Kathy Fitzpatrick and Candace Gauthier (2001) suggest public relations practitioners conceive of themselves as "professionals." They believe public relations people, like attorneys, best serve society by attending to the special interests of their clients or employers. While their first loyalty is always to their client, part of that duty is voicing the opinions and interests of the organization's stakeholders.

They suggest that public relations practitioners should measure their actions against three principles:

1. First, they should carefully consider the harms and benefits of what they propose to do. Harms should be avoided or at least minimized and benefits should be promoted at the lowest cost in terms of potential harms.

2. Second, they should ensure that their actions demonstrate respect for everyone affected. People should be treated with dignity and never solely as means.
3. And third, they should ensure that all rewards and costs implicit in their action should be distributed as fairly as possible.

This tripartite approach promises to bridge the gap between advocacy and social responsibility by giving both roles equal weight. Of course, Fitzpatrick and Gauthier recognize that, in practice, these principles will often conflict with one another. In those cases, they suggest practitioners should fall back on their own values, moral intuition, and character to determine which principle is most important and most controlling. So in essence the theory of professional responsibility includes all three major theories we have discussed—virtue, duty, and consequence.

Kantian Approach

Public relations professor Shannon Bowen has developed an approach that leans heavily on Kant's concepts of autonomy and respect while building on James Grunig's concept of two-way symmetrical communications. In fact, Bowen (2004) proposes that ethics could be seen as the "tenth generic principle" of Grunig's model of public relations excellence. While originally applied to the function of issues management, this approach has obvious relevance to the full practice of public relations.

Bowen's model starts from the implicit assumption that an issue important enough to examine in detail will usually involve a number of managers from different functions, including public relations. She takes pains to caution that before even starting their inquiry, these managers need to satisfy themselves they have sufficient autonomy to address the issue based on their best reasoning, untainted by self-interest or outside interference, such as concern "this could affect my career" or "the client will look for a new agency if I disagree with her on this."

"Autonomy releases the public relations practitioner from blinding subjectivity, worrying about the loss of a job, negative repercussions, reciprocity, or maintaining appearances of loyalty before an employer or client," she writes. "Autonomy frees one to make decisions based on ethics rather than on prudence" (Bowen, 2004, p. 72). Thus freed, the managers can engage in an open discussion of the issue, consulting subject matter experts and even the people affected to gain a clear understanding of the issues at stake. At this stage, managers begin to identify alternative options and can use Kant's categorical imperative to analyze the ethics of the decisions they are contemplating. For example, to reveal any hidden subjectivity in the managers' thinking, they could ask the following:

- Could we obligate everyone else who is ever in a similar situation to do the same thing we are considering?
- Would I accept this decision if I were on the receiving end?
- What is my moral duty in this situation, both in regards to myself and to others?
- Does this decision convey to our publics that we have seriously considered their view on the issue?
- Does this decision make us worthy of earning trust, respect, and support from our publics?

Instead of focusing on an uncertain cost–benefit analysis, these questions would encourage public relations people to consider their ethical duty in the situation, to respect the dignity of the people affected by their decision, and to demonstrate that it comes from a morally good intention. In keeping with the two-way symmetrical model, the participants would communicate with stakeholders about their decision-making process from its initial stages through final decision. "Communication should be ongoing and used to contribute to the decision-making process, as well as to communicate with publics about the decision," Bowen (2004, p. 83) suggests. Indeed, she believes continuous communication with affected publics should be the hallmark of issue management, identifying emerging issues as they arise so they can be addressed and resolved.

Ironically, the principal obstacle Bowen (2004) sees in implementing this approach would be familiar to most senior practitioners—autonomy. "Loyalties to client, employer, the media, and the self as a moral decision maker often conflict in an ethical dilemma," she observes. But the process she recommends requires a practitioner to "diligently strive for an objective view of the situation," removing himself or herself from personal considerations and retributive concerns (p. 84). Indeed that would require an unusual degree of self-confidence rooted not only in an assessment of one's skills and judgment, but also in an unassailable grasp of what is right.

Bowen argues that, "answering the question, 'what is ethically right?' commands consideration of the consequences of a decision, without requiring a decision to be dictated by those consequences." And she adds that "the ramifications of a decision" should be "thoroughly considered" and might even "modify" the decision to do "what duty indicates is ethically right" (Bowen, 2004, p. 86).

Summary

In this chapter, we have considered a range of approaches to ethical decision making, from the starkly pragmatic to the deeply philosophical. Look closely enough and you will see elements of all three major theories we have studied in each—*virtue*, *duty*, and *consequences*. Each approach has advantages and limitations. The lofty principles of codes of conduct, for example, are subject to widely varying interpretation. The TARSE test is most easily applied to persuasive communications, but has limited application to other areas of practice. The six questions and professional responsibility approaches ask the right questions, but offer little help in resolving conflicts when answers inevitably clash. And even though Bowen's approach is deeply rooted in Kantian notions of autonomy and universality, it leaves room for a consideration of consequences.

We agree, but it seems to us the loophole Bowen opens should be the main portal to any ethical decision—*how will this affect the people concerned?* W. D. Ross (1939, 2002) gave us that bridge between duty and consequences. We should use it, which is exactly what we will do in the next chapter.

CHAPTER 13

Constructing a Personal Framework for Ethical Reasoning

Philosophers have been thinking and writing about ethics for thousands of years. Yet their theories boil down to three general approaches that focus primarily on consequences, duty, or virtue. Even feminist ethics, while correcting the patriarchal excesses of the past, principally focuses on duties of justice and care.

Each theory has strengths and weaknesses. The best approach probably borrows from all three. The key, however, is to design an approach particularly suited to the kinds of situations in which you will most likely find yourself in the practice of public relations.

We constructed such a framework based on the principles and theories we have discussed. We are not suggesting you adopt it wholesale. We are just using it as an example of what a framework might look like. It has four parts:

- Issue definition
- Stakeholder Identification
- Evaluation of Options
- Making and Justifying Decision

The real value of any framework is in identifying the questions you should ask *before* you need to ask them. If you do this within the context of your current job, it should be relatively straightforward. In the fog of an ethical dilemma, you won't have to do more than refresh your list of stakeholders and you'll have a head start on identifying the ethical principles most relevant to your function within all three domains of virtue, duty, and consequences.

Framework for Ethical Reasoning

Define the Issue

1. Describe the ethical issue or problem in two or three sentences.
2. List all the salient facts with most immediate relevance. Include any external pressures you feel—political, economic, interpersonal, or social.

Identify Your Stakeholders

3. List the potential stakeholders in this situation (i.e., all the people who might be affected and all the people to whom you owe a duty). Describe their current state of mind and heart.

Define Your Options

4. Develop at least three options to address the situation. List best and worst cases for each.

Evaluate Options

5. For each option, identify the pros and cons (benefits and costs) for each set of stakeholders, including your client. Take into account harms/cares, issues of justice, duties, rights, and personal values.
   - *Harms/Cares*: How would stakeholders benefit, would anyone be harmed, what costs would stakeholders pay?
   - *Duties:* What are your duties in this situation? Does this option respect the integrity and freedom of those affected? Are you using those affected as a means to an end without consideration of their human dignity? Is your decision free of vested interest or ulterior motive? Would you be willing to make this option a rule to be followed by others?
   - *Rights:* What are the stakeholders' rights in this situation? For example, is there a rule, law, or code that would automatically invalidate one of the options? Does your relationship with the stakeholders carry explicit or implicit rights?

- *Values:* Does this option represent behavior and standards for which you would like to be known? Would this option violate your personal values? Is it consistent with the exercise of these values?

Make a Decision

6. Use this analysis to choose your course of action. Select the option that allows you to fulfill your most important duties, is in keeping with your values, and has the best consequences for the people affected. When your only choice is between two harmful actions, choose the one that does less harm. In all cases, be especially careful not to unconsciously justify a decision you had already made.
7. Reexamine your decision until you're sure you have the right balance, then justify it based on ethical precepts as if you were addressing the person least likely to agree.

Ethical decision making calls for great humility. Our understanding of the universal principles underlying ethical choices is almost always flawed in one way or another. We can do our best to conform to our values, do our duty, and produce the most good. But we will seldom be 100 percent certain that we have made the right choice.

Dan Ariely, a columnist for the *Wall Street Journal* and an expert in cognitive behavior,[1] offers some good advice:

> *When we face decisions, we are trapped within our own perspective—our own special motivations and emotions, our egocentric view of the world at that moment. To make decisions that are more rational, we want to eliminate those barriers and look at the situation more objectively. One way to do this is to think not of making a decision for yourself but of recommending a decision for somebody else you like. This lets you view the situation in a colder, more detached way and make better decisions.*

---

[1] Ariely, D. (2013, July 19). Ask Ariely. *Wall Street Journal.* http://online.wsj.com /articles/SB10001424127887324448104578613662185887232. Accessed July 22, 2015.

This framework for ethical reasoning is really not complicated (see Figure 13.1), but it does require some hard thinking. The following example illustrates it well.

Case: Monkey Business at AT&T[2]

Back in the 1980s and 1990s, before the advent of electronic social media, AT&T published a monthly company magazine. It was mailed to all 300,000 employees' homes because the company wanted their families to understand its business goals and performance.[1]

AT&T spent almost $1 million a year, producing and distributing the magazine, which was written by members of the public relations department but designed and printed by an outside company. The magazine won numerous awards and was recognized by many as a world-class publication. Unusually for an internal publication, employees actually read it because the magazine was studiously candid about the company's performance and printed employee letters that were often critical of management. While this was sometimes uncomfortable for line management, the leaders of the public relations department did a good job of insulating the editors from executive complaints and meddling.

In fact, the magazine's editorial staff prided itself on being a self-managed team. What they wrote for the publication was reviewed by subject matter experts for accuracy and by the law department for potential legal issues, but no one else reviewed the magazine in advance of publication. Occasionally, however, the staff had to pull an article at the last minute because a technical reviewer raised issues that could not be resolved by the press deadline. That is what happened as the September 1993 issue was going to bed. A one-page article at the back of the magazine had to be pulled and the editors decided to substitute a fun "quiz" on the company's international business.

The production manager, a young African-American employee new to the magazine staff, called the outside designer and asked him to prepare a

---

[2] For a fuller version of this incident, see Dick Martin. (2004). *Tough Calls: AT&T and the Hard Lessons Learned From The Telecom Wars.* New York: AMACOM, p. 165–167.

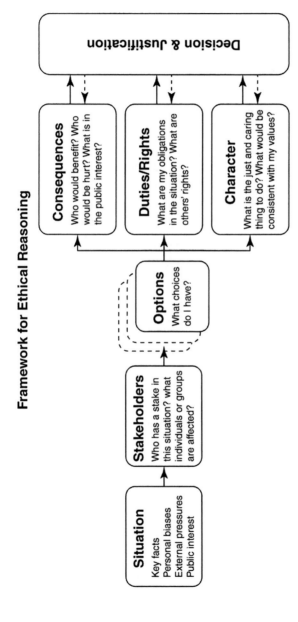

Figure 13.1 When faced with an ethical dilemma, consider all options but select a course of action that produces the most good, fulfills your obligations, and is consistent with your values. Reexamine your decision until you're sure you have the right balance and are not simply rationalizing your initial opinion. Be prepared to justify your decision based on ethical precepts.

layout for the quiz, using the rough copy she was about to fax to him. The designer, in turn, asked a cartoonist he had used many times in the past to prepare some suitable illustrations.

The next day, the cartoonist had faxed some illustrations to the designer, who pasted them into a layout with copy, which he faxed to the production manager. The fax she received was dark and blurry, but she approved the layout. She had already approved the typeset copy, which had arrived the night before, also by fax.

As soon as the first copies arrived in the magazine's offices, the editor knew she had a problem. Each cartoon character illustrating the quiz about the company's international businesses was human except the character in Africa who was a monkey. The cartoon appeared to be a racial slur comparing black people to monkeys. Ashen-faced, she brought it to her boss's attention. The full run of 300,000 copies was already on its way to people's homes, including those of the company's 45,000 African-American employees. What would they think?

There were clearly ethical implications to what started as a sloppy production mistake. AT&T was (and still is) one of the most generous corporate donors to African-American organizations, including the NAACP, the Rainbow/PUSH Coalition, the Urban League, and historically black colleges. At that point, 25 percent of all African-Americans with PhD's in electrical engineering had received financial support and mentoring from AT&T. The company was a pioneer in minority purchasing and spent more than $1 billion a year with firms owned by people of color. Furthermore, even during extensive downsizing following the divestiture of its local telephone companies, AT&T took pains to ensure that the company's diversity profile was not adversely affected. In fact, it actually improved. But, despite all these good efforts, there were still few black executives in top positions. And it had just mailed a cartoon to every employee's home that was at best disrespectful of its African-American employees and at worse was abjectly racist.

What would you do? One of us was faced with that very question. He wishes he could say that he had the benefit of a well-considered framework for ethical reasoning. He did not. But, in the years since, he has applied this situation to the illustrative framework described above. It took only about 1,500 words, though in practice it would also have involved consultation with other managers responsible for relationships with each stakeholder group. That points up the other advantage of developing a framework for ethical reasoning—it can help get everyone on the same page in analyzing what are almost always complex situations with crosscurrents of interests and multiple perspectives.

Sample Framework for Analyzing AT&T Case

Issue: The company magazine has been printed and distributed with what some will consider a racist cartoon. It shows people in different countries talking on the phone. Each cartoon character is human except the character in Africa who is a monkey. The cartoon appears to be a racial slur comparing Blacks to monkeys.

Relevant facts:

- The magazine is already in the mail to the homes of 300,000 employees and cannot be recalled.
- African-American employees account for 15 percent of the workforce.
- White employees believe they are suffering reverse discrimination.
- The company has a very high profile in the community.
- The company has a very good relationship with such organizations as the NAACP and the Urban League. It has a good record on diversity and is considered a corporate leader on the issue.
- The cartoon is relatively small and on the last page of the issue.
- A freelance artist, working for the outside company that designs the magazine, produced the cartoon.
- The woman who approved the art is African American. Her immediate supervisors are both white women.
- The magazine has won numerous awards and is considered one of the best in the industry.
- Some community activists could use the cartoon as an excuse for demanding that AT&T set even more aggressive

goals in hiring and promoting minority employees and purchases from minority suppliers.

Stakeholders:

- *African-American employees:* They already believe they are underrepresented in upper management and continue to suffer discrimination. This cartoon will insult them. At best, it will appear insensitive; at worse, it will appear to reveal unconscious bias.
- *Other employees of color:* They share many of the concerns of African-American employees and will demand an explanation and corrective action.
- *Other employees:* Many will be embarrassed and question the competence of management. Some will be incensed and demand broad corrective action. Some will wonder what all the fuss is about and say employees of color are overreacting.
- *The broader African-American community:* They will be concerned and demand a full explanation as well as corrective action. Some will see this as an opportunity to press for broad action on affirmative action.
- *Magazine staff:* They will be embarrassed and worry about their jobs.
- *Designer and cartoonist:* They will worry that we will throw them under the bus. They may also be defensive and try to deflect blame.
- *Customers:* Some customers who become aware of the situation may question the company's values. A few may write letters of complaint. Some may even threaten to cancel their service. Experience suggests few follow through.
- *Suppliers:* Few suppliers will react negatively. Some will be sympathetic. A few high-profile African-American suppliers such as the editors of *Black Enterprise* and *Ebony* will demand personal explanations, but they are unlikely to do more than criticize the company for allowing this to happen.

Options

1. ***Hunker down.*** Ignore the cartoon. Deal with complaints individually as they come in.

   Best case: the controversy dies after a few weeks.

   Worst case: the controversy gathers steam, involving outside activists.

   a) *Pros/Cons:*
   - *Company:* Potential cost could be loss of employee and community trust, especially among people of color. It could also signal that the company is not serious about racial issues. Potential benefit could be less disruption and lower financial cost. There is always a chance this could blow over before it becomes a problem.
     Net: cost higher than benefit.
   - *Employees:* Potential cost in a missed opportunity to reassert the company's commitment to equal opportunity and intolerance of bias. Potential benefit in avoiding disruption and distraction by allowing the issue to blow over.
     Net: cost higher than benefit given low probability that issue will blow over.
   - *Magazine staff, designer, and cartoonist:* Potential cost includes disruption and tension of waiting for the shoe to drop. Also staff will bear cost of replying to complaints that do emerge. Potential benefit includes possibility that not drawing attention to cartoon may lower its visibility.
     Net: benefit higher than cost.
   - *Customers:* Potential reputational risk.
   - *Suppliers:* High-profile African-American suppliers may be surprised and dismayed if they hear about cartoon from third parties. Cost to them would include a violation of trust if issue blows up, along with criticism from some quarters for their continuing relationship with company. Benefit would include keeping them out of controversy.
     Net: costs are higher than benefits.

b) *Duties:*

- *Harm/Care:* All stakeholders could be harmed in varying degrees by ignoring the issue until it develops. Trust in the company could be undermined. Other stakeholders could be even more offended if it appears the company is ignoring the issue.
- *Justice:* To ignore the issue is to appear to condone it, which violates our employees' right to a bias-free environment.
- *Rules:* The Company's Code of Conduct clearly forbids cartoons that mock people's race. We have a duty to correct harms and to honor people's personal dignity.
- *Categorical Imperative:* I would not be comfortable if "hunkering down" were the universal solution for situations such as this.

c) *Values:* I do not want to work for a company that ignores harms committed against employees until forced to pay attention.

2. **Take responsibility.** Issue an immediate apology to our employees, explaining how it happened and describing steps to ensure similar mistakes never happen again, including sensitivity training for all involved, reassigning the production manager who approved the artwork, and never using the cartoonist who executed it again.

Best case: African-American employees accept our apology and corrective action. *Worse case:* African-American employees do not accept our apology and are outraged that we seem not to understand the depth of their concerns. They enlist outside help to force real corrective action.

a) *Pros/Cons:*

- *Company:* Potential cost could include giving the cartoon greater visibility. Potential benefit could include retaining employee trust.
  Net: benefit higher than cost.
- *Employees:* Potential cost in disruption and distraction. Those who consider response an overreaction will feel we are playing favorites. Those who consider response insufficient will feel betrayed. Potential benefit includes deepening

feelings of trust and pride in company by taking concrete action to reassert company's intolerance of bias and commitment to equality.

Net: benefit higher than cost.

- *Magazine staff, designer, and cartoonist:* Potential cost includes shame of responsibility for racist cartoon and having to spend time in training. Potential benefit includes pride in being part of positive response.

    Net: cost higher than benefit.

- *Customers:* Potential reputational costs. Little upside.

- *Suppliers:* High profile African-American suppliers could feel that their trust in company has been vindicated. Still, cost could include criticism from some quarters for their continuing relationship with company. Benefit would include credible response to criticism.

    Net: benefit higher than cost.

b) *Duties:*

- *Harm/Care:* Action corrects harm and cares for affected employees.

- *Justice:* Respects our employees' right to a bias-free environment.

- *Rules:* Adheres to Company's Code of Conduct. Honors people's personal dignity.

- *Categorical Imperative:* I would be comfortable if responding in this way were the universal solution for similar situations.

c) *Values:* I would be proud to work for a company that takes its employees' dignity seriously and responds aggressively to violations of its Code of Conduct.

3. *Take definitive action.* In addition to apologizing, announce that we have ceased publication of the company magazine. Also announce concrete goals for increasing the representation of minority employees in management and for increasing purchases from minority suppliers.

Best case: All employees consider this action appropriate and are willing to put the issue behind them.

Worse case: African-American employees consider the action inadequate and some white employees consider it another example of preferential treatment.

a) *Pros/Cons:*

- *Company:* Potential costs and benefits same as in Option 2. In addition, cost of developing new employee communications vehicles. Additional benefit includes signaling the seriousness of the company's corrective actions.
  Net: benefit higher than cost.

- *Employees:* Same costs and benefits as in Option 2, with greater weight on the side of benefits despite the potential cost of a suit brought by the designer for wrongful termination.
  Net: benefit higher than cost.

- *Magazine staff, designer, and cartoonist:* Benefit of shifting employee communications to electronic and face-to-face media earlier than planned. Costs include transition expenses and serious blow to morale within public relations department.
  Net: immediate cost higher than benefit; long-term costs and benefits in balance.

- *Customers:* Potential reputational cost. Little upside benefit.

- *Suppliers:* Same costs and benefits as Option 2 with higher weight on benefit side.
  Net: benefit higher than cost.

b) *Duties:*

- *Harm/Care:* Action corrects harm and cares for affected employees.

- *Justice:* Respects our employees' right to a bias-free environment.

- *Rules:* Adheres to Company's Code of Conduct. Honors people's personal dignity.

- *Categorical Imperative:* I would be comfortable if responding in this way were the universal solution in similar situations.
  c) *Values:* I would be proud to work for a company that takes its employees' dignity seriously and responds aggressively to violations of its Code of Conduct.

Decision

Which recommendation would you pick? Or is there another, preferable option?

Justification

How would you justify your recommendation? What combination of ethical principles seems most relevant?

What We Did

In fact, we choose Option Two (though we did not know it at the time since we had not consciously conducted the analysis outlined above). We were simply operating on instinct and our best judgment, heavily influenced by the fact that the public relations organization itself had been the cause of this problem. For example, a group of African-American executives urged us to follow what is identified above as Option Three—closing down the magazine and "firing" (i.e., reassigning) the editors of the magazine. We resisted their entreaties out of loyalty to the employees responsible for the magazine, who we were confident had not intentionally expressed racist attitudes.

So we did not wait for people to complain. We issued an immediate apology and sent it to all employees. In fact, we sent three apologies. The first was from the editor, the second about 2 days later was from the head of public relations, and the third by mail to employees' homes was from the company's Chairman and CEO. He not only apologized, he pointed out that we fired the artist who drew the cartoon, asked the designer who hired him to go through diversity training, committed to increase the diversity of the magazine's staff (not mentioning that the production manager who approved the cartoon was African American), and formed a committee of minority employees to advise the publication's editors. **It did not work.**

By a stroke of bad luck, about a week after the magazine came out, the Congressional Black Caucus held its annual legislative weekend in Washington, DC. More than 2,000 public officials and African-American leaders were in town to discuss race relations. And the *Washington Post* ran a front-page story about the cartoon on the first day of the meeting. Speaker after speaker used the cartoon as an example of corporate America's sorry diversity record. The Caucus called for hearings, Rev. Al Sharpton picketed AT&T headquarters, and local NAACP chapters launched boycotts.

The furor did not subside until we closed down the magazine, reassigning all the staff. We actually had been planning to close down the print publication anyway in favor of electronic and face-to-face communications. But the decision still stung, especially for the magazine's staff. They had not done anything ethically wrong, but our decision to throw in the towel certainly made them look guilty.

Now, here is the irony. The very month in which that monkey cartoon ran in our employee magazine—September 1993—the alumni magazine of Rutgers University ran a cartoon by the same artist. It showed Rutgers alumni around the world flying the school banner. The alum in Nigeria? A monkey. No one said anything about it. So ethical decisions are not always cut and dry exercises of checking actions against a list of guidelines. *Context matters.*

That does not mean Rutgers's cartoon was ethical while AT&T's was not. Both cartoons were disrespectful, if only because their creator and distributors did not anticipate how African Americans, still stung by decades of racial slurs and insults, would interpret them. AT&T's misfortune was to have a much higher profile than Rutgers. And its African-American employees harbored more serious grievances than the company knew. The cartoon gave vent to the company's actual ethical problem—15 percent of its employees felt disenfranchised and neglected.

Some argue the company brought condemnation down on itself by calling attention to the cartoon in its string of apologies. There may be something to that, but if the company erred, it was in issuing multiple apologies from increasingly higher level people. Had the CEO immediately issued a single apology, backed up with the forceful action the company eventually took, he could have avoided weeks of turmoil. And that points up another lesson: the person or organization responsible for an unethical act is seldom the right one to address it.

Summary

Three decades later, it is hard to believe something as trivial as a sloppy production mistake could bring a company like AT&T to its knees for more than a month. That it did demonstrates both the combustibility of deeply felt grievances and the unpredictable friction that can ignite them. Of course, one of the public relations practitioner's principal duties is to anticipate such events by tracking the currents of public opinion and scanning the environment for potential disruptions.

Arguably, that was our fundamental failure. We misread the depths of our African-American employees' discontent, and we underestimated the extent to which outside groups would leverage our employees' anger and the shallowness of our response. To compound matters, our *ad hoc* approach, careening from apology to apology, culminating in a full-bore CEO apology tour, drew attention to the problem without really solving it.

There is no guarantee the illustrative framework presented in this chapter would have resulted in an earlier resolution of the crisis. But having such a framework would have better organized our efforts, directing attention to important areas requiring analysis and surfacing issues for debate. This illustrative framework may not be appropriate for every organization in every situation. But AT&T's experience does point up the importance of having *some* predetermined framework in place to address ethical issues that threaten the company as a whole. And it suggests what principles might guide decision making.

In the next chapter, we will sum up our discussion of ethical theories and suggest how public relations practitioners can apply them, both in the conduct of their own function and in counseling their clients.

CHAPTER 14

Conclusion

In the ethics classes and workshops we have taught, we have noticed a tendency for public relations people to address ethical issues in terms of "what works?" rather than "what's right?" That is sometimes because it is often more difficult to figure out what ethics *requires* than what good public relations practice *demands*. Sometimes they are the same thing, and it is simply good business to behave ethically. Enlightened self-interest suggests that businesses will do well financially by doing good ethically. Developing a reputation for ethical behavior—deserved or not—can forestall government regulation; it almost certainly gives companies a competitive edge among many consumers and business people.

But sometimes what works is not right; it is just expedient and might even go unnoticed for a long period of time. It took five years for the Federal Trade Commission to take action against Legacy Learning's bogus endorsements. And the tobacco companies used various public relations campaigns to delay regulation of cigarettes for more than two decades. In fact, many of those campaigns continue to this day, as regulation has moved from package warnings to outright bans that limit where people can smoke, and the warnings themselves are getting more graphic. These efforts are roundly criticized as a continuation of a discredited disinformation campaign. Yet, we see echoes of the tobacco industry's campaign in soft drink company research suggesting obesity is caused by lack of exercise, not by over-consumption of sugary beverages.[1]

As we have suggested, many of the great financial scandals of recent years began as perfectly legal attempts to manage earnings. One might say they got out of control, but the real issue is whether anyone was ready to ask not "will it work?" but "is it right?"

---

[1] O'Connor, A. (2015, August 9). Coca-Cola Funds Scientists Who Shift Blame for Obesity Away From Bad Diets. *The New York Times.* http://well.blogs.nytimes.com /2015/08/09/coca-cola-funds-scientists-who-shift-blame-for-obesity-away-from-bad-diets/?_r=0

Ethical Issues Can Be Difficult

To be honest, ethical issues are not easy to resolve. As we write this, a Japanese manufacturer of automobile air bags has appeared before two Congressional committees trying to explain why its products have been exploding and seriously injuring drivers. The company's case has not been helped by the discovery that its engineers knew about the problem ten years ago but did nothing about it. Meanwhile, federal safety agencies have asked the company to declare a nationwide recall on the air bags, which have been installed in more than 8 million cars. The company, which believes the problem is related to high heat and humidity, has agreed to recall the air bags in 11 states with that kind of climate and where all the previous problems occurred. To broaden the recall to all 50 states, the company claims, would create a parts shortage that would make it more difficult to replace the air bags in the most vulnerable states. Now, this is a public relations problem wrapped in an ethical problem, wrapped in an engineering and logistics problem. Clearly, the company, the media, Congress, and the chattering class are attacking both ends. But who is tackling the core issue—what is the right thing to do?

That issue is wrapped in considerations of virtue, duty, and consequences, none of which stands alone but is in a hydraulic relationship to the others. Our goal in this book has been to equip public relations people with the essential elements of ethical theory so they can function effectively as counselors and as practitioners.

As members of senior management, public relations leaders increasingly have a voice in the development of business strategy and policies. This will almost inevitably touch on ethical issues, from the safety and social impacts of a company's products to the fairness and care with which it conducts its affairs. And the scope of that ethical inquiry will range far beyond the company's formal borders into its chain of suppliers and dealers.

In addition, public relations leaders are responsible for the ethical conduct of their own organizations across functions such as media relations, employee communications, speechwriting, community relations, social media, investor relations, marketing communications, and so forth. And they are responsible for the ongoing management of stakeholder relationships, ideally through open and candid dialog capable of surfacing, addressing, and resolving issues before they become an ethical dilemma.

In both roles, as counselor and practitioner, we hope public relations people look at ethical behavior not only as the avoidance of doing wrong. But also as actually doing good. Scholars like James Grunig (e.g., Grunig and White, 1992) and Shannon Bowen (2004) have suggested that the very act of establishing an open dialog between an organization and its publics makes the practice ethical. That may be so, but we do not believe it is necessary to sidestep public relations practitioners' more prosaic work. As *The New York Times* columnist David Brooks once noted, "Aristotle teaches us that being a good person is not mainly about learning moral rules and following them. It is about performing social roles well—being a good parent or teacher or lawyer or friend." To that we can add, "being a responsible company."[2] And public relations practitioners play a critical role in fulfilling that responsibility through the very exercise of their function.

An Electronic Extension

Participating in communities of interest through social media can be an electronic extension of the two-way symmetrical dialog that scholars like Grunig and Bowen consider inherently ethical. In fact, it can be a service to customers in its own right, answering their questions, advising them on everything from product usage to industry trends. Similarly, spreading the word about a product or service of genuine utility and value to consumers is ethical in itself. Bringing employees information they need to do their job and to understand a company's role in society, as well as the state of its financial performance, shows them respect in a Kantian, as well as a common, sense. Helping senior executives express themselves accurately and truthfully in the arena of public opinion is good work in every sense of the word. Maintaining cordial and mutually supportive relationships

---

[2] Brooks, D. (2014, December 5). Why elders smile. *The New York Times.* http://www.nytimes.com/2014/12/05/opinion/david-brooks-why-elders-smile.html?_r=0

with members of the local community recognizes both our corporate duty to care for those affected by our behavior and their right to know what we are up to. Exercising corporate responsibility through works that benefit the community and serve the common good are unquestionably ethical. All these actions are examples of what W. D. Ross would call *prima facie* duties of beneficence.

Is Public Relations Inherently Unethical?

So we end where we started, asking whether public relations is inherently unethical. By now, we hope our answer is obvious: there is no fundamental dichotomy between the purpose of public relations and the best ethical thinking of the last 2,500 years. Nor is it an amoral function, ethical or unethical, depending entirely on how it is used. On the contrary, public relations professionals and practitioners may never be recognized as any company's "chief ethics officer" or even its "conscience," but their proper role in any organization is profoundly ethical. It is to collaborate with colleagues in senior management to identify and nurture their company's very *character*.

That is a particularly Aristotelian view of ethics, but it is also, in fact, how the Arthur W. Page Society defines a senior public relations leader's role. The Society is a professional association of the world's leading public relations people, from academia, government, and business. It is named after AT&T's first public relations officer. (Full disclosure: one of us worked at Page's desk for 6 years, while the other served on the society's Board of Trustees for 24 years.)

The members of the Page Society define their job as their namesake did—more broadly than simple wordsmithing or story pitching. They even consider it more than caring for the company's reputation, quoting Abraham Lincoln on the subject. "Character is like a tree and reputation a shadow," Lincoln is reputed to have said. "The shadow is what we think of it; the tree is the real thing."

A company's character is manifest in everything it does, from strategy to marketing, and especially in how it serves all the people who contribute to its success and bear the cost of its failures. No public relations person—not even Arthur Page—can do that single-handedly. But the Page model calls for a company's public relations leader to serve as a catalyst for C-suite collaboration in shaping a distinctive corporate character rooted in its values and higher purpose. As the Page White Paper puts it, "to ensure that our companies and institutions *look like, sound like, think like* and *perform like* our stated corporate character."[3]

After all, as we noted at the beginning of this book, most public relations crises begin as an ethical lapse, a failing of character. Johnson & Johnson, for example, has always been a company people feel good about. Those feelings may be stimulated by all the freshly powdered babies with whom the company has carefully associated itself. Or it may reflect memories of its forthright actions 32 years ago when some still unidentified lowlife laced Tylenol capsules with cyanide, killing seven people. Whatever the reason, J&J always lands in the upper ranks of reputation surveys.

Yet, in 2013, J&J became the biggest scofflaw in the pharmaceutical industry, racking up more than $6 billion in fines and penalties to settle an array of civil and criminal charges.[4] The Tylenol crisis, which cost J&J a few hundred million dollars, was the work of persons unknown. But the Department Of Justice suit, which cost orders of magnitude more, was self-inflicted. Some will argue J&J admitted to no more than a misdemeanor for misinterpreting confusing labeling rules and the biggest chunk of the fines were related to a product recall.[5] In both cases, the company paid up simply to put expensive litigation behind it. That may be true. And J&J is a familiar, if not exactly good, company.

---

[3] Page, A.W. (2012, March 22). Building Belief: A New Model For Activating Corporate Character And Authentic Advocacy. *Society* See: http://www.awpagesociety.com/wp-content/uploads/2012/11/Building-Belief-New-Model-for-Corp-Comms.pdf

[4] J&J Is Now Top-Fined Company in the Pharma Criminal & Civil Settlement Planetary System: A Blot on Gorsky's Leadership. (2013, November 13). *Pharma Marketing Blog.* http://pharmamkting.blogspot.com/2013/11/j-is-now-top-fined-company-in-dojs.html Accessed August 25, 2015.

[5] The Huffington Post documented one case J&J settled in a multi-part series with links to FDA findings, court filings, and depositions. See Brill, S. (2015). America's Most Admired Lawbreaker. *Huffington Post Highline.* http://highline.huffingtonpost.com/miracleindustry/americas-most-admired-lawbreaker/

But they will have wasted their money if they do not do something about the culture that spawned these crises in the first place.

Ethical Compliance

Every major company has a senior officer who is supposed to ensure that employees comply with laws and regulations. In the spirit of all things C-suite, call him or her the Chief Compliance Officer. Usually, he or she is a lawyer, which makes practical sense—lawyers are trained in the nuts and bolts of the law, know how to interpret regulations, and can keep their work product away from prying eyes.

But compliance is not the same as ethics. Compliance is concerned with the letter of the law; ethics, with its spirit. Compliance is rooted in statutes; ethics flows from a company's character. Compliance and ethics overlap somewhat, but not completely. J&J, for example, was under no legal obligation to take Tylenol off the shelves back in 1982; the company did so because it decided it would be unethical to expose its customers to such risk. More recently, someone at J&J apparently decided regulations did not prevent it from marketing an antipsychotic drug for off-label purposes. The Department of Justice felt differently. But the bigger question is "Was it ethical?" Did it reflect the company's character as expressed in its famous credo that, "our first responsibility is to the doctors, nurses and patients, to mother and fathers and all other who use our products and services"?[6]

We believe a company's public relations leader is best positioned to help answer questions like that. But the qualifications necessary to fulfill that role do not come with the other perks of the job. They are earned in working with colleagues across the C-suite to define and activate corporate character, not only in marketing and communications, but also across all operations and management systems.

---

[6] J&J proudly displays the Credo, written by Chairman and member of the founding family Robert Wood Johnson, on its web site. See http://www.jnj.com/about-jnj/jnj-credo/??sitelink=The+JJ+Credo&utm_campaign=J%26J+Love&utm_source =google&utm_medium=cpc&utm_term=j%26j%20credo&utm_content=J%26J+-+Heritage+-+E Accessed Sept. 7, 2015

Author David Brooks draws a distinction between what he calls "résumé virtues" (Brooks, 2015, x) and "eulogy virtues." Résumé virtues are the skills on which we build a career—intelligence, creativity, eloquence, and so forth. Eulogy virtues are the characteristics by which we will be remembered after we die—whether we were brave, trustworthy, honest, and so forth. The eulogy virtues, he says, are "the ones that exist at the core of your being." And their measure is "what kind of relationships you formed," suggesting that in the practice of public relations, eulogy virtues *are* the best résumé virtues.

Curators of Character

As the Arthur W. Page Society sees it, public relations leaders must be "curators of corporate character," capable of ensuring that the company's communications and its people remain true to their core identity. And in helping to define and protect that identity, they must be "masters of data analytics" capable of building common understanding of customers, employees, investors, citizens, and other stakeholders as individuals rather than as amorphous "publics," "target audiences," or "demographic segments." And they have to be "students of behavioral science" to inform and sustain an ongoing dialog with company stakeholders. But their goal is not to manipulate the beliefs, attitudes, and opinions of people outside the company; it is to shape the behavior of the company itself, consistent with its values and identity. That, it seems to us, is the essence of ethics—and the way to practice public relations without losing your soul.

References

Andrews, K.R. (1989). *Ethics in Practice: Managing the Moral Corporation.* Boston, MA: Harvard Business School Press.

Andsagera, J.L. and Hustb, S.J.T., (2005). Differential gender orientation in public relations: Implications for career choices. *Public Relations Review, 31,* 85–91.

Aristotle. (c. 350 BCE, trans. Jowett, B. 1999). *Politics.* Kitchener, Ontario: Batoche Books. http://socserv2.socsci.mcmaster.ca/econ/ugcm/3ll3/aristotle /Politics.pdf. Accessed September 8, 2015.

Aristotle. (c. 350 BCE, trans. Hammond, W.A., 1902). *On the Soul.* New York: Macmillan. https://archive.org/details/aristotlespsych00aris. Accessed September 8, 2015.

Aristotle. (c. 350 BCE, trans. Ross, W.D., 1999). *Nicomachean Ethics.* Kitchener, ON: Batoche Books. http://socserv2.socsci.mcmaster.ca/econ/ugcm/3ll3/ aristotle/Ethics.pdf. Accessed July 22, 2015.

Avenanti, A., Sirigu, A., & Aglioti, S.M. (2010). Racial Bias Reduces Empathic Sensorimotor Resonance with Other-Race Pain. *Current Biology,* 20(11) 478–480. http://ac.els-cdn.com/S0960982210005154/1-s2.0-S0960982210 005154-main.pdf?_tid=f4b27ab8-559d-11e5-9310-00000aab0f6c&acdnat =1441657440_dd78cce3305343fc6f91f46c39cb90dd Accessed September 7, 2015.

Axelrod, A. (2008). *Profiles in Folly.* New York, NY: Sterling Publishing.

Baier, A. (1995). The need for more than justice. In *Justice and Care: Essential Readings in Feminist Ethics,* ed. V. Held, pp. 47–60. Boulder, CO: Westview Press.

Bakan, J. (2004). *The Corporation: The Pathological Pursuit of Profit and Power.* New York, NY: Free Press.

Baker, S., & Martinson, D. (2001). The TARES test: Five principles for ethical persuasion. *Journal of Mass Media Ethics, 16,* 148–175. http://philpapers .org/rec/BAKTTT. Accessed July 22, 2015.

Bargh, J., Chen, M., & Burrows, L. (1996). Automaticity of social behavior. *Journal of Personality and Social Psychology, 71,* 230–244. http://www.ncbi .nlm.nih.gov/pubmed/8765481. Accessed July 22, 2015.

Barnum, P.T., (1866). *The Humbugs of the World,* New York: Carlton. http: //www.gutenberg.org/ebooks/26640. Accessed September 4, 2015.

Baron, R. (1997). The sweet smell of helping. *Personality and Social Psychology Bulletin, 25,* 498–505. http://web.natur.cuni.cz/~houdek3/papers/Baron% 201997.pdf. Accessed July 22, 2015.

Batson, C.D., Lishner, D.A., Carpenter, A., Dulin, L., Harjusola-Webb, S., Stocks, E.L., Gate, S., Hassan, O., & Sampat, B. (2003). As you would have them do unto you: Does imagining yourself in the other's place stimulate moral action? *Personality and Social Psychology Bulletin, 29*, 1190–2010. http://www .overcominghateportal.org/uploads/5/4/1/5/5415260/imagining_yourself_in_ the_others_place.pdf. Accessed July 22, 2015.

Bernays, E.L. (1923). *Crystalizing Public Opinion.* New York, NY: Bonni and Liveright.

Bernays, E.L. (1928). *Propaganda.* New York, NY: Horace Liveright.

Bernays, E.L. (1928, June 26). *Metropolitan Life Insurance Company in the Library of Congress.* http://memory.loc.gov/cgi-bin/query/r?ammem/cool:@field(DOC ID+@lit(me191). Accessed July 22, 2015.

Bernays, E.L. (1940). *Speak Up for Democracy.* New York, NY: Viking.

Bernays, E.L. (1941). *Morale: First Line of Defense.* Whitefish, MT: Kessinger Publishing, 2010.

Bernays, E.L. (1945). *Public Relations.* Boston, MA: Bellman Publishing.

Bernays, E.L. (1947). The engineering of consent. *American Academy of Political and Social Science, 250*, 113–120. http://provokateur.com/wp-content/uploads /2012/01/The-Engineering-of-Consent.pdf. Accessed July 22, 2015.

Bernays, E.L. (1961/2010). *Your Future in Public Relations.* Whitefish, MT: Kessinger Publishing, 2010.

Bernays, E.L. (1965). *Biography of an Idea.* New York, NY: Simon and Schuster.

Bernays, E.L. (1979). *Your Future in a Public Relations Career.* New York, NY: Rosen Publishing.

Bernays, E.L. (1986). *The Later Years: Public Relations Insights.* Rhinebeck, NY: Howard Penn Hudson Associates.

Bertrand, M., & Mullainathan, S. (2004). Are Emily and Greg more employable than Lakisha and Jamal? A field experiment on labor market discrimination. *The American Economics Review, 94*, 991–1013.

Bivins, T.H. (2004). *Mixed Media: Moral Distinctions in Advertising, Public Relations, and Journalism.* Hillside, NJ: Lawrence Erlbaum.

Bivens, T.H. (2006). Responsibility and accountability. In *Ethics in Public Relations: Responsible Advocacy*, eds. Fitzpatrick, K., & Bronstein, C., 19–38. Thousand Oaks, CA: Sage.

Bivens, T.H. (2009). *Mixed Media: Moral Distinctions in Advertising, Public Relations, and Journalism.* New York, NY: Routledge.

Blackburn, S. (2001). *Ethics: A Very Short Introduction.* New York, NY: Oxford University Press.

Bok, S. (1989). *Secrets: On the Ethics of Concealment and Revelation.* New York, NY: Vintage.

Bowen, S.A. (2004). Expansion of ethics as the tenth generic principle of public relations excellence: A Kantian Theory and Model for Managing Ethical Issues. *Journal of Public Relations Research, 16,* 65–92.

Bowen, S.A., Rawlins, B., & Martin, T. (2010). *The Public Relations Function.* New York, NY: Business Expert Press.

Brandt, A. (1996, January–April). Recruiting women smokers: The engineering of consent. *Journal of the American Medical Women's Association, 51,* 63–66.

Brooks, D. (2015). *The Road to Character.* New York, NY: Random House.

Brooks, J. (1976). *Telephone: The First Hundred Years.* New York, NY: Harper & Row.

Broom, G.M., & Dozier, D.M. (1986). Advancement for public relations role models. *Public Relations Review, 7,* 37–56.

Brunn, E. (2001). *The Forbes Book of Great Business Letters.* New York, NY: Black Dog and Leventhal Publishers.

Budziszewska, M., Hansen, K., & Bilewica, M. (2014). Backlash over gender-fair language: The impact of feminine job titles on men's and women's perception of women. *Journal of Language and Social Psychology, 33,* 681–691.

Callahan, J.C. (ed.) (1988). *Ethical Issues in Professional Life.* New York, NY: Oxford University Press.

Campbell, F.E. (2010). *Backs to the Wall: How Public Relations Carries Discomfort for Organizations.* UHBS Working Paper, University of Hertfordshire.

Carr-Saunders, A.M., & Wilson, P.A. (1933). *The Professions.* Oxford: Clarendon Press.

Caruso, E., Rahnev, D., & Banaji, M. (2009). Using conjoint analysis to detect discrimination: Revealing covert preferences from overt choices. *Social Cognition, 1,* 128–137. http://faculty.chicagobooth.edu/eugene.caruso/docs/Caruso%20et%20al.%20(2009)%20Conjoint%20Analysis%20and%20Discrimination.pdf. Accessed September 7, 2015.

Chialdini, R.B., Reno, R.R., & Cailgren, C.A. (1990). A focus theory of normative conduct: Recycling the concept of norms to reduce littering in public places. *Journal of Personality and Social Psychology, 58,* 1015–1026.

Christensen, W. (2012, February 27). Torches of freedom: Women and smoking propaganda. *Sociological Images.* http://thesocietypages.org/socimages/2012/02/27/torches-of-freedom-women-and-smoking-propaganda/. Accessed July 22, 2015.

Clark, R.C. (1986). *Corporate Law.* London: A Balkema Textbook Treatise Series.

Cline, B. N. and Walkling, R. A. and Yore, A. S. (2015, July 31). The Agency Costs of Managerial Indiscretions: Sex, Lies, and Firm Value. http://ssrn.com/abstract=1573327 orhttp://dx.doi.org/10.2139/ssrn.1573327

Coates, J.C., IV. (2015, February 27). Corporate speech and the First Amendment: History, data, and implications. *Constitutional Commentary,* Forthcoming. http://dx.doi.org/10.2139/ssrn.2566785. Accessed July 22, 2015.

Cogan, M.L. (1955). The problems of defining a profession. *Annals of the American Academy of Political Science, 297*, 105–111.

Coleman, R., & Wilkins, L. (2009). The moral development of public relations practitioners: A comparison with other professions and influences on higher quality ethical reasoning. *Journal of Public Relations Research, 21*, 318–340. http://www.academia.edu/7832252/The_Moral_Development_of_Public_Rel ations_Practitioners_A_Comparison_With_Other_Professions_and_Influence s_on_Higher_Quality_Ethical_Reasoning. Accessed July 22, 2015.

Cutlip, S.M. (1994). *The Unseen Power*. Mahwah, NJ: Lawrence Erlbaum.

Cutlip, S.M. (1981, November 8). *Thoughts about the Public Relations Curriculum*. Unpublished paper presented to the Educators Section, Public Relations Society of America, Chicago.

Cutlip, S.M., Center, A.H., & Broom, G.M. (1985). *Effective Public Relations*. 6th ed. Englewood Cliffs, NJ: Prentice-Hall.

Damasio, A. (1994). *Descartes' Error: Emotion, Reason, and the Human Brain*. New York, NY: Penguin Group.

De Dreu, C., Greer, L., Handgraaf, M., Shaul, S., Van Kleef, G.A., Baas, M., Ten Velden, F., Van Dijk, E., & Feith, S.W. (2010). The neuropeptide oxytocin regulates parochial altruism in intergroup conflict among humans. *Science, 328*, 1408–1411.

DeGeorge, R.T. (2000, September). Ethics in international business—A contradiction in terms? *Business Credit, 102*, 50.

Donaldson, T. (1996, September–October). Values in tension: Ethics away from home. *Harvard Business Review*. https://hbr.org/1996/09/values-in-tension-ethics-away-from-home.

Donaldson, T., & Preston, L. (1995). The stakeholder theory of the corporation: Concepts, evidence, and implications. *Academy of Management Review, 20*, 65–81.

Drucker, P. (1984, Winter). The new meaning of corporate social responsibility. *California Management Review, 26*(2), 53–63.

Drucker, P. (1993). *Management: Tasks, Responsibilities, Practices*. New York, NY: Harper and Row.

Edmond, D. (2013). *Would You Kill the Fat Man?* Princeton, NJ: Princeton University Press.

Ellsworth, J.D. (1936, December). *The Twisted Trail*. Unpublished memoir, AT&T Aechives, Warren, N.J.

Evan, W.M., & Freeman, R.E. (2012). A stakeholder theory of the modern corporation: Kantian capitalism. In *Ethical Theory and Business*, 9th ed. eds. D. Arnold and T. Beauchamp. New York, NY: Pearson.

Ewen, S. (1996). *PR! A Social History of Spin*. New York, NY: Basic Books.

Festinger, L. (1962). Cognitive dissonance. *Scientific American, 207*, 93–107.

Fitzpatrick, K., & Gauthier, C. (2001). Toward a professional responsibility theory of public relations ethics. *Journal of Mass Media Ethics, 16,* 193–212.

Flexner, A. (1915, June 26). Is social work a profession? *National Conference on Social Welfare Proceedings. 576* http://www.socialwelfarehistory.com/social-work/is-social-work-a-profession-1915/ Accessed September 9, 2015.

Freeman, C. (2007, May 23). *Who's Harming Whom? A PR Case Study of PETA's Holocaust on Your Plate Campaign.* Paper presented at annual meeting of International Communication Association, San Francisco. https://www.academia.edu/645889/Whos_Harming_Whom_A_PR_Ethical_Case_Study_of_PETAs_Holocaust_on_Your_Plate_Campaign. Accessed July 22, 2015.

Freeman, R.E. (1984). *A Stakeholder Theory of the Modern Corporation. General Issues in Business Ethics, Strategic Management: A Stakeholder Approach.* New York, NY: Harper Collins.

Freeman, R.E. (2001). Stakeholder theory of the modern corporation. In *Ethical Issues in Business: A Philosophical Approach,* eds. T. Donaldson, P. H. Werhane, and M. Cording, Englewood Cliffs, NJ: Prentice Hall.

Freeman, R.E. (2009, October 1). Shareholders vs. stakeholders—Friedman vs. Freeman debate. *Business Roundtable Institute for Corporate Ethics.* www.youtube.com/watch?v=_sNKIEzYM7M&NR=1. Accessed July 22, 2015.

Freeman, R.E. (2009, October 1). What is stakeholder theory? *Business Roundtable Institute for Corporate Ethics.* www.youtube.com/watch?v=bIRUaLcvPe8. Accessed July 22, 2015.

Friedman, M. (1995). Beyond caring: The de-moralization of gender. In *Justice and Care: Essential Readings in Feminist Ethics,* ed. V. Held, pp. 61–77. Boulder, CO: Westview Press.

Gallicano, T.D., Yoon, Y., Cho, Y.Y., & Bivens, T. (2013). What do blog readers think? A survey to assess ghost blogging and commenting. *Research Journal of the Institute for Public Relations Research, 2.* http://www.instituteforpr.org/wp-content/uploads/Tiffany.pdf. Accessed July 22, 2015.

Gellerman, S.W. (1998). *How People Work: Psychological Approaches to Management Problems.* Westport, CT: Greenwood Publishing Group.

Gifford, W.S. (1926, June). The changing character of big business. *World's Work, 5,* 166–168.

Gilligan, C. (1977). In a different voice: Women's conceptions of self and morality. *Harvard Educational Review, 47,* 481–517.

Gilligan, C. (1982). *In a Different Voice: Psychological Theory and Women's Development.* Boston, MA: Harvard University Press.

Gino, F., Shahar, A., & Ariely, D. (2009). Unethical behavior: The effect of one bad apple on the barrel. *Psychological Science, 20,* 393–398. http://people.duke.edu/~dandan/Papers/Cheating/contagion.pdf. Accessed July 22, 2015.

Gino, F., Shu, L.L., & Bazerman, M.H. (2010). Needless + harmless: When seemingly irrelevant factors influence judgment of (un)ethical behavior. *Organizational Behavior and Human Decision Processes, 111*, 102–115.

Goffman, E. (1974). *Frame Analysis: An Essay on the Organization of Experience.* Boston: Northeastern University Press. http://is.muni.cz/el/1423/podzim 2013/SOC571E/um/E.Goffman-FrameAnalysis.pdf. Accessed September 9, 2015.

Goodpaster, K.F., & Matthews, J.B, Jr. (1989). Can a corporation have a conscience? In *Ethics in Practice: Managing the Moral Corporation*, ed. K.R. Andrews, pp. 115–167. Boston, MA: Harvard Business School Press.

Gordon, J.C. (1997). Interpreting definitions of public relations: Self-assessment and a symbolic interactionism-based alternative. *Public Relations Review, 23*, 57–66.

Green, A.R., Carney, D.R., Pallin, D.J., Ngo, L.H., Raymond, K.L. Iezzoni, L.I., & Manaji, M.R. (2007). Implicit bias among physicians and its prediction of thrombolysis decisions for black and white patients. *Journal of Internal General Medicine, 22*, 1231–1238. http://www.refdoc.fr/?traduire=en &FormRechercher=submit&FormRechercher_Txt_Recherche_name_attr=l isteTitreSerie:%20(Journal%20of%20general%20internal%20medicine). Accessed July 22, 2015.

Grunig, J.E., (1991, September). Excellence in Public Relations and Communication Management Executive summary/Initial Data Report, San Francisco: International Association of Business Communicators. http://jobaccess.iabc .com/researchfoundation/pdf/Excellence.pdf

Grunig, J.E., & White, J. (1992). The effect of worldview on public relations. In *Excellence in Public Relations and Communications Management*, ed. J. Grunig, pp. 31–64. Mahwah, NJ: Lawrence Erlbaum Associates.

Grunig, J.E., & Hunt, T. (1984). *Managing Public Relations.* New York, NY: Holt, Rinehart & Winston.

Grunig, L.A., Toth, E. & Hon, L.C. (2000). Feminist Values in Public Relations, Public Relations Research, *12(1)*, Issue 1, pp. 49–68.

Habermas, J. (1984). *The Theory of Communicative Action: Volume 1, Reason and the Rationalization of Society.* Boston, MA: Beacon Press.

Habermas, J. (1987). *Theory of Communicative Action: Volume 2, Lifeworld and Reason—A Critique of Fundamentalist Reason.* Boston, MA: Beacon Press.

Haidt, J. (2012). *The Righteous Mind.* New York, NY: Pantheon.

Haidt, J., Greene, J.D., Sommerville, R.B., Nystrom, L.E., Darley, J.M., & Cohen, J.D. (2001). An fMRI study of emotional engagement in moral judgment. *Science, 293*, 2105–2108.

Haidt. J. (1992). *Moral Judgment, Affect, and Culture: Or Is It Wrong To Eat Your Dog.* Unpublished doctoral dissertation. University of Pennsylvania.

http://people.stern.nyu.edu/jhaidt/articles/haidt.1992.dissertation.pub001b
.pdf. Accessed September 9, 2015.

Hallahan, K. (2002). Ivy Lee and the Rockefellers' response to the 1913–1914
Colorado coal strike. *Journal of Public Relations Research, 4*, 265–315.
http://lamar.colostate.edu/~pr/ivylee.pdf. Accessed July 22, 2015.

Haney, C., Banks, C., & Zimbardo, P. (1973, September). A study of prisoners
and guards in a simulated prison. *Naval Research Reviews*. http://www
.zimbardo.com/downloads/1973%20A%20Study%20of%20Prisoners%20
and%20Guards,%20Naval%20Research%20Reviews.pdf. Accessed July 22,
2015.

Harris, E. (1969, Spring). Respect for persons. *Daedalus, 122*, 113.

Held, V. (1993). *Feminist Morality: Transforming Culture, Society, and Politics.*
Chicago: University of Chicago Press.

Hill, J., II. (1992). *Health and Morality—Tobacco's Counter Campaign*. Philip
Morris; Billey. http://legacy.library.ucsf.edu/tid/eso87e00. Accessed July 22,
2015.

Hill, J.W. (1958). *Corporate Public Relations: Arm of Modern Management*. New
York, NY: Harper & Brothers.

Hill, J.W. (1993). *The Making of a Corporate Public Relations Man*. Wausau,
WI: NTC Business Books.

Hinman, L.M. (2012). Kant and Kantian ethics. *Ethics Updates*. http://ethics
.sandiego.edu/theories/Kant/index.asp. Accessed July 22, 2015.

Hofstede, G. (2010). *Cultures and Organizations: Software of the Mind*. New
York, NY: McGraw-Hill. www.geerthofstede.nl

Huff, D. (1954/1993). *How to Lie with Statistics*. New York, NY: W. W. Norton.

Hughes, E.C. (1965). The professions. In *The Professions in America*, eds. Lynn,
K.S., & the Editors of Daedalus. Boston, MA: Houghton Mifflin.

Jaggar, A. (2000). Ethics naturalized: Feminism's contribution to moral episte-
mology. *Metaphilosophy, 31*, 452–468.

Johannesen, R. L. (1983). *Ethics in Human Communication*. 2nd ed. Prospect
Heights, IL: Waveland Press.

Jowett, G., & O'Donnell, V. (1999). *Propaganda and Persuasion*. Thousand
Oaks, CA: Sage Publications.

Kahneman, D. (2011). *Thinking Fast and Slow*. New York, NY: Farrar, Straus,
& Giroux.

Kahneman, D., & Tversky, A. (1970). Prospect theory: An analysis of decision
under risk. *Econometrica, 47(2)*, 263–292.

Kant, I. (1763, trans. Frierson, P and Guyer, P., 2011). *Observations on the
Feeling of the Beautiful and the Sublime*. Oakland, CA: University of California Press, http://ebooks.cambridge.org/chapter.jsf?bid=CBO978051197
6018&cid=CBO9780511976018A011. Accessed September 9, 2015.

Kant, I. (1781, 1787, trans. J.M.D. Meiklejohn, 2014). *The Critique of Pure Reason.* http://www.gutenberg.org/files/4280/4280-h/4280-h.htm. Accessed July 22, 2015.

Kant, I. (1785, trans. James Ellington, 1993). *Grounding for the Metaphysics of Morals.* 3rd ed. Indianapolis/Cambridge: Hackett Books. https://wiki.zirve.edu.tr/sandbox/groups/economicsandadministrativesciences/wiki/ad713/attachments/d0f5f/Immanuel_Kant-Grounding_for_the_Metaphysics_of_Morals.pdf?sessionID=f41ac06a0b59605c792cf5a128702ccd74421411. Accessed September 9, 2015.

Keizer, K., Lindenberg, S., & Steg, L. (2008). The spreading of disorder. *Science, 322*, 1681–1685.

Knight, K. (1998). *The MacIntyre Reader.* Notre Dame: University of Notre Dame Press.

Klein, N. (2001, May–June). Reclaiming the commons. *New Left Review, 9*, 81–89.

Kohlberg, L. (1958). *The Development of Modes of Thinking and Choices in Years 10 to 16.* Unpublished Dissertation, University of Chicago.

Kruckeberg, D. (1989). The need for an international code of ethics. *Public Relations Review, 15*, 6–18.

Latman, R.K. (2012). *The Good Fail.* New York, NY: Wiley.

Le Bon, G. (1895). *The Crowd: A Study of the Popular Mind.* http://www.gutenberg.org/cache/epub/445/pg445.html. Accessed July 22, 2015.

Lee, I. (1925). *Publicity.* New York, NY: Industries Publishing.

L'Etang, J. (2004). The myth of the "ethical guardian:" An examination of its origins, potency and illusions. *Journal of Communication Management, 8*, 53–67.

Levy, R. (1999). *Give and Take: A Candid Account of Corporate Philanthropy.* Cambridge, MA: Harvard Business School Press.

Lieberman, M. (1956). *Education as a Profession.* Englewood Cliffs, NJ: Prentice-Hall.

Lieber, P. (1998). *Ethics in Public Relations: Gauging Ethical Decision-Making Patterns of Public Relations Practitioners.* Unpublished Masters' Thesis, Syracuse University. http://195.130.87.21:8080/dspace/bitstream/123456789/904/1/Ethics%20in%20Public%20Relations.pdf. Accessed July 22, 2015.

Lieber, P. (2008). Moral development in public relations: Measuring duty to society in strategic communication. *Public Relations Review, 34*, 244–251. http://www.sciencedirect.com/science/article/pii/S0363811108000507. Accessed July 22, 2015.

Long, R. (2013, February 19). Thinking our anger. *Center for a Stateless Society.* http://c4ss.org/content/17334.

Macintyre, A. (1998). *A Short History of Ethics: A History of Moral Philosophy from the Homeric Age to the Twentieth Century.* South Bend, IN: University of Notre Dame Press.

Martin, D. (1977). *The Executive's Guide to Handing a Press Interview.* New York, NY: Pilot Books.

Martin, D. (2004). *Tough Calls: AT&T and the Hard Lessons Learned from the Telecom Wars.* New York, NY: AMACOM.

Mautner, T. (ed.). (1997). *The Penguin Dictionary of Philosophy.* London: Penguin Books.

Messina, A. (2007). Public relations, the public interest, and persuasion: An ethical approach. *Journal of Communications Management, 11,* 29–52.

Michaelson, D., & Stacks, D.W. (2011). *A Professional and Practitioner's Guide to Public Relations Research, Measurement, and Evaluation.* New York, NY: Business Expert Press.

Milgram, S. (1963). Behavioral study of obedience. *Journal of Abnormal and Social Psychology, 67,* 371–378. http://www.radford.edu/~jaspelme/_private/gradsoc_articles/obedience/Migram_Obedience.pdf. Accessed July 22, 2015.

Milgram, S. (1973, December). The perils of obedience. *Harper's, 62–77.* https://www.nmmi.edu/academics/leadership/documents/Milgram-Obedience2.pdf. Accessed July 22, 2015.

Mill, J.S. (1863, edition of 2001). *Utilitarianism.* Kitchener, Ontario: Batouche Books. http://socserv.mcmaster.ca/econ/ugcm/3ll3/mill/utilitarianism.pdf. Accessed September. 9, 2015.

Mill, J.S. (1869). *The Subjection of Women.* London: Longmans, Green, Reader, and Dyer, http://www.gutenberg.org/ebooks/27083?msg=welcome_stranger. Accessed July 22, 2015.

Miller, K.S. (1999). *The Voice of Business: Hill & Knowlton and Postwar Public Relations.* Chapel Hill: University of North Carolina Press.

Moore, G.E. (1903). *Principia Ethica.* Cambridge: Cambridge University Press. http://fair-use.org/g-e-moore/principia-ethica. Accessed July 22, 2015.

Morris, M., Podolny, J., & Sheira, A. (2001). Culture, norms, and obligations: Cross-national differences in patterns of interpersonal norms and felt obligations toward coworkers. In *The Practice of Social Influence in Multiple Cultures,* eds. W. Wosinska, D. Barrett, R. Cialdini, and J. Reykowski, pp. 97–123. Mahwah, NJ: Lawrence Erlbaum. http://www1.gsb.columbia.edu/mygsb/faculty/research/pubfiles/1913/1913.pdf. Accessed July 22, 2015.

Morse, S. (1906). An awakening in Wall Street: How the trusts, after years of silence, now speak though authorized and acknowledged press agents. *The American Magazine, 62,* 457–463.

Nisan, M. (1991). The moral balance model: Theory and research extending our understanding of moral choice and deviation. In *Handbook of Moral Behavior and Development*, eds. K. Williams and J. Gerwitz, pp. 213–249. Mahwah, NJ: Lawrence Erlbaum Associates.

Noddings, N. (1995). Caring. In *Justice and Care: Essential Readings in Feminist Ethics*, ed. V. Held, pp. 7–30. Boulder, CO: Westview Press.

Nosek, B., & Hansen, J. (2008). The associations in our heads belong to us: Searching for attitudes and knowledge in implicit evaluation. *Cognition and Emotion, 4*, 553–594.

Oreskes, N., & Conway, E. (2010). *Merchants of Doubt.* New York, NY: Bloomsbury Press.

Otteson, J.R. (2006). *Actual Ethics.* Cambridge: Cambridge University Press.

Page, A.W. (1941). *The Bell Telephone System.* New York, NY: Harper & Row. http://wedophones.com/TheBellSystem/pdf/thebelltelsys.pdf. Accessed July 22, 2015.

Page, A.W. (1956, June). *Reminiscences of Arthur W. Page.* The Columbia Oral History Archives, Rare Book & Manuscript Library, Columbia University in the City of New York.

Parsons, P. (2004). *Ethics in Public Relations.* Philadelphia: Kogan Page Publishers.

Paul, R.N. (1994). Status and outlook of the chain-restaurant industry. *Cornell Hotel & Restaurant Administration Quarterly, 35*, 23–27.

Peters, J.D. (1999). *Speaking into the Air: A History of the Idea of Communication.* Chicago: University of Chicago Press.

Plaisance, P.L. (2014). *Media Ethics: Key Principles for Responsible Practice*, 2nd ed. Thousand Oaks, CA: Sage.

Porter, M., & Kramer, M. (2006, December). Strategy & society. *Harvard Business Review.* http://www.stockholmresilience.org/download/18.aeea469 11a31274279800090883/1381790092816/susannesweet.pdf. Accessed July 22, 2015.

Porter, M., & Kramer, M. (2011, January). Creating shared value. *Harvard Business Review, 62–77.*

Price, J., & Wolfers, J. (2010). Racial discrimination among NBA referees. *Quarterly Journal of Economics, 125*, 1859–1887. http://ftp.iza.org/dp2863.pdf. Accessed July 22, 2015.

Rachels, J. (1999). *The Elements of Moral Philosophy*, 3rd ed. New York, NY: McGraw-Hill.

Rawls, J. (1985). Justice as fairness: Political not metaphysical. *Philosophy and Public Affairs, 14*, 223–251.

Redelmerier, D., & Tibsgirani, R. (1997). Association between cellular-telephone calls and motor vehicle accidents. *The New England Journal of Medicine, 336*, 453–458.

Riley, L.A., & Brown, S.C. (1996). Crafting a public image: An empirical study of the ethics of ghostwriting. *Journal of Business Ethics, 15,* 711–720. http://www.businessinsider.com/pr-agencies-agree-to-stop-wikipedia-edits-2014-6.

Ritzer, G. (2014). *The McDonaldization of Society,* 8th ed. Thousand Oaks, CA: Sage.

Rooth, Dan-Olof. (2010). Implicit discrimination in hiring: Real-world evidence. *Labour Economics, 17,* 523–524. https://ideas.repec.org/p/iza/izadps/dp2764.html. Accessed July 22, 2015.

Rosenhan, D.L., Salovney, P., Karylowski, J., & Hargis, K. (1981). Emotion and altruism. In *Altruism and Helping Behavior,* eds. J.P. Rushton and R.M. Sorrentino, pp. 233–248. Mahwah, NJ: Lawrence Erlbaum Associates.

Ross, W.D. (1930/2002). *The Right and the Good.* New York, NY: Oxford University Press.

Ross, W.D. (1939). *Foundations of Ethics.* New York, NY: Oxford University Press.

Schmertz, H. (1986). *Good-Bye to the Low Profile.* New York, NY: Little Brown & Co.

Schwartz, M., & Carroll, A. (2003). Corporate social responsibility: A three domain approach. *Business Ethics Quarterly, 13,* 503–530.

Schwitzgebel, E. (2009). Do ethicists steal more books? *Philosophical Psychology, 22,* 711–725.

Shaw, W. (2013). *Business ethics,* 8th ed. Boston, MA: Cengage Advantage Books.

Shu, L., Gino, F., & Bazerman, M. (2009). Dishonest deed, clear conscience: Self-preservation through moral disengagement and motivated forgetting. *Harvard Business School,* Working Paper 09-078. http://hbswk.hbs.edu/item/6112.html. Accessed July 22, 2015.

Simon, H. (1982). *Models of Bounded Rationality and Other Topics in Economics.* Cambridge, MA: MIT Press.

Smith, A. (1759/1976). The theory of moral sentiments (Vol. 1). In *Works and Correspondence of Adam Smith* (The Glasgow Edition). New York, NY: Oxford University Press. https://direitasja.files.wordpress.com/2012/02/theory_of_moral_sentiments.pdf. Accessed September 7, 2015.

Solomon, R. (1992). Corporate roles, personal virtues: An Aristotelian approach to business ethics. *Business Ethics Quarterly, 2,* 317–339.

Stacks, D.W. (1983). Toward the establishment of a preverbal stage of communication. *Journal of Communication Therapy, 2,* 39–60.

Stacks, D.W., & Anderson, P.A. (1989). The modular mind: Implications for intrapersonal communication. *Southern Speech Communication Journal, 54,* 273–293.

Stauber, J., (2002). *Toxic Sludge Is Good for You: The Public Relations Industry Unspun.* Northampton, MA: Media Education Foundation.

Steiner, L. (1989). Feminist theorizing and communications ethics. *Communication, 12*, 157–173.

Stocker, K., & Tusinski Berg, K. (2006). Reconsidering public relations' infatuation with dialogue: Why engagement and reconciliation can be more ethical than symmetry and reciprocity. *Journal of Mass Media Ethics, 21*, 156–176. http://epublications.marquette.edu/cgi/viewcontent.cgi?article=1013&conte xt=comm_fac. Accessed July 22, 2015.

Strine, L., Jr. (2015, March 20). The Dangers of Denial: The Need for a Clear-Eyed Understanding of the Power and Accountability Structure Established by the Delaware General Corporation Law. Research Paper No. 15–08. Institute for Law and Economics, University of Pennsylvania. http://papers .ssrn.com/sol3/papers.cfm?abstract_id=2576389. Accessed July 22, 2015.

Strohminger, N. & Nichols, S. (2014). The essential moral self. *Cognition, 131*, 159–171. http://static1.squarespace.com/static/520cf78be4b0a5dd07f51048 /t/52f57354e4b008f86b8a52b6/1391817556763/Strohminger.Nichols.201 4.pdf

Svetozar Pejovich, P. (1990). *The Economic of Property Rights: Towards a Theory of Comparative Systems*: Dordrecht, NL: Kluwer Academic Publishers.

Tajfel, H., Billig, M.G., Bundy, R.P., & Flament, C. (1971, April–June). Social categorization and intergroup behavior. *European Journal of Social Psychology, 1*, 149–178.

Tedlow, R. (1979). *Keeping the Corporate Image: Public Relations and Business, 1900–1950*. Greenwich, CT: JAI Press.

Trotter, W. (1916). Instincts of the *H*erd in *P*eace and *W*ar. New York, NY: Macmillan.

Van Hook, S.R. (2011). Modes and models for transcending cultural differences in international classrooms. *Journal of Research in International Education, 10*, 5–27.

Vollmer, H.M., & Mills, D.L. (Eds.). (1966). *Professionalization.* Englewood Cliffs, NJ: Prentice-Hall.

Wang, G., Wilson, C., Zhao, X., Zhu, Y., Mohanial, M., Zheng, H., & Zhao, B. (2011). Serf and turf: Crowdturfing for fun and profit. *Proceedings of the World Wide Web Conference.* http://arxiv.org/PS_cache/arxiv/pdf/1111 /1111.5654v1.pdf. Accessed July 22, 2015.

Warren, S., & Brandeis, L. (1890, December 15). The right to privacy. *Harvard Law Review. IV(5)*, http://groups.csail.mit.edu/mac/classes/6.805 /articles/privacy/Privacy_brand_warr2.html Accessed September. 9, 2015.

Waytz, A., Dungan, J., & Young, L. (2013). The whisteblower's dilemma and the fairness-loyalty tradeoff. *Journal of Experimental Social Psychology, 49*,

1027–1033. http://moralitylab.bc.edu/wp-content/uploads/2011/10/Waytz DunganYoungWB.pdf. Accessed July 22, 2015.

Weaver, K., Motion, J., & Roper, J. (1996). Rhetoric, ethics, propaganda, and publics. In *Critical Perspectives in Public Relations,* J.L'Etang and M. Pieczka. Boston, MA: Cenage Learning EMEA.

Wehmeir, S. (2013). Habermas, Jurgen and public relations. In *The Encyclopedia of Public Relations,* ed. Heath, R., pp. 410–411. Thousand Oaks, CA: Sage Publications.

Williams, A. (2008, January 6). The falling-down professions. *New York Times,* K-1. http://www.nytimes.com/2008/01/06/fashion/06professions.html?ex=1357275600&en=e6188de13887a970&ei=5124&partner=permalink&exp rod=permalink&_r=0. Accessed July 22, 2015.

Wilson, E.O. (1999). *Consilience: The Unity of Knowledge.* New York, NY: Vintage, Reprint Edition.

Wollstonecraft, M. (1792) A Vindication of the Rights of Woman. Boston: Thomas and Andrews. www.earlymoderntexts.com/pdfs/wollstonecraft17 92.pdf

Wright, D.K. (1996). Communication Ethics. in *An Integrated Approach to Communication Theory and Research,* eds. M.B. Salwen and D.W. Stacks, pp. 523–537. Mahwah, NJ: Lawrence Erlbaum.

Yorker, V.C., Kizer, K.W., Lampe P., Forrest, A.R., Lannan, J.M., & Russell D.A. (2006). Serial murder by healthcare professionals. *Journal of Forensic Science, 16,* 301–309.

Index

OTHER TITLES IN OUR PUBLIC RELATIONS COLLECTION

Don W. Stacks and Donald K. Wright, Editors

- *The Social Media Communication Matrix: A New Direction in Public Relations* by Kenneth D. Plowman and Beki Winchel
- *The Public Relations Firm* by Stacey Smith and Bob Pritchard
- *Leadership Communication: How Leaders Communicate and How Communicators Lead in Today's Global Enterprise* by E. Bruce Harrison and Judith Muhlberg
- *A Professional and Practitioner's Guide to Public Relations Research, Measurement, and Evaluation, Second Edition* by David Michaelson and Donald W. Stacks
- *Crisis Management in the Age of Social Media* by Louis Capozzi and Susan Rucci
- *An Overview of the Public Relations Function* by Shannon A. Bowen, Brad Rawlins and Thomas Martin

Announcing the Business Expert Press Digital Library

Concise e-books business students need for classroom and research

This book can also be purchased in an e-book collection by your library as

- a one-time purchase,
- that is owned forever,
- allows for simultaneous readers,
- has no restrictions on printing, and
- can be downloaded as PDFs from within the library community.

Our digital library collections are a great solution to beat the rising cost of textbooks. E-books can be loaded into their course management systems or onto students' e-book readers.

The **Business Expert Press** digital libraries are very affordable, with no obligation to buy in future years. For more information, please visit **www.businessexpertpress.com/librarians**. To set up a trial in the United States, please email **sales@businessexpertpress.com**.